Hollyw

American 1

How do Hollywood filmmakers construct and interpret American history? Is film's visual historical language inherently different from the traditions of written history? What are the contexts and consequences of nostalgia? This definitive collection of essays by leading scholars probes the full range of theoretical and historical contexts of films made about the American past from the silent era to the present.

Interdisciplinary in approach, chapters explore a series of issues deeply connected with the problems of historical filmmaking, from historiography to censorship to race, gender, and sexuality. The book discusses a wide range of films and genres, from Westerns to film noir, including classics such as *The Virginian, Gone with the Wind, Citizen Kane, Some Like it Hot,* and *Chinatown. Hollywood and the American Historical Film* offers a fresh assessment of the transgeneric phenomenon of studio-era historical filmmaking and its legacy, and will be essential reading for anyone interested in, studying, or researching American history and film.

Includes essays by Susan Courtney, David Culbert, Nicholas J. Cull, Vera Dika, David Eldridge, Marcia Landy, Mark W. Roche and Vittorio Hösle, Robert Rosenstone, Ian Scott, Robert Sklar, J.E. Smyth, and Warren I. Susman.

J.E. SMYTH is Associate Professor of History and Comparative American Studies at the University of Warwick. She is the author of *Reconstructing American Historical Cinema: From* Cimarron *to* Citizen Kane and *Edna Ferber's Hollywood: American Fictions of Gender, Race, and History.*

Hollywood and the American Historical Film

Edited by

J.E. SMYTH

palgrave
macmillan

First published 2012 by
PALGRAVE MACMILLAN

Palgrave Macmillan in the UK is an imprint of Macmillan Publishers Limited, registered in England, company number 785998, of Houndmills, Basingstoke, Hampshire RG21 6XS.

Palgrave Macmillan in the US is a division of St Martin's Press LLC, 175 Fifth Avenue, New York, NY 10010.

Palgrave Macmillan is the global academic imprint of the above companies and has companies and representatives throughout the world.

Palgrave® and Macmillan® are registered trademarks in the United States, the United Kingdom, Europe and other countries.

ISBN 978–0–230–23092–7   hardback
ISBN 978–0–230–23093–4   paperback

This book is printed on paper suitable for recycling and made from fully managed and sustained forest sources. Logging, pulping and manufacturing processes are expected to conform to the environmental regulations of the country of origin.

A catalogue record for this book is available from the British Library.

A catalog record for this book is available from the Library of Congress.

10 9 8 7 6 5 4 3 2 1
21 20 19 18 17 16 15 14 13 12

Printed in China

For Katharine Park
and in memory of Noel Taylor (1917–2010)

Contents

List of Illustrations   ix

Notes on Contributors   xiii

Introduction   xvi

1 Film and History: Artifact and Experience   1
Warren I. Susman

2 Film History, Reconstruction, and Southern Legendary
History in *The Birth of a Nation*   11
David Culbert

3 The Hollywood Western, the Movement-Image,
and Making History   26
Marcia Landy

4 Ripping the Portieres at the Seams: Lessons from
Streetcar on *Gone with the Wind*   49
Susan Courtney

5 Hollywood about Hollywood: Genre as Historiography   71
Robert Sklar

6 *Some Like It Hot* and the Virtues of Not Taking History
Too Seriously   94
David Eldridge

7 Vico's Age of Heroes and the Age of Men in John Ford's
The Man Who Shot Liberty Valance   120
Mark W. Roche and Vittorio Hösle

8 Anatomy of a Shipwreck: Warner Bros., the White House,
and the Celluloid Sinking of *PT 109*   138
Nicholas J. Cull

9 The Long Road of Women's Memory:
   Fred Zinnemann's *Julia*   165
   J.E. Smyth

10 Inventing Historical Truth on the Silver Screen   183
   Robert Rosenstone

11 "This Is Not America: This Is Los Angeles": Crime, Space,
   and History in the City of Angels   192
   Ian Scott

12 Between Nostalgia and Regret: Strategies of Historical
   Disruption from Douglas Sirk to *Mad Men*   208
   Vera Dika

Further Reading   234
Index   238

List of Illustrations

I.1 *The Godfather* (1972) and the image of frontier
     capitalism © Paramount Pictures Corporation   xxii

2.1 The "overrun" Senate in D.W. Griffith's *Birth of a
     Nation* (1915) © Epoch Producing Corporation/
     David W. Griffith Corporation   19

4.1 Blanche DuBois (Vivien Leigh), the leaky subject of
     A Streetcar Named Desire (1951) © Charles K. Feldman
     Group Productions   66

4.2 Unreliable psychic and spatial borders: *A Streetcar
     Named Desire* (1951) © Charles K. Feldman Group
     Productions   66

4.3 Open windows, lost pasts, and plantations: *A Streetcar
     Named Desire* (1951) © Charles K. Feldman Group
     Productions   66

4.4 The contrast of spatial order in *Gone with the Wind*
     (1939) © Selznick International Pictures in association
     with Metro-Goldwyn-Mayer   66

4.5 Silhouetted master and mistress (Leslie Howard and
     Olivia de Havilland): *Gone with the Wind* © Selznick
     International Pictures in association with
     Metro-Goldwyn-Mayer   66

4.6 Ashley offers Melanie, and the spectator, the master's
     view from the Big House *Gone with the Wind* ©
     Selznick International Pictures
     in association with Metro-Goldwyn-Mayer   66

4.7 Antebellum spatial perfection: *Gone with the Wind*
     © Selznick International Pictures in association with
     Metro-Goldwyn-Mayer   66

4.8 Resisting the chaos of war in 1864: *Gone with the Wind*
     © Selznick International Pictures in association with
     Metro-Goldwyn-Mayer   66

4.9 The "reconstructed" space: *Gone with the Wind*
     © Selznick International Pictures in association with
     Metro-Goldwyn-Mayer   66

4.10 Plantation windows through which Scarlett (Leigh)
     views the destruction of her dreams: *Gone with the Wind*
     © Selznick International Pictures in association with
     Metro-Goldwyn-Mayer   67

4.11 The end of her world—Scarlett (Leigh) watches
      Ashley (Howard) depart: *Gone with the Wind* © Selznick
      International Pictures in association with Metro-
      Goldwyn-Mayer   67
4.12 Scarlett (Leigh) perceives her father's (Thomas Mitchell)
      mental collapse: *Gone with the Wind* © Selznick
      International Pictures in association with
      Metro-Goldwyn-Mayer   67
4.13 Facing the threat of eviction from the Big House,
      Scarlett confronts the boarded windows and portieres
      which will be her "reconstruction" project (with Hattie
      McDaniel): *Gone with the Wind* © Selznick International
      Pictures in association with Metro-Goldwyn-Mayer   67
4.14 Melanie (de Havilland) closes the window and
      comforts Rhett (Clark Gable): *Gone with the Wind*
      © Selznick International Pictures in association with
      Metro-Goldwyn-Mayer   67
4.15 The end of a marriage: *Gone with the Wind*
      © Selznick International Pictures in association with
      Metro-Goldwyn-Mayer   67
4.16 Unstable spaces and vanishing dreams—Rhett's
      departure in the fog: *Gone with the Wind* © Selznick
      International Pictures in association with
      Metro-Goldwyn-Mayer   67
4.17 A window that neither fully shuts out nor clearly
      opens onto a world outside: *A Streetcar Named Desire*
      © Charles K. Feldman Group Productions   67
4.18 Contrasting feminine spaces in *A Streetcar Named Desire*
      © Charles K. Feldman Group Productions   67
5.1   *Sunset Boulevard* (1950): Hollywood's vampire
      (Gloria Swanson) projects her version of the silent
      film past © Paramount Pictures Corporation   73
5.2   Two from the "Waxworks": Harry B. Warner and
      Buster Keaton in *Sunset Boulevard* © Paramount
      Pictures Corporation   79
5.3   Vicki Lester's (Judy Garland) small image at the Academy
      Awards now competes with television's larger picture:
      A Star Is Born (1954) © Warner Bros.   89
6.1   Wilder's playful "intertitle": *Some Like It Hot* (1959)
      © Ashton Productions   95

6.2 Daphne (Jack Lemmon) has stopped leading
     and plays the lady with Osgood (Joe E. Brown):
     Some Like It Hot (1959) © Ashton Productions   103
7.1 The unacknowledged view of the legend:
     The Man Who Shot Liberty Valance (1962) © Paramount
     Pictures Corporation/John Ford Productions   124
9.1 Separation of word and image: Lillian Hellman
     (Jane Fonda) in *Julia* © Twentieth Century-Fox   173
9.2 Divided in the frame: Lillian with Hammett
     (Jason Robards) in *Julia* (1977) © Twentieth Century-Fox 175
9.3 Together in the frame: young Lillian (Susan Jones)
     with young Julia (Lisa Pelikan) in *Julia* © Twentieth
     Century-Fox   175
9.4 An overdetermined and overframed image of beauty:
     Vanessa Redgrave as Julia in *Julia* © Twentieth
     Century-Fox   177
12.1 Laurie Simmons, "Woman Listening to Radio," 1978
     © Laurie Simmons   209
12.2 *Far From Heaven* and the constructed space (2002)
     © Vulcan Productions/Focus Features   226

Notes on Contributors

Susan Courtney is Associate Professor in the Film and Media Studies Program and the Department of English at the University of South Carolina. She was a visiting fellow at the Tanner Humanities Center at the University of Utah in 2010–11. She is the author of *Hollywood Fantasies of Miscegenation: Spectacular Narratives of Gender and Race, 1903–1967* (2005).

David Culbert is John L. Loos Professor of History, Louisiana State University, Baton Rouge, and former editor of the *Historical Journal of Film, Radio and Television*. His many books include *News for Everyman* (1976), *Mission to Moscow* (1980), *Film & Propaganda in America* (5 vols, 1990–93), *World War II, Film, and History* (1996) with John Chambers; *Propaganda and Mass Persuasion* (2003) with Nicholas J. Cull and David Welch, and the translation of Leni Riefenstahl's *Behind the Scenes of the National Party Convention Film* (2009). Culbert was director of historical research and associate producer for Ken Burns's *Huey Long* (1985), co-producer of *Television's Vietnam* (1986), and the American consultant for Ray Mueller's *The Wonderful Horrible Life of Leni Riefenstahl* (1993).

Nicholas J. Cull is Professor of Public Diplomacy and Director of the Masters Degree in Public Diplomacy at the University of Southern California. He has taught at the University of Birmingham and the University of Leicester (UK). He is the author of *Selling War* (1995), *The Cold War and the United States Information Agency: American Propaganda and Public Diplomacy, 1945–1989* (2008), and *Projecting Empire: Imperialism and Popular Cinema* (2009) with James Chapman. He is the President of the International Association for Media and History (IAMHIST).

Vera Dika teaches at New Jersey City University and is the author of *Games of Terror: Halloween and the Films of the Stalker Cycle* (1991) and *Recycled Culture in Contemporary Art and Film: The Uses of Nostalgia* (2003). Her work has appeared in *Artforum* and the *Los Angeles Times*. She also contributed to Nick Browne's *The Godfather Trilogy* (2001) and several other edited collections on film. She is a founding editor of the *Millennium Film Journal*.

Notes on Contributors

David Eldridge is Director of American Studies at the University of Hull, where he has lectured in American history and cinema since 2000. He is the author of *Hollywood's History Films* (2006) and *American Culture in the 1930s* (2008). His articles have appeared in the *Journal of American Studies* and the *Historical Journal of Film, Radio and Television*. Eldridge's "Dear Owen: The CIA, Luigi Luraschi and Hollywood in 1953" (*Historical Journal of Film, Radio and Television*, 2000) exposed the identity of a "mole" in Paramount Studios who was reporting to the CIA at the height of the Cold War.

Vittorio Hösle is Paul Kimball Professor of Arts and Letters at the University of Notre Dame (with concurrent appointments in the Departments of German, Philosophy, and Political Science). He is the author of numerous books and articles, including *Hegel's System* (1987), *Objective Idealism: Ethics and Politics* (1998), *The Dead Philosopher's Café: An Exchange of Letters for Children and Adults* (with Nora K., 2000), and *Woody Allen: An Essay on the Nature of the Comical* (2007).

Marcia Landy is Distinguished Professor of English and Film Studies, with a secondary appointment in the French and Italian Department at the University of Pittsburgh. Her publications include *British Genres* (1991), *The Folklore of Consensus: Theatricality in Italian Cinema* (1998), *Italian Cinema* (2000), *The Historical Film: History and Memory in Media* (2001), *Stars: The Film Reader* (with Lucy Fischer, 2004), and *Stardom Italian Style: Screen Performance and Personality in Italian Cinema* (2008), and essays in *Screen*, the *Journal of Film and Television*, the *Quarterly Review of Film and Video*, the *Historical Journal of Film, Radio, and Television*, *KinoKultura*, and *boundary 2*.

Marc W. Roche is the Rev. Edmund P. Joyce, CSC, Professor of German Language and Literature and Concurrent Professor of Philosophy at the University of Notre Dame. He has written six books, including *Tragedy and Comedy: A Systematic Study and a Critique of Hegel* (1998), *Die Moral der Kunst: Über Literatur und Ethik* (2002), and *Why Literature Matters in the 21st Century* (2004). His film publications explore the work of Alfred Hitchcock, Woody Allen, John Ford, and Clint Eastwood.

Robert Rosenstone, novelist, memoirist, biographer, historian, and theorist of film and history, is Professor of History at the California Institute of Technology. He is the founding editor of *Rethinking History: The Journal of Theory and Practice* and associate editor of *Film Historia*. Rosenstone is the author of *Mirror in the Shrine: American Encounters* *with Meiji Japan* (1991), *Visions of the Past: The Challenge of Film to Our Idea of History* (1995), *Romantic Revolutionary: A Biography of John Reed* (1981; rev. 2001), *The Man Who Swam into History* (2005), *History on Film / Film on History* (2006), *The King of Odessa* (2007), and *Crusade on the Left: The Lincoln Battalion in the Spanish Civil War* (2009).

Ian Scott lectures in the American Studies Department at the University of Manchester (UK). He is the author of *American Politics in Hollywood Film* (2000) and *In Capra's Shadow: The Life and Career of Robert Riskin* (2006). His articles have appeared in *Film Historia*, the *Journal of American History*, *Film and History*, and in Peter Rollins and John E. O'Connor's *Why We Fought: America's Wars in Film and History* (2008).

Robert Sklar is Professor Emeritus of Cinema at New York University, where he taught in the Cinema Studies Department for 32 years. Among his books are *Movie-Made America: A Cultural History of American Movies* (1975; rev. 1994), *Resisting Images: Essays on Cinema and History* (with Charles Musser, 1990), *City Boys: Cagney, Bogart, Garfield* (1992), *Silent Screens: The Decline and Transformation of the American Movie Theater* (2000), and *A World History of Film* (2003; an updated edition of his *Film: An International History of the Medium*). He is a member of the National Film Preservation Board and of the National Society of Film Critics, and is a contributing editor and film reviewer for the quarterly magazine *Cineaste*.

J.E. Smyth is Associate Professor in the School of Comparative American Studies and the History Department at the University of Warwick (UK). Smyth is the author of *Reconstructing American Historical Cinema from Cimarron to Citizen Kane* (2006) and *Edna Ferber's Hollywood: American Fictions of Gender, Race, and History* (2009). Her articles have appeared in *Rethinking History*, *American Studies*, the *Historical Journal of Film, Radio and Television*, and several edited collections on Hollywood cinema.

Warren I. Susman (1927–85) taught at Cornell, Northwestern, Reed College, and finally Rutgers University, where he chaired the History Department from 1973 to 1979. Susman's work continues to have a profound impact on American Studies research and writing. His numerous books include *History and the American Intellectual: Uses of a Usable Past* (1964), *Culture and Commitment, 1929–1945* (1973), *American History: Selected Topics in Twentieth-Century History* (1983), and *Culture as History* (1985).

Introduction

[T]he filmmaker, simply because he operates directly in terms of the actual manipulation of time and space, because in his editing he makes arrangements of time and space that shatter simple chronology, the traditional unities of time and space act as an historian faced with the same problem of finding the proper arrangement of materials to provide a view of the process which is his history. Thus films demonstrate—even if unconsciously and even when the subject matter is not specifically historical—a vision of history as process.

Warren I. Susman (1983)

Given the often acrimonious and repetitive contemporary debates about whether filmmakers are capable of constructing and interpreting history, it may come as a surprise to read Warren Susman's words, now nearly thirty years old. In "Film and History: Artifact and Experience," reproduced in Chapter 1, Susman maps the field of American cinema and history, arguing that films engaged the past on several levels: as products of wider historical events, as reflections of their production eras, as self-conscious interpreters of history, and as powerful historical agents for change. Susman acknowledges that while all films are more or less products of their production years, they are not necessarily passive reflections of the social milieu. He warns social historians interested in cinema, "This is the question most often asked and most often too simply answered." He continues:

Too often historians fail to be alert to the warning Vico provides us: the words and images may contain disguised or unconscious assumptions and perceptions, clues to issues and concerns often fundamental to the filmmakers, but not obvious because we fail in our effort to see as they saw, feel as they felt.[1]

It was a call for more rigorous cinema scholarship, an analytical, historically adapted eye that both anticipates the tenets of the "new film history" of the mid-1980s and argues for a renewed attention to the complexities of visual discourse.

But while Susman outlines four major areas of interaction between American film and American history, it is his discussion of Hollywood cinema's potential to articulate self-conscious, historiographic discourse and engage critically with the past which resonates most powerfully with the chapters in this book. Susman puts it very simply: "John Ford is perhaps the most influential *historian* of the United States in the twentieth century." Here, Susman was effectively clashing with a generation of film scholars and historians who claimed Ford was an auteur and mythmaker, but never a historian. Until very recently, film studies was still living with the legacy of *Cahiers du cinéma*'s article on Ford's *Young Mr. Lincoln* (1939), in which the authors famously claimed that the film made only an unconscious critical intervention about Lincoln's personality.[2] *Cahiers*'s view of even an acknowledged auteur like Ford mirrored the consensus on all American historical films made in studio-era Hollywood—namely, that they reflected the conservative agendas of corporate entities and old-fashioned, unchallenged myths. Because Hollywood films allegedly reflected dominant historical ideas and passively replicated national myths, historians similarly argued that Hollywood could not "do" history.

Several years after Susman's intervention, the English translation of Marc Ferro's *Cinema and History* appeared.[3] Ferro's question, "Does a Filmic Writing of History Exist?", has haunted Hollywood's historical work for decades. Film scholars and historians, almost always divided in their evaluations of historical cinema, have been united in denying Hollywood, and especially studio-era Hollywood, the ability to create a new "film historiography" or, as Hayden White so uneuphoniously coined the term in 1988, "historiophoty."[4] But what is meant by "a filmic writing of history"? Robert Rosenstone has argued for certain filmmakers' self-conscious ability to engage with and critique the past and its relationship to the present, but states that cinema has a different "filmic" language quite apart from the one historians write. Ferro and Rosenstone's work, key in widening interest in historical filmmaking, has also tended to perpetuate a separate but equal formulation of cinematic history and traditional historiography.

Yet, Susman again provides a methodological bridge between written and visual historical discourse and between the concerns of historians and film scholars. As he argues:

> because [the filmmaker] operates directly in terms of the actual manipu-
> lation of time and space, because in his editing he makes arrangements
> of time and space that shatter simple chronology, the traditional unities
> of time and space act as an historian faced with the same problem of
> finding the proper arrangement of materials to provide a view of the
> process which is his history.

There is a long tradition in film theory of equating a "shot" with a "word," and a sequence with a sentence, but here Susman also invests the editing process with an overarching historical argument. As historians cut and paste to suit their historical perspectives or ideological agendas, so too do filmmakers cut and paste their historical material. At a more mundane level, one might argue that a filmic "writing" of history is certainly possible, since all historical films are essentially adapted texts (in that they originate as researched scripts) and frequently employ projected text, document inserts, voiceover narration, and flashbacks as hallmarks of the genre. It is fitting that the scholar most associated with American Studies in the twentieth century provided the study of American historical filmmaking with an interdisciplinary path away from polarizing debates and methodological canons.

Rather than fostering a separate but equal formulation for Hollywood's films about the American past, this book argues for a mixed visual historiography for Hollywood. It is also a fundamentally interdisciplinary volume. The contributors all approach Hollywood cinema and the American historical film from different academic fields and backgrounds. Many hold joint appointments in already deeply interdisciplinary departments. Each approach is different, and none is valorized over another. There is also no intention here of collecting a "canon" of acceptable or lionized historical films about the American past, and then neatly assessing their historical peccadilloes and discourses. Although some of films discussed here would fit the most stringent historian's criteria for historical analysis, the scholarly spectrum is necessarily broad and inclusive.

If the collection spans a wide range of films, from the first silent versions of *The Virginian* and D.W. Griffith's *Birth of a Nation* to Todd Haynes's *Far From Heaven* (2002) and Clint Eastwood's *Changeling* (2008), then the genres they also "belong" to are equally wide-ranging. For this is the key to the richness of the field: historical filmmaking—regardless of whether the topic is American, African, European, or Asian history—is transgeneric. From the early studio era, Hollywood genre films with predominantly American settings—among them Westerns, musicals, war films, women's melodramas, literary adaptations, biopics, film noirs, and gangster pictures—often doubled as films about the American past. Filmmakers and critics in John Ford's generation often referred to films with American historical content as "Americana" or "U.S. historical melodramas," yet the vocabulary of historical filmmaking included sagas, generational dramas, biopics and biodramas, women's sentimental dramas, and classic adaptations. When contemporary films had historical prologues, flashback narration, projected textual touches or visual sequences that alluded to the past or past film productions, American trade critics usually drew attention to them, noting a variety of historical resonances in an inclusive manner. Studio publicity also made efforts to relate the films to historical currents and trends outside the confines of mainstream Hollywood discourse. American history was a prestigious style choice that connected Hollywood to broader historical and cultural discourses.

Yet, when film historians and cultural critics have relied upon individual genre histories to impose order on Hollywood filmmaking, the tendency has been either to ignore the historical contexts within the films or isolate them as "bad" examples of the genre due to their historical content and non-"timeless" qualities. As I've argued elsewhere, this practice had a negative critical impact upon Westerns as diverse as *Cimarron* (1931), *Duel in the Sun* (1946), and *Giant* (1956).[5] At the risk of sounding polemical, "genre cleansing" has prevented scholars and students from acknowledging Westerns like *The Man Who Shot Liberty Valance* (1962), gangster films like *Some Like It Hot* (1959), women's historical pictures like *Julia* (1977), nostalgia films like *Far From Heaven* (2002), and even classic Civil War epics like *Gone with the Wind* (1939) as complex historical films. As David Eldridge argues persuasively in his study of *Some Like It Hot*, while some scholars are in favor of

> consigning to "the waste heap" any movie that would "simplify history, trivialize it, or bend it to shape the needs of the artist" . . . such a waste heap would include thousands of melodramas, comedies, Westerns, musicals, swashbuckling adventures, and other period-set films, especially those made in the "classical" Hollywood studio era.

Ironically, while academic and mainstream scholarship has separated and graded Hollywood films in their adherence to often artificial genre elements and equally artificial assumptions of historical objectivity, studio-era filmmakers and film critics approached history, and particularly American history, with a nuanced and flexible appreciation of its cultural impact.[6] The studio era witnessed the creation of research libraries, the mass purchase of historical novels and properties for script development, targeted publicity campaigns, and the first important critical recognition of historical films as Hollywood's main realm of "prestige cinema." Historical issues and a unique historical film language developed to link all of these mainstays of the Hollywood genre system. In the post-studio era, these production practices and genres became other sites of nostalgic speculation and debate.

★ ★ ★

Hollywood and the American Historical Film is the first interdisciplinary attempt in over thirty years to probe the full range of theoretical and historical contexts of films made about the American past from the silent era to the present.[7] It is also unique, in that the majority of chapters consider films made during the studio era; even those chapters which discuss films released beyond the historical borders of the studio system are haunted by its shifting contexts and legacies. Most offer distinctly revisionist perspectives. As Warren Susman and Robert Rosenstone have argued, the time is past for questioning whether films *can* reflect upon their production eras or serious historical issues. Although it has taken longer to recognize Hollywood's powerful and nuanced contributions to the adaptation, narration, and marketing of national history than the cinemas of Europe, in this volume, film historians take Hollywood, the American historical film, and its legacy to new levels.

In Chapter 2, David Culbert re-examines the origins of perhaps the most notorious American historical film, *The Birth of a Nation* (1915), and the degree to which its historical pretensions engaged mainstream historiography and public opinion. Culbert's deft analysis exposes many tenacious public assumptions about Griffith's alleged investment in the Lost Cause myth, representation of Civil War and Reconstruction history, and the impact of the musical score. But in Marcia Landy's study of the pre-Second World War Western, theories of the history of cinema and historiographic debate follow a similar arc, where the movement-image and the tenets of progressive history upholding the frontier discourse are fractured by the crisis of war. Susan Courtney's exploration of the "plantation suture," developed in *Gone with the Wind* and deconstructed by *A Streetcar Named Desire*, looks at a similar visual crisis, in which the spatial formulation of the "Big House" and its accompanying racial narrative and historical certainty are destabilized by the spatial "violation" of Blanche DuBois in Elia Kazan's adaptation of *Streetcar*. Courtney's approach not only formulates a powerful visual argument about Southern history through suture and spatial positioning, but also looks at the ways one film can speculate on the past constructed by another historical film text. Ensuing chapters by myself, Ian Scott, and Vera Dika explore variations of this approach.

Warren Susman was one of the first major critics to even notice there were conflicting Hollywood stories about the silent era and to suggest this as an area for future research. It was a controversial viewpoint. For when it comes to historical subject matter, films about Hollywood's past might appear to be the most historiographically corrupt material imaginable. In an industry where stars' biographies were freely invented by the columnists and where you were only "as good as your last picture," historical speculation was equated with

failure. Hollywood's safety lay in modernity and youth. But as Robert
Sklar points out in Chapter 5, like any vampire, Hollywood's youthful
image masked a varied past. In "Hollywood about Hollywood," Sklar
takes up the challenge of assessing the film industry's own attitudes
toward its past in the 1950s, effectively engaging alternate historiog-
raphies of Hollywood. As he points out, Hollywood's postwar "crisis"
forced several filmmakers to

> offer up the Hollywood industry not as an entity unaltered in form
> throughout time, but as a malleable subject amenable to critical analysis
> and evaluation.

In particular, Billy Wilder's *Sunset Boulevard* (1950),Vincente Minnelli's
The Bad and the Beautiful (1952), and George Cukor's remake of *A Star
Is Born* (1954)

> are rare instances of their genre: works that inscribe as well as foster a
> historiographical approach to U.S. motion picture history.

Wilder's work is also the subject of David Eldridge's chapter on *Some
Like It Hot* (1959). Although most critical assessments of studio-era
gangster pictures refuse to consider them as American historical films,
Some Like It Hot seems deliberately to "not take history seriously." In fact,
it is probably, like so many Hollywood "historical" films, the one in
this collection most guaranteed to raise the hackles of historians writing
about American cinema. Yet, as Eldridge demonstrates, Billy Wilder
and co-writer I.A.L. Diamond's manipulation of 1920s gang history
in *Some Like It Hot* enabled the director to get Legion of Decency
approval for a film about homosexuality and transsexuality, controversial
historical subjects for both 1920s and 1950s audiences.

   Mark W. Roche and Vitorrio Hösle first joined forces to explore
John Ford's *The Man Who Shot Liberty Valance* in 1993. Though many
scholars have written about this late Western, and some have acknowledged Ford's critical view of the West, no one, in my opinion, comes
closer to understanding the depth of Ford's historical philosophy than
they. In Chapter 7, Roche and Hösle, like Warren Susman, draw on
the historical philosophy of Giambattista Vico. In this case, Vico's
critical perspective on what is lost between the transition from the
heroic age to the reasoned modern age of men is used to illumi-
nate Ford's disillusionment with the frontier past and its written
and falsified memorialization. Historians have viewed Vico's work
as a precursor of the postmodern disaffection with conventional,
progressive, "Whiggish" philosophies of history; yet one wonders,

given Roche's and Hösle's scholarship, not only whether Ford was America's most popular Western historian, but also whether he was an early, popular proponent of the revisionist New Western History more recently associated with the historical writings of Patricia Nelson Limerick and Richard White.

Ford's juxtaposition of the museum-piece stagecoach and the dreaded progress of the railroad was a brilliant visual historical motif; its critical implications would be used not only in future Westerns, but also in Coppola's *The Godfather* (1972), when Mafia chiefs shake hands in front of a massive painting of an approaching train, signalling the end of innocent, "drug-free" crime in America, and the beginning of no-holds-barred, amoral capitalism (Illustration I.1). This historical shorthand not only invokes the critique of American corporate capitalism, but also proves that even the most classic of genre films is never mummified in its mythic construction of the past.[8]

While the chapter by Roche and Hösle chapter shows a master filmmaker paying loving, if critical, tribute to the Hollywood film tradition that fostered his unique brand of historical filmmaking, in Chapter 8, Nicholas J. Cull shows the aging studio system in another light. Although the biopic, like the Western, has been a critical mainstay of the study of historical filmmaking in Hollywood, Cull presents

Illustration I.1   The Godfather (1972) and the image of frontier capitalism © Paramount Pictures Corporation

a highly complex, revisionist interpretation of Hollywood's efforts
to "construct public history" through the trope of the great male
life—in this case, Warner Bros.'s biography of John F. Kennedy, *PT
109* (1963). As Cull shows, the link between Hollywood and government power should never be taken for granted; studio efforts to court
Washington and Washington's efforts to control Hollywood often
ended in disaster.

Fred Zinnemann's *Julia* shows yet another way of interpreting
history. Though long overshadowed by androcentric Westerns, gangster films, war pictures, and biopics, the women's historical film represented a longstanding, powerful component of Hollywood production
and paid heed to the contemporaneous market research legitimizing
women as America's main reading and cinema-going audience.[9]
Often, these films were tied to the market of women's historical fiction,
a tradition which certainly extends to *Gone with the Wind* (1939). In
"The Long Road of Women's Memory," I explore Zinnemann's *Julia*
as a product of and response to the troubled adaptation of women's
cinematic history. In *Julia*, Zinnemann breaks all the rules of traditional
biopics and uses oral narration and a non-chronological structure to
dramatize the lives of two women, playwright Lillian Hellman and her
friend, American antifascist leader, "Julia." Robert Rosenstone explores
something similar in his discussion of *Glory* (1989). Here, Rosenstone
points out contemporary and still almost entirely white Hollywood's
sporadic ability to visualize the history of African Americans via this
"biopic" of Civil War hero Robert Gould Shaw. *Glory*'s use of diaries
and letters, related in a predominantly "white" voiceover, in some
measure articulates the problems of documenting the lives of marginalized Americans.

The contributors in this book challenge the ahistorical or modern
critical formulation of Hollywood films about Hollywood and
gangster pictures; they interrogate easy "mythic" formulations of the
Western, and refocus debates on racial and gender dynamics in the
biopic. But can that bastion of modern America, film noir, embody
a distinct attitude toward the American past? Certainly, neo-noir
films can be seen as part of the "nostalgia" trend in recent cinema
discussed by Vera Dika in Chapter 12. But one might also argue that
Philip Marlowe and his private-eye colleagues inhabit a powerful,
anti-progressive metaphor for the consequences of American history.
As Ian Scott argues in his study of Clint Eastwood's *Changeling* (2008)
and Roman Polanski's *Chinatown* (1974), the search for objective truth,
for law and order, is also the search through a corrupt and tangled
past. As Herman Mankiewicz and Orson Welles's reporter, Thompson,

discovers in *Citizen Kane* (1941), no story is ever completely found, and much key evidence is lost. That so many culprits in the classic and neo-noir novels and films are Americans escaping to the Western landscapes of Los Angeles and San Francisco, remaking their identities in an "empty" frontier past, says as much about America's obsession with the frontier myth as it does about its moral bankruptcy (*The Maltese Falcon*, 1941; *Murder, My Sweet*, 1944; *Out of the Past*, 1947; *Vertigo*, 1958; *L.A. Confidential*, 1997).[10]

In the final two chapters, Ian Scott and Vera Dika look at the legacies of Los Angeles and the postwar studio era as sites of disturbing nostalgia, challenging Fredric Jameson's original model for the historically and visually harmless nostalgia picture.[11] Dika's unique formulation of regret, a historically-critical variant of the original "nostalgia" impulse in 1970s cinema, draws upon many historical contexts—not only postwar American social history, but postwar Hollywood's genre of women's melodrama, dominated by Douglas Sirk and later reconfigured through the world of Rainer Werner Fassbinder. As Dika argues, Todd Haynes's *Far From Heaven*, and even the enormously popular "nostalgia" television series, *Mad Men* (2007–), look back on a past overburdened with excessively perfect Hollywood images. Contemporary female spectators, however mesmerized, are more than happy to stay outside that historical frame.

This book emerged thanks to the cooperation and generous support of Kate Haines and Palgrave Macmillan. I am indebted to Kate's flexibility, thoughtful criticism, and commitment to the project's interdisciplinarity. Jenni Burnell, Jenna Steventon, and Felicity Noble have been a pleasure to work with. I would also like to acknowledge my copyeditor, Keith Povey. I am especially grateful to the contributors for their original belief in the project and their commitment to rethink and challenge traditional definitions and approaches to Hollywood's American historical films. I also want to thank Kim Wade, Alistair and Isobel Galloway, and Rebecca Earle for their patience and sympathy. Zachary and Zoe were neither patient nor sympathetic, but managed to drag me away from the screen for my own good. Many of us in this book owe debts of thanks to archivists and friends Ned Comstock, Linda Mehr, Barbara Hall, Jenny Romero, Lauren Buisson, and Sandra Joy Lee—in this case, particularly, "the names *behind* the title." Through several years of teaching courses on American historical filmmaking in Hollywood's studio era, my students have helped me to pinpoint areas in need of new perspectives and research. This book is for them and others like them who want to look back at the system and remember with affectionate regret.

J.E. SMYTH

Notes

1. Susman refers here to the text of Giambattista Vico, *The New Science* [1725], trans. David Marsh (London: Penguin, 2000).

2. Editors of *Cahiers du cinéma*, "John Ford's *Young Mr. Lincoln*" [1970], reprinted in Philip Rosen (ed.), *Narrative, Apparatus, Ideology: A Film Theory Reader* (New York: Columbia University Press, 1986): 444–82. See J.E. Smyth, *Reconstructing American Historical Cinema: From* Cimarron *to* Citizen Kane (Lexington: University Press of Kentucky, 2006), 15–17, 176, 181.

3. Marc Ferro, trans. Naomi Greene, *Cinema and History* (Detroit: Wayne States University Press, 1988): 161–3.

4. Hayden White, "Historiography and Historiophoty," *American Historical Review* 93(5) (December 1988): 1193–9; Ferro: 161–3.

5. These films also share the double burden of being "women's" Westerns in a film genre and historical space traditionally defined as masculine (Smyth, 2006: 116). For a sample of critic Bosley Crowther's contempt for Westerns which step outside too many boundaries, see Crowther, "*Duel in the Sun:* Selznick's Lavish Western That Stars Jennifer Jones, Gregory Peck, Opens at Loew's Theatres," *New York Times* (May 8, 1947).

6. David Eldridge, *Hollywood's History Films* (London: IB Tauris, 2006); Smyth (2006).

7. John E. O'Connor and Peter C. Rollins (eds.), *American History/American Film* (New York: Ungar, 1979).

8. Fredric Jameson and many of the scholars in Nick Browne's anthology (Berkeley: University of California Press, 2000) have argued the first *Godfather* lacks the Marxist dialectic and critical attitude toward history in part two, yet Coppola's awareness of the insidious frontier legacy operating within the world of the twentieth-century Mafia is obvious throughout part one. See also Jameson, "Reification and Utopia in Mass Culture" [1979], in *Signatures of the Visible* (London: Routledge, 1990): 9–34.

9. See, for example, Jason Joy, "Introducing—A Shopping Guide to the Movies," [1929], Los Angeles: MPPDA, Crawford Collection, Yale University; Robert and Helen Lynd, *Middletown* (New York: Harcourt Brace, 1929); Tino Balio, *Grand Design: Hollywood As a Modern Business Enterprise, 1930–1939* (Los Angeles: University of California Press, 1993): 1; J.E. Smyth, *Edna Ferber's Hollywood: American Fictions of Gender, Race, and History* (Austin: University of Texas Press, 2009): 8–28.

10. David Fine, *Imagining Los Angeles: A City in Fiction* (Reno: University of Nevada Press, 2000).

11. Fredric Jameson, "Postmodernism and Consumer Society," in Hal Foster (ed.), *The Anti-Aesthetic: Essays on Postmodern Culture* (Port Townsend: Bay Press, 1983): 111–25.

1

Film and History: Artifact and Experience[1]

Warren I. Susman

For most historians films are first and foremost artifacts, human-made objects for particular human use much like the many other objects with which man fills his environment. For some historians these artifacts, again like many others, can become, in the historians' limited special vocabulary, "documents" or "sources"—works that can be read in such a way as to provide knowledge of the history of the people who make and use such objects. Not all historians are comfortable with such sources: they appear too slippery, too easily manipulated. Others confine their use to service as additional evidence confirming what they have already learned from the use of "harder" data: films of the Depression era "document" social tensions that historians know initially from social surveys; science fiction films of the 1950s "demonstrate" the anxieties of the period of McCarthy and the Cold War, already common knowledge as the result of research on Congressional investigations or detailed study of newspapers.

Yet historians do have, in their own pre-professional past, a major work that offers at least encouragement for a wider view of such artifacts. In *The New Science*, Giambattista Vico argued that there were, in fact, only three "totally incorruptible" sources for true historical knowledge: language, mythologies, and antiquities. Antiquities—literary monuments and the like—embodied the "beliefs of the age," the "common sense" of a people, the unquestioned and unreflected-upon assumptions held by all. Mythologies revealed the real "civic history" of the first peoples and expressed the way they saw, understood, and reacted to the world around them. Words and images were natural symbols by which men expressed their feelings, attitudes, and thoughts. In analyzing these, the historian might witness "the development of the morphology of the symbolic system" which was "one with the growth of a culture of which it is the central organ." Thus,

1

as Isaiah Berlin, one of Vico's ablest interpreters, sums up, "language, myths, antiquities reflect the various fashions in which the social or economic or spiritual problems or realities were refracted in the minds of our ancestors." They were—primitive and distorted as they might often be—important ways of recognizing social facts and reacting to them. If historians asked of them the right questions—always treating them seriously, if not literally—they might find that they had raised a curtain on the past enabling them to reconstruct, not simply a parade of famous men, significant events, and major institutions, but the very way of life, the very "style" of an entire society. But the new questions to be asked of old familiar data were what was important:

> What kind of men can have talked, written . . . created as these men did? What must the natures and lives of such men have been, and what kind of social experiences must have shaped them, to have generated the successive stages through which they developed? Can a fixed order or pattern of such stages be shown to follow . . . from the changing nature of such men, or, may it be, of all men and societies as such? . . . What comes into being, at what time, in what fashion?

I am, of course, aware that Vico is speaking of ancient peoples, peoples without our modern exceptional self-consciousness and our sophisticated command of powerful technology. Further, I am not fully prepared to commit myself to the idea that film may be one of the "incorruptible" historical sources, as later comments on the problems of film text and contexts will suggest. But I am convinced that, as artifact, the individual film and the sequence of films that makes the history of the moving-image media can be analyzed in very much the way that Vico uses languages, myth, and antiquities. The result would offer us—along with the study of other cultural products—clues to the symbolic system basic to the culture, the fundamental patterns of belief, stated and unstated, the ways of responding to problems and realities that define the essence of a society, its style.

To move in this direction, historians must probe at least four questions that key on the relationship between "history" and "film." Each provides a special problematic of its own; each raises methodological issues centering on the complex relationship between "text" and "context," "film" and "history."

First, in what sense can film be seen as a *product* of history, and what do we learn as we treat it this way? We know that film and what we associate with the modern media is a function of a particular time and a particular place: they became possible at a given moment historians have designated the Communication Revolution, a period when the application of new sources of power produced a series of remarkable inventions that facilitated an incredibly rapid movement of men, goods, services, and ideas. One of the most amazing consequences of these developments was the liberation of sound and image from any grounding in a specific time or a particular place. This was related to new ways of perceiving the world itself, and even new ideas about perception: an intellectual revolution with radically different ideas about time and space. But there was, as well, a significant transformation of the social order: historians speak of an Organizational Revolution, new forms of human organization that became characteristic of the culture, including the vital corporate form that a whole economic order depended upon. This Organizational Revolution, made possible in large part by the revolution in communications itself, produced a New Class: a growing group within the social order with considerable power who were neither traditional workers nor owners of the productive operations of the society. Rather, these were salaried or self-employed professionals, engineers, managers, experts, technicians, white-collar workers, providers of service and ideas rather than goods. These changes were also accompanied by alterations in ideology or, at the very least, a movement toward a system of values and beliefs that challenged the long-established views of the traditional world of the Republican, Puritan, Pioneer, Producer-Capitalist. All of these transformations created tensions within and between each of the orders, changes often proceeding at different rates in the different orders.

If film is, in fact, the product of these changes—and that proposition is worth a firm effort to establish—it may be possible to examine individual films, groups of films, or the total sequences of all films in such a way as to discover the particular relationship that prevailed between the various orders at any particular moment in time or in any specific place. A film represents a significant arrangement of technology, social organization, and moral ideas; it comes into existence within the particular boundaries of a polity and an economy. The production history of a film itself thus often re-enacts the larger historical movement of forces, and the examination of a film can inform us of these developments. Moreover, the system of representation the filmmaker uses is a key to his ideological vision; in knowing how he perceives his world, we may have some insight into the view of a whole class, if not a whole culture. He may select certain technical devices (of narrative, for example) from the "past" but use them in ways that reveal something of the changes in the three orders that have or have not occurred. A technically avant-garde art may be used to present a content that is morally traditional. A culture can be most easily recognized in terms of a series of words, images, sounds, rhythms, that are characteristically its own; each of these has a history and a careful examination of these histories—the changes in words, images, sounds, and the possible interrelationships between such changes—may give us the fundamental clues about the changes in the culture itself. Images and even sequences of images, for example, have their histories; how they are used and changed may tell us a good deal about the emerging symbolic system. A film *and* its many aspects each has its own history; those histories, in turn, can be examined as products of a larger history as well.

The second question may appear but a variant on the first: in what sense does a film *reflect* the society in which it is made and therefore tell us something about that time and that place that is of value for the historian? This is the question most often asked and most often too simply answered. In the most elemental sense—if not by definition—it is impossible to imagine any cultural product that doesn't "reflect" the culture. The issues ought, rather, to be the special or significant way in which this is, in fact, the case. In the most basic sense, films as source serve the historian as a museum does: providing vivid data about the way people looked, how they dressed, what they did and how they loved. Historians continue to mine this record. (Interestingly, in one most obvious area historians have failed to use their source: films provide a brilliant record of human movement, human speech, human gesture, and in terms of what we know about the significance of such operations in various cultures, it is surprising that historians have not devoted attention to these changing aspects of the human body in social arrangements and movements as they changed over time.) Historians also use films as a vital source of information on what people believed, their basic interests, values, and concerns at a particular moment in time. Films become an index to the key problems of a period and even more importantly, the way those problems were perceived. Too often historians fail to be alert to the warning Vico provides us: the words and images may contain disguised or unconscious assumptions and perceptions, clues to issues and concerns often fundamental to the filmmakers, but not obvious because we fail in our effort to see as they saw, feel as they felt. Obvious sociological reference frequently obscures less obvious but even more vital psychological reference. Recent re-examinations of the gangster films of the 1930s show an overwhelming concern about the nature and meaning of manhood that was often overlooked by those who picked up the more immediate clues to social issues they were already aware of as a consequence of the Depression. And, finally, the very nature of the film, form as well as content, image as well as idea, reveals the "period" of which it comes—a vision of style. Historians can refer to a film of the 1930s or the 1960s and we can be aware of certain visual, technical, and thematic similarities that make such allusions meaningful. Yet, we need to work toward a more precise realization of questions of historical style and its meaning. There are here, too, methodological dangers that make it difficult for us to deal with often brutal conflicts of style and theme within a so-called period that go often unattended. Wilder's *Sunset Boulevard* (1950) and Kelly and Donen's *Singin' In the Rain* (1952) offer us not only two different Hollywoods, but also two different *histories* of Hollywood; both are early 1950s films that achieved considerable critical acclaim, professional awards, and enthusiastic audience responses. How can the same culture claim both?

Third, this suggests the even more significant issues that are involved in the question of how film operates as an *interpreter* of history, the provider of an explanation of historical development, and an analysis of the process of history itself. This is not only a question of subject matter. There are few major events and developments and fewer major historical figures from the American and European past that have not been translated into words and images on both the large and the small screen. But even more important than this, the filmmaker, simply because he operates directly in terms of the actual manipulation of time and space, because in his editing he makes arrangements of time and space that shatter simple chronology, the traditional unities of time and space act as an historian faced with the same problem of finding the proper arrangement of materials to provide a view of the process which is his history. Thus, films demonstrate—even if unconsciously and even when the subject matter is not specifically historical—a vision of history as process. Master directors who are self-conscious in their craft impose a vision of history—how it happens and what it means—that may have a significant impact on those who see his films. John Ford is perhaps the most influential *historian* of the United States in the twentieth century. Not only do his films provide a particular view of American development through his treatment of a variety of major historical experiences, but they provide as well a philosophy of history, a vision of the process and its meaning that I suspect many Americans, at least in Ford's lifetime, held or came to hold in some measure because of his art.

With the issue of interpretation, we begin to move with film itself to the larger culture where we began. Our fourth question concerns itself with the possible role of film as agent in history: how does film *shape* history? If it is a product of the historical process, a reflection of historical development, an interpretation of that history, can it also be said to be itself a transformer or maker of history? Again, the answers range from the simple to the most problematic. Films can have an impact on lifestyles: establishment of fashions in dress and home design; patterns of behavior; characteristic language and speech. The idea of audiences *imitating* films, using films as a standard by which to judge one's own life, offers an exceptional area for investigation that must lead us beyond the Payne studies' obsession with the fact that young boys like to be like Little Caesar. The public involvement with the roles stars play on the screen and the "real" lives of the stars—the whole world of fans and gossip that color our vision of the world—raises important questions: why is this so and what are the cultural consequences? Life may indeed imitate art, but such imitations are not trivial. That kind of behavior can often reveal even ideological matters of considerable importance: everyday life often provides major clues to the structure of consciousness and the symbolic and moral order. What audiences select—and what they choose *not* to imitate—makes the issue even more complex, for neither all stars nor all roles become sources for imitation. From films, as well, come many of the major icons that are fundamental to the culture. It is possible to begin to think in terms of a set of images, words, and sounds that form the basis for an iconography crucial in particular eras or fundamental in specific ways to the life of the culture in our century. Some film images, for example, develop and retain a special meaning outside the "text" of the film itself. The image of King Kong atop the Empire State Building remains a significant American icon to generations who have never seen the film and to millions of non-Americans who continue to associate that image with American life and culture. Further, the "independent" role of such icons provides a special problem: it is part of the "context" from which we now must view the text. It impinges upon what we may mean by the text.

Thus, with the question of film as agent in history, the historian has moved away from the traditional vision of the film as artifact and has moved specifically toward the second aspect of the historian's involvement with the film: as significant experience of women, men, and children in the twentieth century. Film is an important and, for some, a fundamental aspect of life in our time, and we must understand it as part of that huge field of interest, itself as invention and concern of our century, as Henri LeFebvre has brilliantly argued.[2] (It should be noted, of course, that film is one of the most important agents in our desire to explore and record every aspect of that very everyday life, a fact that provides an ideological rationale for the entire film enterprise itself.) For an understanding of the film as experience, the historian must ask a completely new set of questions, and even seek a whole new set of materials for investigation. Here, the scholar's interest in no longer in the "document" or the text; rather, it centers on the context in which that document is experienced, the environment that may help shape the response and, even, meaning of the text and relate it to other aspects of life experience in the larger culture. Only a few examples should, at least, suggest the range of questions this raises: films themselves offer calculated images of their own worlds and work that may shape audience perceptions of film efforts: a particular view of Hollywood and what it is about; the publicity campaigns, the advertising, the promotions that sharply color our experience of a particular film; posters and still photographs (sometimes scenes not in the final film text as released); the glamour and the gossip; the fan apparatus—all of these have consequences of major importance. There is, as well, that contribution made by the particular manner and location of presentation or performance: the majestic and dimly-lighted movie palace and the comfortable well-lighted living room. There may even be, after all, a fundamental relationship between the question of viewing space and time (season as well as time of day) and the issue of social or ideological concern. Motion pictures were, in some sense, a response to the urgent social question much debated in the period in which the movies were born: how can an individual survive in a world of the crowd? Not only were the technical devices ideally suited to illustrate effectively and dramatically the problem (crowd "splendor" versus the close-up), but the huge theatre in which a patron sat among that very crowd heightened the audience's feeling of the problem. Filmmakers were aware of what was happening: the final moments of King Vidor's *The Crowd* (1928) make this clear. The camera pulls back and the family, central to Vidor's drama, is finally realized by the audience to be only a very small element in a huge audience doing precisely the same thing. Television operates, often, on a very different premise. At least since the brilliant developments of the 1950s, television has frequently concentrated its cameras on the American family and its problems and joys. In a world increasingly concerned about the maintenance of a strong family life in the United States, television devoted much of its attention to that unit. As if to heighten the effect, the viewing area for much of TV is the living room—or better yet, in the special language of the 1950s, family room.

The question of audience, difficult as it always is, is an imperative for the historian of the film experience. This issue is especially complex. The experience we are discussing is social: if we do not share it with others in a theatre, in a bar, or living room, we share it by exchanging notes with others about our experience of it. Sometimes we have films specifically crafted for a particular audience; perhaps no films ever made could have such specific knowledge of its intended audience as Capra's *Why We Fight* series. But the producers' intentions represent only one aspect of the larger issue—where, when, with whom was the film seen?

The whole question of attendance raises the issue of film as ritual: that people go (or don't go) to the movies or watch (or don't watch) television, may be more important than what they see. The whole system of distribution colors that question of ritual attendance as well— what is available to whom and when and how? This, in turn, suggests the problem of programming and how it affects our experience. More work has been done on this important question for television—when and where do news programs appear and with what effect—than programming in films: how does continuous performance (with the audience wandering in and out), double features, the ritual bill (short subjects, previews of coming attractions, newsreels, cartoons, etc.) affect the experience of certain films? But the success of various films should never lead the historian to forget those who refuse to become an audience not only for particular films, but for all films: there was, from the start, a vigorous resistance to the world of moving images, a series of critical debates, a continuous effort at censorship—all of which are crucial in any effort to analyze the film experience or even frequent particular film texts.

Any examination of audience immediately raises the question that those who undergo any film experience are also operating at the same time in a culture in which they are being affected by other popular cultural instruments as well. Students of film need to pay attention to all aspects of the popular culture, especially those born out of the same universe as film, not as a special academic exercise in inter-disciplinary studies but rather because the audience for one is usually the audience for all; and because the media borrow from one another, reinforce one another, play upon significant shared relationships. Sound was always part of the film experience, and the aim to record both sound and image centered even in the same inventor—Edison. The still photograph and photographer haunts the world of film; figures from the comics show up constantly; the world of radio and, especially, the world of the newspaper and newspaperman form almost a genre; the changing world of popular music is a common film subject. These are but a few examples. There is a world of popular culture in which films function and which films comment upon. Those interrelationships are important in any cultural analysis. There is, of course, at the same time, an increasingly self-conscious interest of filmmakers in the so-called high arts and an interesting continuing story of their use of images and perceptions from that area as well: the relationship between the various cultural forms becomes essential if we are to know the full meaning of the experience of Americans with the moving image itself.

It must be remembered that film in all its forms developed as a part of a series of aspirations of a class which wished somehow to be able to preserve for time a world of sound, motion, and color. Thus, in an important way, film is but an aspect of a cultural drive basic to the experience of everyday life so fundamental as to form the base of a new culture itself. Furthermore, the historian can never forget that, in this world—ever-dependent on an increasingly complex technology and therefore requiring ever more sharp divisions of labor, specialization, and professionalization—the possibility for the individual or amateur has grown, rather than disappeared, with ever-increasing consequences. There are home-movies and movie video-tapes (as well as amateur photographers and wide sales of tape recorders) and this very fact raises questions, not only about professionals and amateurs, but also about the interrelationship between the two worlds: everyman his own filmmaker while at the same time the audience for the work of others. This aspect of participation—the vast increase of participation as maker as well as audience—is too important an aspect of the experience with moving images in our time to be ignored.

All of this suggests important questions about the relationship between text—the film as artifact—and the context—the film as experience. History too, represents two separate things: it is the ongoing flux of human experience over time and space, *and* the effort by men and women to order and structure that experience in an effort to provide special meaning. That work itself—the history—also becomes an artifact and it, in turn, operates within a context as it becomes part of that flux of experience again. The historian sees the film in order, first, to reconstruct the major symbolic system that is at the core of the culture. But this very involvement becomes itself a part of the context, part of the world of experience. Thus, the text never remains static or even constant: text and context interrelate in history itself, and in the work of the historian.

Notes

1. This paper was originally presented at the Astoria Foundation in New York in November 1983. It was then reprinted for *Film and History* (1985) and is reprinted here with permission of the editor.
2. Henri LeFebvre (1901–91), French sociologist, wrote *The Critique of Everyday Life* (1947) and *The Production of Space* (1974), among other works.

2

Film History, Reconstruction, and Southern Legendary History in *The Birth of a Nation*

David Culbert

The timing was right: 1915 was the fiftieth anniversary of the end of the Civil War. D.W. Griffith's notorious film masterpiece, *The Birth of a Nation*, purports to reveal the truth of America's Civil War and Reconstruction from 1861 to 1877. The film is mostly set in a small town in the Piedmont part of South Carolina, although there are scenes which take place in Washington, DC, and a series of battles which purport to show some of the bitterest parts of the war, such as the burning of Atlanta or the final siege at Petersburg, Virginia. The film itself was shot entirely in California, so its geographical location is at best intended to suggest an approximate terrain. There are no location shots, although a number of scenes, such as the assassination of Abraham Lincoln, are taken—intertitles insist—directly from actual historic engravings or photographs.

Griffith's film has four claims on history. First, it is a brilliant piece of filmmaking, demonstrating the new medium of film deserved serious attention as an art form. Second, it is the lavish, feature-length film which transforms American cinema-going, showing distributors the possibility of tickets at previously undreamed-of prices, and in its commercial success suggesting an upscale audience largely untapped before 1915. Third, the film's notorious racial stereotypes—and their seeming acceptance by most viewers at the time—suggest that the film, at a minimum, reflects widespread attitudes in white America about African Americans. Fourth, the film seems to present a Southern legendary view of the Civil War and Reconstruction, in which the Lost Cause is wedded to an assessment of Reconstruction as "the tragic era."[1]

The bibliography on *The Birth of a Nation* is unrivaled by that of any other feature film. Three recent books are of particular value.

Melvyn Stokes published a comprehensive history of the film in 2007, in which he treats the film in terms of film history, and in terms of social history, that is, the changing societal attitudes towards racial stereotyping in the film. Paolo Cherchi Usai's eighth volume in *The Griffith Project*, published in 2004, provides valuable information about the film's production, its racial stereotyping, and the complicated history of extant copies of the film, plus problems in creating an authoritative original print from surviving variants. In 1997, Martin Miller Marks published *Music and the Silent Film*, an authoritative study of the musical score for the film.[2]

Griffith's film was previewed at the Loring Opera House, in Riverside, California, on January 1, 1915. It premiered in Los Angeles on February 8, still called *The Clansman*; the New York opening occurred on March 3, at which time a score by Joseph Carl Breil was added. A special screening for cabinet members and Supreme Court justices took place at the Raleigh Hotel in Washington, DC, on February 19, 1915. A special screening took place in the White House, before Woodrow Wilson, President of the United States, on February 18. It was after this private screening that Wilson is alleged to have said, "It is like history written with lightning. And my only regret is that it is all so terribly true." Though few historians have resisted accepting Wilson's words as accurate, Wilson's biographer discovered that the first use of this statement seems to have been in an article published in 1937. Wilson's Southern attitudes towards African Americans are documented in many other places, but he was anything but an enthusiast for film, so the statement would be more interesting—if true—as an example of a president's acceptance of a new mass medium than as a conclusive statement as to Wilson's attitude about race. Wilson's press secretary issued a stern warning to Griffith not to try and exploit the president's name as an endorsement for the film. Wilson certainly was hostile to any attempt to use his name for commercial endorsements.[3]

The New York release of Griffith's film coincided almost exactly with a landmark United States Supreme Court decision, *Mutual Film Corporation v. Industrial Commission of Ohio* (1915), in which a unanimous court argued that film was akin to vaudeville shows, "a business, pure and simple," but with a "capacity for evil," which should indeed be subject to prior censorship and was therefore not protected by First Amendment free speech guarantees. This validated a series of state and municipal boards of censorship, giving local authorities the right to suppress a film entirely, or to demand various deletions.[4] Griffith advanced his free speech case in a celebrated (or notorious) intertitle advocating free speech for the inflammatory contents of his film.

Right from the start, the National Association for the Advancement of Colored People (NAACP) tried to use state and city censors to block the showing of a film so filled with racial stereotypes. Melvyn Stokes is the most recent film historian to explore this exhaustively studied censorship campaign by the NAACP. His conclusion about the effectiveness of the protest seems persuasive:

> There can be little doubt that the attitudes expressed in the film were unexceptional to the vast majority of the white American population. Most critics who viewed the film could not understand why it generated such controversy, and it is probable that ordinary spectators reacted in much the same way. As the twentieth century moved on, however, racial attitudes began to change: the increasing success of the obsessive NAACP campaign against the film functioned as a barometer of this evolution.[5]

It is perhaps worth noting, for example, that when the film played in Boston, the site of the powerful NAACP opposition, the program distributed to viewers noted proudly that the theater was safe from something clearly on many a theater-goers' mind: "Equipped with three celebrated Regan water curtains which are positive in their action. Also an Asbestos Curtain."[6]

David Wark Griffith (1875–1948) was born in Kentucky. He often spoke of stories of the Civil War and Reconstruction which he had heard from his father. Another Southerner, Thomas Dixon, Jr., (1864–1946) a Baptist minister, successful playwright and novelist, and one-time classmate of Woodrow Wilson in the new doctoral program in history at Johns Hopkins University, enjoyed great commercial success with historical novels, including *The Leopard's Spots* and *The Clansman*, both vehicles which glorified the Ku Klux Klan (KKK), and which used plots obsessively dwelling on miscegenation. Anyone who wants to see where the actions of Gus and Silas Lynch come from need go no further than the earlier novels, and, in particular, the highly-successful play based on *The Clansman*.[7]

By now, scholars recognize that the film's entire treatment of Reconstruction, with its lurid, obsessive Negrophobia, comes directly from Thomas Dixon's novels and play. A representative example is not hard to find. "The Riot in the Master's Hall," chapter 8 in *The Clansman*, is directly incorporated by Griffith in his film, as can be seen by one of Griffith's so-called historical tableaux, the House of Representatives, State of South Carolina. In Dixon's words:

> As he passed inside the doors of the House of Representatives, the rush of foul air staggered him. The reek of vile cigars and stale whiskey, mingled with the odor of perspiring Negroes, was overwhelming. He paused and

gasped for breath. The space behind the seats of the members was strewn
with corks, broken glass, stale crusts, greasy pieces of paper, and picked
bones. The hall was packed with Negroes, smoking, chewing, jabbering,
pushing, perspiring . . . The remains of Aryan civilization were represented
by twenty-three white men from the Scotch-Irish hill counties.[8]

Dixon's Negro-dominated legislature approves anti-white measures,
including, predictably, bills "to permit the intermarriage of whites and
blacks; and to enforce social equality."[9] This scene is also reproduced
directly in *The Birth of a Nation*, where many of the extras are African
Americans, along with a number of whites in blackface.

Griffith makes a point, in his intertitles, to emphasize the accuracy
of his historical tableaux, citing, with intertitles, such authorities as
Woodrow Wilson and Albion Tourgee, the author of *A Fool's Errand*,
one of the most successful historical novels about Reconstruction.
His photographic source, he says, is the pioneering ten-volume
Photographic History of the Civil War, published in 1911, and edited by
Francis T. Miller. The volumes are still impressive. Miller sent a young
Yale graduate, Roy M. Mason, through the South, to locate photo-
graphic images in homes and photographic studios. "My quarry,"
said Mason, "was any and all photographs of war scenes taken by
Southerners within the Confederate lines during the war."[10] Francis
T. Miller, in turn, was simply bowled over by Griffith's films. He
wrote of his 1918 film, *Hearts of the World*:

> You—Mr. Griffith—are the First of the great Cinema historians. This is
> the position that you will occupy in the records of human progress. This
> letter, then, is a greeting from an historian of the old school of typography,
> to a historian of the New School of Cinematography.[11]

Dixon's obsession with miscegenation reflects a wartime Southern
phobia. The word first appears in an 1864 book title: *Miscegenation: The
Theory of the Blending of the Races, Applied to the American White Man
and Woman*. The OED defines the word as "mixture of races, especially
the sexual union of whites with Negroes." The American Heritage
Dictionary says something more: "cohabitation, sexual relations, or
marriage involving persons of different races." This obsession with miscegenation, of course, is at best a code word for rape, and rape of white
women by black men, and that is both Dixon's obsession and Griffith's
obsession, and lies at the heart of modern objections to *The Birth of a
Nation*. Mulattoes, notoriously Silas Lynch, are the result of miscegenation. In Griffith's film, the traitor to both blacks and whites is a mulatto.

The Supreme Court criminalized miscegenation in *Pace v. Alabama*
(1883). The Court upheld an Alabama law punishing fornication more

severely than had the plaintiffs been of the same race. The Court held that since both partners were punished equally, the Alabama statute did not violate the equal protection clause of the Fourteenth Amendment. Anti-miscegenation laws were on the books in sixteen Southern states. Not until 1967, in *Loving v. Virginia*, did a unanimous Supreme Court overturn its earlier ruling, this time agreeing that, indeed, anti-miscegenation laws did violate the equal protection clause of the Fourteenth Amendment.[12]

Southern Legendary History in *The Birth of a Nation*

Southern history is treated in an idiosyncratic fashion in Griffith's film, though many have presumed that it simply popularized beliefs already widespread, and that the film, with its enormous commercial success, allowed a Southern view of the Civil War and Reconstruction to triumph in Progressive America's marketplace of ideas. This is not totally incorrect, but ignores the ways in which Griffith departs from received wisdom, circa 1900.

Griffith sets his scene in the years just before 1861, with a functioning social order. White masters are kindly, and care deeply for the wellbeing of their slaves. Slaves, happy and content, and needing the oversight of kindly masters, work in the fields, but then enjoy a three-hour lunch break. Then follows the Civil War. Griffith is no enthusiast for the Lost Cause. His vision of the Civil War is anti-militarist, and pacifist. He shows the burning of Atlanta, and the grim desperate last days for Confederate forces in the siege of Petersburg, Virginia. He shows antebellum chums from both the North and South dead on the battlefield, side by side. True, during the climactic scenes in the Battle of Gettysburg, Colonel Ben Cameron (Henry B. Walthall) charges through Union lines to spike a canon with the standard of a Confederate flag, but this is a rare moment in the carnage. No one should imagine that *The Birth of a Nation* enthuses over the bloodiness of Civil War battles.

Nothing indicates Griffith's take on the Civil War more clearly than his treatment of Abraham Lincoln. Lincoln is depicted, in wooden, religious fashion, as the one great leader of all America. His assassination, based, according to intertitles, on actual images of Ford's Theater, is termed the greatest blow to chances for a defeated South to return peacefully to the Union. In the film, truly, Lincoln can do no wrong.

There is no President of the United States once Lincoln is assassinated in April 1865. The actual new president, Andrew Johnson of Tennessee, is never mentioned, either by name or in a

fictional guise.[13] In a film where one half of the duration is given
to Reconstruction, and we know that Johnson's impeachment trial
in 1868 was a major part of Reconstruction, there is no mention
of impeachment either. Instead, leadership of the plan to punish the
white South, by destroying the social order of the antebellum South,
is given to two characters, Senator Charles Sumner of Massachusetts,
and Pennsylvania Representative Thaddeus Stevens, the latter clearly
functioning as both President of the United States, and vindictive
leader of the Radical Republicans in Congress. Austin Stoneman
is Stevens. Thaddeus Stevens died on August 11, 1868, so in some
respects the film's treatment of Reconstruction not only gets rid of
any actual president, but relies on a fictional character to promote
extreme anti-Southern measures. Stoneman finally comes to his
senses when the mulatto Silas Lynch (George Siegmann) tries to force
Stoneman's beautiful daughter (Lillian Gish) to marry him.

In many respects, one might think of *The Birth of a Nation* as two
separate films. That dealing with the Civil War is a series of individual
set pieces, made according to the requirements of films lasting no
more than twenty minutes, such as Griffith had made hundreds of
before 1915. Part II, Reconstruction, is a diatribe, but also a piece of
brilliant cinematography. It shows a vindictive radical congressman
punishing the white South, in the process totally destroying the functioning social order, by using the power of the federal government to
force blacks into leadership roles, and making white Southerners the
helpless pawns of misguided or venal rule. The film's central argument
is made outrageously clear: whites must control blacks, because if not,
the black man's insatiable desire for sex with a white woman will
not be contained. This is made clear in the actions of Gus (played by
Walter Long, a white man in blackface) who pursues a terrified little
Flora (Mae Marsh), and in Griffith's intertitles. Flora leaps to her death
rather than become a victim of miscegenation.

Salvation for the white South comes from an extralegal vigilante
organization, the KKK. In the film, it is the traditional aristocratic
elite's representative, Colonel Ben Cameron, who gets the inspiration
for the KKK after seeing some white children frightening black children
by the river with sheets.

The KKK is called into being after Flora's death. It is an organization led by the same aristocracy which had controlled the South in
1860, and which provided the military leadership for the war.[14]
We see Gus murder another white man. Only then is Gus captured
by the Klan and put on trial in the middle of the forest, lacking any
sort of legal representation. We then see Gus's body dumped on the

front porch of the home where Silas Lynch lives. The KKK rides
to the rescue of a cabin full of both white Southerners and white
Northerners, and then the KKK oversees elections in which blacks
run from the ballot place back to the fields. The Klan puts Silas Lynch
out of business. In a romantic plot lifted from Shakespeare, the aristocratic
Southerner, Ben Cameron, gets the beautiful Northern daughter
of Austin Stoneman, and a double wedding ceremony marks the
return of a functioning social order.[15] The film never mentions
the Fourteenth or Fifteenth Amendments, but it is obvious that,
as love conquers sectional animosities, neither amendment will be
enforced in Dixie.

   The historic record of the KKK is very much at odds with that
depicted in Griffith's film. It is true that the Klan was wildly popular
all over the South; it is true that the women of the South were
complicit, in that it was they who made the robes, and who kept the
secret of their husbands' nocturnal duties quiet. It is not true that
the Klan "saved" the South. There was no central organization to the
Klan. In some districts, multiple Klans competed for what could be taken
by force. The Klan's actions actually lengthened military reconstruction, because the North was forced to send more federal troops to
combat the Klan, sometimes in daylight skirmishes. Some Klansmen
were deserters, or common criminals, who used Klan regalia for
personal gain. But never did Griffith's film include a castration scene
for Gus. This claim seems to have been advanced by Seymour Stern,
the idiosyncratic official biographer of Griffith, who never got much
beyond an issue of *Film Culture* from 1965 in which he combined
documents with unproven assertion. This has not kept such scholars
as Michael Rogin from assuming that the original film did include
a castration scene.[16]

Thaddeus Stevens and The Riot in the Master's Hall

What might be said as to the historical figure of Thaddeus Stevens
compared with how he is treated in Griffith's film? Certainly, in the
film, Austin Stoneman is given a gorgeous daughter which he did
not have in real life. He has a poorly fitting wig which he removes to
wipe perspiration from his head; he walks with a very pronounced
limp. He has a mulatto housekeeper, Lydia Brown, and the film clearly
suggests that Stoneman has a sexual relationship with Lydia Brown.
Given the film's notorious racial stereotyping, modern viewers may
well presume that the depiction of Stoneman is simply a convention
of drama, in which the villain both looks villainous and acts villainous.

Fawn Brodie's *Thaddeus Stevens: Scourge of the South* was published in 1959; it is her later *Thomas Jefferson: An Intimate History* which raised the very real possibility of Jefferson's having fathered children by Sally Hemmings.[17] Brodie does not by any means attempt to place the historic figure of Stevens in a manner which would meet with Griffith's approval, but she has information which may strike some persons as surprising, if one does not know much about Stevens as an historic figure, or presumes that because Silas Lynch is a stock mulatto villain, that Austin Stoneman must be exactly the same sort of fictional character.

Stevens was born with a club foot, so his entire life he walked with a pronounced limp. He lost all of his hair after an illness as a young man, and spent the rest of his life wearing the sort of ill-fitting wig that was the best money could buy in his lifetime. He had an African American housekeeper. He was morally-driven, humorless, and determined to punish the white South. Before his death in August 1868, he had forced through Congress the legislation making military reconstruction of the South a requirement. The punitive clauses of the Fourteenth Amendment, and the requirement that Southern states elect legislatures which approved the Fourteenth Amendment, were part of his final legislative achievement. Brodie describes Stevens in mid-1867: "With increasing age he grew more irascible, waspish, and defiant. His skin was gray, his voice hollow and empty. The dark brown wig, sitting carelessly on his head . . . gave him 'the visage of an undertaker.'"[18]

Brodie has important information about the reality of "The Riot in the Master's Hall," a chapter title taken over directly into Griffith's film as an intertitle (Illustration 2.1). We read that the tableau is based on a historic photograph of the South Carolina House of Representatives from 1870. Brodie, citing the work of Paul Lewinson, states that the requirements of the Fourteenth Amendment meant that "at least 100,000 white men were disfranchised or chose to stay away from the polls in the summer of 1867."[19] Brodie notes that Negro voters outnumbered white voters in Florida, Alabama, South Carolina, Mississippi, and Louisiana. Only in Louisiana and South Carolina did blacks outnumber whites in the total population. "Only in South Carolina and Louisiana did the Negroes participate in proportion to their population in the electorate. South Carolina elected 48 white delegates and 76 Negroes. Two-thirds of the latter had been slaves."[20]

In sum, the film uses vicious innuendo to suggest that Stevens's obsession with equality was based on his sexual desire for his housekeeper. The film uses outrageous stereotyping to indicate that the Stevens plan put the South Carolina State House under the control of illiterate blacks who literally were incapable of governing, and fell

Illustration 2.1 The "overrun" Senate in D.W. Griffith's *Birth of a Nation* (1915) © Epoch Producing Corporation/David W. Griffith Corporation

prey to the actions of Silas Lynch, elected lieutenant governor. Today's viewer cannot possibly endorse the innuendo and racial stereotyping. But this should not lead a viewer, uncritically, to presume that Thaddeus Stevens was a kindly, gentle law-maker, or that the lower house in South Carolina was never under black control.

Carl Breil's Musical Score

The Birth of a Nation is easily downloaded for free these days; it is easily rented from *netflix*; it can be seen in the version released by D.J. Spooky. In each of endless versions, many incomplete, most with poor quality transfers from 16mm, the racial stereotypes are easy to see—and deplorable. But very rarely do modern viewers see a version of the film which makes use of Carl Breil's score, the one which he created in consultation with D.W. Griffith, nor do viewers see a version of the film which employs the various color tints found in the original. Of all the versions available today, the one released on DVD by Kino Video in 2002 is the one to use.[21]

Carl Breil's career is listed in one of Marks's appendices.[22] Breil was born in Pittsburgh, in 1879. He was a tenor, who studied voice in Leipzig and Milan. He was a tenor with a touring American opera

company, and for five years served as choir director at St. Paul's
Cathedral in Pittsburgh.[23] He was an editor of classical music for
various New York publishers, including Remick. He wrote the music
for *Queen Elizabeth*, a film from 1912, and claimed to have thus written
the first score for a film. His music for the Italian feature-length film
Cabiria (1914) helped bring him to Griffith's attention. Breil had an
opera performed once at the Metropolitan Opera in 1919; he died in
Los Angeles in 1926.

Martin Marks has done a remarkable job of explaining exactly
what Breil did in providing the music for Griffith's film. It might be
helpful to think of Breil as being part composer, part arranger, and
part borrower of very familiar popular tunes and notable orchestral
excerpts in creating his score for a film lasting over three full hours.
The difficulty with Marks's book is simply that his numerous musical
examples will be totally unintelligible to someone who does not read
music. And his arrangement of material does not always make for
ease of comprehension. Marks argues that Breil was a serious, creative,
long-forgotten presence in the development of feature film scores as
we know them. This does not mean that the reader is presented with
a succession of musical triumphs—much of the music in *The Birth of a
Nation* simply makes use of melodies and classical orchestral excerpts
already staples in accompanying silent films before 1915.

In 1914, G. Martaine published two volumes entitled *An Album
of Photo-Play Music*, with its intended use in large typeface on the
cover: "a large variety of photo-play music for almost any occasion
and the pieces are arranged in such a way that they may be repeated
as often as desired." The arrangement of "The Hunting Chorus" from
Weber's *Der Freischutz* (a source used by Breil the next year) is recom-
mended for almost everything but love scenes: "For Battle, Hurry,
Pursuit, Attack, Noise, Running, Riding, Chase, Hunt, Horsemen,
Mounted Troops, Cavalry, etc."[24] Part of Breil's assignment was simply
to select appropriate popular songs, such as "My Old Kentucky
Home;" patriotic tunes, such as "Dixie;" and, for the ride of the
KKK, Richard Wagner's *Rienzi* overture which segues into his "Ride
of the Valkyries." He even made use of a spurious piece of Mozart's
church music, a Gloria from the so-called *Twelfth Mass*, which is used
in the Kino Video DVD for an overture to accompany the main titles.
Breil also composed a series of themes (not really Leitmotifs in the
Wagnerian sense, but inspired by Wagner) for such things as a theme
to accompany the spirit of the "African slave;" or the spirit of Austin
Stoneman; or the lust of Lydia Brown, Stoneman's mulatto housekeeper. These are worked into appropriate scenes, along with a good

bit of connecting music, basically musical sounds to keep the viewer's ears filled with something. One Breil song became a genuine commercial hit, "The Perfect Song," with words provided by Clarence Lucas. "The Perfect Song" was published by Chappell in three keys for solo voice and piano; and also as a piano solo, as well as for cello and piano, and band. The song lived on for decades as the theme song of Amos 'n' Andy, a highly successful radio program of the 1930s, and an unsuccessful television program of the 1950s.[25]

The music for "The Riot in the Master's Hall" is instructive in terms of Breil's technique. To accompany the gross stereotyping of the South Carolina House of Representatives, Breil composes a couple of cheerful tunes, which might well seem to be another instance of a borrowed orchestral favorite. Not so. Breil is simply adopting the conventions of countless nineteenth-century light overtures, and it might seem an odd choice for a legislature in session. But the music adds an enforced gaiety which provides an ironic foretaste of what the acts of the legislature are going to bring. When the "grim reaping" begins, we are introduced to the menacing figure of Gus, and the music returns to the theme of the African slave with which the film begins. Marks casts doubt on the claims of memoirists that Griffith selected the music for his film.[26] It seems much more likely that Griffith had plenty of opinions about the music, but that Breil made the selections. If one wants to try and view the film countless persons saw in 1915, it has to make use of Breil's score, not the totally-unsuited music put out with various versions of The Birth of a Nation in which pretty much any old bit of music will do—and never "The Ride of the Valkyries" to accompany the Klan.

The Social Impact of The Birth of a Nation

In 1916, the NAACP reported the case of a teenager from Kentucky who viewed The Birth of a Nation, and then shot and killed a Negro. This story received wide publicity. We know that the film helped inspire the KKK of the 1920s, and was used into the 1950s as a recruiting vehicle for successor Klan groups. When I started teaching at Louisiana State University in 1971, and used The Birth of a Nation in my survey class in American history, students told me of the film's continued use for Klan recruitment in New Orleans and in Livingston Parish, not more than twenty miles from Baton Rouge.[27]

Melvyn Stokes examines the 1916 NAACP report, which he suggests may be apocryphal, and then turns to Payne Fund studies from the 1930s about the impact of Griffith's film on adolescent perceptions of Negroes. Sociologists Ruth Peterson and L.L. Thurstone examined the impact of *The Birth of a Nation* on 434 schoolchildren from Crystal Lake, Illinois. The children, from grades six through twelve, were shown the new sound version of the film, and asked in May 1931 to fill out a questionnaire about their racial attitudes before and after seeing the film. As Stokes explains, "The children's attitude had changed enormously by the time of the second survey; they were now far more hostile to, and prejudiced against, black people . . . A follow-up survey suggested that much of the changed attitude persisted some five months after the film was first shown."[28] Stokes notes that in 1971 a sociologist returned to the same school to test the impact of the film again, and found its power had vanished. Of course, Stokes is unable to say whether the creaky dramatic conventions of a film from 1915 might have failed to inflame adolescent viewers in 1971.[29]

Stokes cites the best book on the Payne Fund, Garth Jowett's *Children and the Movies*, published in 1996, but, in his 2007 study of the film, ignores what Jowett, Ian Jarvie, and Kathryn Fuller intended to demonstrate—the conflicting research agendas of the Payne Fund scholars, and the conflict between most of the scholars and the one-volume popularization of their work, Henry James Forman's *Our Movie-Made Children* (1933). For example, sociologist Herbert Blumer collected amazingly candid interviews with selected University of Chicago undergraduates, revealing titillating ways in which respondents claimed to have warmed to sexual adventures by copying what they had seen on movie screens. Jowett shows how Blumer changed the religious affiliation and sex of his respondents, indicating that researchers should not take Blumer's research as either statistically-representative of adolescent behavior in the 1930s, or even accurate for the small number of respondents, however salacious the material.[30]

Jowett, Jarvie and Fuller note the valuable contributions to the Payne Fund made by Paul Cressey, whose Payne Fund study remained unpublished. Cressey's doctoral thesis also seems to have disappeared from New York University. Nevertheless, Cressey, in published and surviving unpublished work, suggests the limits of a feature film, no matter how ugly its content, in and by itself to create changes in the behavior of individual spectators. Cressey's impressive research remained largely unpublished, in part because his conclusions directly contradicted what Henry James Forman was so keen to demonstrate. To Cressey, "the photoplay, upon the basis of data available upon Intervale, cannot be said, strictly speaking, to be a 'causative factor' in delinquency."[31] This continues to be what research into adolescent behavior indicates as accurate.

In sum, *The Birth of a Nation*, for all of its vicious racial stereotypes, cannot alone be held responsible for the murder or lynching of innocent blacks. It cannot alone be held responsible for intensifying, by itself, societal prejudice towards blacks. It is a brilliant piece of filmmaking. But today's world rejects the viciousness of the film's stereotyping, with good reason, and because of that, the film is now seen mostly in classrooms, and almost never in a film society's series. It is a modest irony, but a fact of life, that Griffith's most significant achievement is one of his least-seen and least-admired films. As Russell Merritt reminds us, "were the film no more complicated than Dixon's play on which it was based, it would have been forgotten long ago . . . The disturbing fact is that Griffith invests even his most offensive sequences with skillfulness that repays minute examination."[32]

Notes

1. William A. Dunning, *Reconstruction: Political & Economic, 1865–1877* (1905); C.W. Ramsdell, *Reconstruction in Texas* (1910); W.W. Davis, *The Civil War and Reconstruction in Florida* (1913); J.G. de Roulhac Hamilton, *Reconstruction in North Carolina* (1914); for contemporary assessments of the Dunning School, see Peter Novick, *That Noble Dream* (Cambridge: Cambridge University Press, 1988): 74–7; Eric Foner, *Reconstruction: America's Unfinished Revolution, 1863–1877* (New York: Harper & Row, 1988).

2. Melvyn Stokes, *D.W. Griffith's* The Birth of a Nation: *A History of "The Most Controversial Motion Picture of All Time"* (New York: Oxford University Press, 2007); Paolo Cherchi Usai, general editor, *The Griffith Project: Volume 8 Films Produced in 1914–15* (London: BFI Publishing, 2004); Martin Miller Marks, *Music and the Silent Film: Contexts & Case Studies, 1895–1924* (New York: Oxford University Press, 1997).

3. For Wilson's biographers' efforts to locate Wilson's alleged words, see the discussion in John Whiteclay Chambers II and David Culbert (eds.), *World War II, Film, and History* (New York: Oxford University Press, 1996): n.1, 158–9. Neither Wilson nor Chief Justice Edward White trusted Dixon's attempts to collect endorsements by hook or by crook. See Arthur S. Link, *Wilson: The New Freedom* (Princeton: Princeton University Press, 1956): 252–4: "He did, however, let [Press Secretary] Joseph Tumulty say that he had at no time approved the film." In addition, see Arthur S. Link (ed.), *The Papers of Woodrow Wilson, 32* (January 1–April 16 1915) (Princeton: Princeton University Press, 1980): 142, 267, 310–11, 454–5, 487.

4. Garth Jowett, *Film: The Democratic Art* (Boston: Little, Brown, 1976): 119–22.

5. Stokes: 285.

6. Program, Tremont Theatre, Boston, August 9, 1915. Laid into signed, limited edition of Terry Ramsaye, *A Thousand and One Nights*, (1926) offered for sale by Appledore Books, Waccabue, NY, at the New York Antiquarian Book Fair, New York City, April 2009.

7. Michele K. Gillespie and Randal L. Hall (eds.), *Thomas Dixon Jr. and the Birth of Modern America* (Baton Rouge: Louisiana State University Press, 2006).

8. Thomas Dixon, Jr., *The Clansman: An Historical Romance of the Ku Klux Klan* [1905] (Ridgewood, NJ: Gregg Press, 1967): 263–4, 268. For tensions between black and white in South Carolina, see Joel Williamson, *After Slavery: The Negro in South Carolina During Reconstruction, 1861–1877* (New York: Norton, 1975): 257–3, 259–60, 260–6.

9. *Ibid.*

10. William C. Davis (ed.), *Shadows of the Storm, Volume One of The Image of War 1861–1865* (Garden City, NY: Doubleday, 1981), introduction: 10–11.

11. Francis T. Miller to David Wark Griffith, April 23, 1918, in Richard Wood (ed.), *Film and Propaganda in America: A Documentary History, Volume I World War I* (Westport, CT: Greenwood Press, 1990), document 70: 166.

12. Kermit L. Hall (ed.), *The Oxford Companion to The Supreme Court of the United States* (New York: Oxford University Press, 1992), entries for *Pace v. Alabama* and *Loving v. Virginia*; Douglas Martin, "Mildred Loving, Pioneer, Dies at 68; Battled Ban on Mixed-Race Marriage," *New York Times* (May 6, 2008): C13.

13. Eric L. McKitrick, *Andrew Johnson and Reconstruction* (Chicago: University of Chicago Press, 1960).

14. Allan T. Trelease, *The Ku Klux Klan* (New York: Harper, 1970).

15. Griffith and Dixon borrowed their plot from Albion Tourgee, whose *A Fool's Errand* (New York: Harper & Brothers, 1879) made obvious use of *Much Ado About Nothing*.

16. Seymour Stern, *The Birth of a Nation, Film Culture* (36, spring–summer, 1965): 123–4; Michael Rogin, "'The Sword Became a Flashing Vision': D.W. Griffith's *The Birth of a Nation*," *Representations* (9, winter, 1985): 150–95; Richard Schickel, *D.W. Griffith: An American Life* (New York: Touchstone, 1985): 602.

17. Fawn M. Brodie, *Thaddeus Stevens: Scourge of the South* (New York: Norton, 1966); *Thomas Jefferson: An Intimate History* (New York: Norton, 1975). Brodie's Jefferson volume was dismissed by many historians when it first appeared, but has since been re-evaluated.

18. Brodie (1966): 309.

19. *Ibid.*: 314.

20. *Ibid.*: 315.

21. Kino Video DVD, K266, 2002. This version, on a second accompanying DVD, also includes the 1930 filmed prologue featuring Griffith and David Shepherd's instructive *The Making of* The Birth of a Nation [1992] (24 mins.).

22. Marks: 198.

23. For photographs of the 1903–06 replacement to the building in which Breil served, see *The Tracker: Journal of the Organ Historical Society* 54:1 (winter, 2010): 2, 21–2.

24. G. Martaine, *Album of Photo-Play Music* (New York: Academic Music, 1914).

25. Joseph Carl Breil, "The Perfect Song, The Love Strain from D.W. Griffith's Gigantic Spectacle *The Birth of a Nation*" (New York: Chappell, 1915).

26. Marks: 132–41.

27. I also received an anonymous piece of hate mail from my students, a return ticket to Africa, for "Nigger lovers," distributed by George Lincoln Rockwell.

28. Stokes: 252.

29. *Ibid.*

30. Garth S. Jowett *et al.*, *Children and the Movies: Media Influence and the Payne Fund Controversy* (New York: Cambridge University Press, 1996): 237–301.

31. *Ibid.*: 218.

32. Quoted in Usai: 62.

3

The Hollywood Western, the Movement-Image, and Making History

Marcia Landy

The Hollywood Western from the silent era through the Second World War is, in many ways, the pre-eminent genre to trace the rise and fall of a mode of American history-making through cinema. Key pre-Second World War Westerns—*The Covered Wagon* (Cruze, 1923), *The Iron Horse* (Ford, 1924), *The Virginian* (De Mille, 1914; Forman, 1923; Fleming, 1929), *Stagecoach* (Ford, 1939), and *Destry Rides Again* (Marshall, 1939)—are tied to a historical project of nation-building. These films convey a form of historicizing based on the nineteenth-century faith in the constancy and universality of Truth, the efficacy of enlightened moral action, and chronological progress invoking the ultimate aim of history. Historians Francis Parkman, Frederick Jackson Turner, and Theodore Roosevelt were the most eloquent exponents of Western history and its powerful ties to American nationhood.[1] In the first few decades of the twentieth century, their vision of the Western frontier world was expressed onscreen through an organic montage that inspired awe and confidence in the imperative of moral purpose through progressive action on the natural and social environment. By the late 1930s, if not earlier, a lack of confidence in cinema's capacity for transforming the world through action became evident. Certain Westerns—*The Ox-Bow Incident* (1943) and the 1946 version of *The Virginian*—are symptomatic of an uncertainty, if not loss of belief, in national unity, identity, and ethical purpose symbolized by the frontier.

Gilles Deleuze's writings on cinema are an engagement with philosophical concepts that account for the power of the cinematic image to animate confidence in historical agency, as well as symptoms of its decline. His is not an empirical study of history proper, but an analysis of cinema's expressive uses of the body, of faces, and of spaces that engender affects that are organized around action. Nevertheless, his formulations resonate with the Western's historiographic trajectories between 1915 and 1945. In *Cinema 1*, Deleuze focuses on the "movement-image" that relies on sensory-motor responses based on perception-, affection-, and action-images to create a consonance between "movement as physical reality in the external world, and psychic reality as consciousness" through an examination of "images and signs . . . [and] their pre-verbal intelligent content."[2] Relying on Friedrich Nietzsche's delineation of monumental history as belonging to the man of deeds and power . . . who fights a great fight . . . for a nation or for mankind as a whole," Deleuze describes this view of history as considering "effects in themselves" in which "the only causes it understands are simple duels opposing individuals."[3] Deleuze explores how this form of history inspired the American cinema of the pre-Second World War years:

> The American cinema constantly shoots and re-shoots a single fundamental film, which is the birth of a nation-civilization, whose first version was provided by Griffith . . . The ancient or recent past must submit to trial, go to court, in order to disclose what it is that produces new life; what the ferments of decadence and the germs of new life are, the orgy and the sign of the cross, the omnipotence of the rich, and the misery of the poor. A strong ethical judgment must condemn the injustice of "things," bring compassion, and herald the new civilization on the march, in short, constantly to rediscover America.[4]

This form of narration relies on images that are assembled through montage, through a form of linkage defined as a "movement-image" that situates the protagonists in a situation where they must overcome a threatening milieu and establish (or restore) a moral order to the community (the large form). Time is indirect, composed of continuous segmentations of space whose parts are commensurate with the whole of the film, producing universal, linear, and teleological conceptions of history.[5] This is, in many ways, the narrative of traditional Western history and particularly of the "classic" Western, where history's narrative of "change over time" is replayed again and again in a set of mythic, binary conflicts and resolutions.[6]

Deleuze argues that the perception of images derives from a blank screen and light that involves a "diffused *prehension*" of things . . . that are incomplete and prejudiced,"[7] since they entail a subtraction, elimination, of unnecessary information. While the perception-image is one side of the process, the other side is action (the images to be acted upon). The affection-image conveys the emotional intensity that animates the "domain of the action-image" and serves, on the one hand (as in close-ups), to "tear the image away from spatio-temporal coordinates in order to call forth the pure affect as the expressed."[8] On the other hand, the affection-image can also convey emotional states in a determinate space-time, "actualized in a state of things," producing real connections and tensions among objects people and events. In relation to the Western, "the principal quality of the image is breath, respiration. It not only inspires the hero, but brings things together in a whole of organic representation and contracts or expands depending on the circumstances."[9] Thus, the cinema of the movement-image is not a merely a matter of style: it is a visceral process that characterizes the spectator's encounter with this earlier form of history-making.

The Large Form of the Foundational Narrative: *The Covered Wagon* and *The Iron Horse*

The Covered Wagon: "The Plow that Broke the Plain"

One expression of the movement-image is a large form in which actions are determined by monumental figures and situations, going from a general to a modified situation resolved by action.[10] The affect generated by this form arises from the vast natural landscape and the hero's passionate commitment to contend with epic forces that lie in the way of realizing the ethical goals of subduing natural and social obstacles. James Cruze's *The Covered Wagon* (1923) was cast in the large form in its narration of the conquest of the American West, described in the inter-titles as "empire building." The film solicits the viewer's perception of a world structured through the intermediary role of affection-images that animate action through a series of duels with men, with the milieu, and with other hostile forces that arouse sensations of curiosity, wonder, and admiration.

In Kevin Brownlow's assessment of the film's spectacular treatment, "the filming of the epic Western . . . was an epic in itself."[11] Even the intertitles are more than dialogue, description, or explanation: they "gain an almost epic poetry, exactly fitting the mood of the film" and evoke the vivid prose of Parkman and Roosevelt.[12] The vastness of the production combined with a minute attention to historical detail. According to the publicity booklet, the film employed the services of 1,000 Native Americans from reservations in Wyoming and Mexico (under the direction of a military officer); 40,000 feet of canvas were used for the Conestoga wagons; numerous "wild" bison for the hunt were hired from a firm known as Buffalo Livestock Corporation; cowboys managed the animals, including 150 steers and 1,000 horses.[13] In a sense, the film bears comparison with Buffalo Bill's Wild West (1883–1913), and the director, Cruze, a former traveling actor in road shows, was the perfect impresario for this type of spectacle.

Through the panoramic long shots, the viewer perceives the vastness of the country and of the natural obstacles to be overcome. The photography of the landscape is monumental, with its high mountains and dangerous waterfalls, and visualizes the trials the pioneers encounter in the movement westward in the various obstacles entailed in such a long and arduous trek: the dangerous and dramatic crossing of a deep river by the wagons, buffalo hunting, an attack by Native Americans, and fights between individuals and factions. And yet, the film's epic style also covers the protagonists' relentless day-to-day struggles with childbirth, death, shortages of food supplies, and dissension among groups, culminating in a split between those men who seek gold in California and the "men of the plow" who want to settle the land and create a community.

The choreography of the large cast filmed against this landscape also contributes to its "epic" character. Woodhull (Alan Hale) is the antagonistic and obstructionist figure who attempts to turn the journey into a personal duel between himself and Bannion (J. Warren Kerrigan), the "natural" leader of the pioneers capable of bringing them to the "promised land." Cruze's casting of actors is consistent with the focus on the physical ordeals of the journey. The dominant figures are the pioneers, and J. Warren Kerrigan as their deliverer. While the film presents Bannion as playing a critical role in the trek westward, he is less an individual hero distinguished from his men than a social type dependent on others for the collective good. Slight of figure and short, less athletic, and visibly older than many heroes, without benefit of low-angle shots, Banion is a nurturing figure, a chivalrous defender of women and children, a maligned hero fighting untrue reports about his military past, and a man of honor who refuses to use violence unjustly. What is significant about Kerrigan's physical appearance as Bannion is that he does not eclipse the physical trials confronted by the pioneers. His physiognomy distinguishes him from the traditional wilderness scout exemplified by James Fenimore Cooper's Leatherstocking and by the hunter-hero image of Theodore Roosevelt and his "Rough Riders," composed of aristocrats and cowboys.[14]

Unlike Tom Mix and Fred Thomson in other Westerns of the time, Kerrigan lacks the distinctive identity associated with heroes of this action-oriented genre, but Cruze's emphasis is not on the actor's unique performance (a star quality), but on Bannion's interactions with the other figures. Bannion is often grimy and disheveled, hardly a larger-than-life portrait. Tully Marshall's Bridger and Ernest Torrence's Jackson, who provide comic interludes, often overshadow Kerrigan's role. Moreover, the antagonism between Bannion and Woodhull, while integral to the conflicts in the narrative, does not threaten to overwhelm the larger "imperial" mission. In a film that uses close-ups sparingly, Molly, as played by Lois Wilson, a former schoolteacher, receives the largest share of close-ups. She is often framed by the arched front of the Conestoga wagon akin to an iris-shot that situates her in the emotional position of threatened femininity. Molly embodies the image of an attractive pioneer woman, not glamorous, exotic or clinging, but wholesome-looking and adventurous—The Prairie Madonna. She is the object of contention between Bannion and Woodhull, and the duel between the men involves the quality of the political and domestic fate of the pioneers.

Cleared of false charges brought by Woodhull and with his antagonist eliminated, Bannion has become a wealthy man, thanks to his also having prospected for gold after going west. He is united with Molly to form the basis of a new society, and the plow that Bannion and the other pioneers employ to break the plains becomes the instrument of civilization. *The Covered Wagon* anticipated Westerns to come in its stirring portraits of adventure and heroic action, consistent with the large form of the epic, to link "the world of nature and man, nature, and thought" in such films as Ford's *The Iron Horse* (1924), DeMille's *Union Pacific* (1939), *Dodge City* (1939), *Arizona* (1940), *Santa Fe Trail* (1940), and *American Empire* (1942).[15]

The Iron Horse: The Railroad and Founding Myths

In the following year, John Ford's *The Iron Horse* (1924) offered another large form of the journey westward, in which the railroad and its movement through space is also exemplary of the large form of the epic. "What *The Covered Wagon* does for the wagon train," writes David Lusted, "*the Iron Horse* does for the locomotive by placing the railroad within the foundation myth."[16] From *The Great Train Robbery* (1903) to *Once Upon a Time in the West* (1968), the "iron horse" played a critical role in establishing the large form of the Western and its contribution to monumental historicizing. Aside from its choreography of the workers in the ordeal of constructing the railroad and its insertion of actual political figures (e.g. President Lincoln), the film places greater emphasis on the importance of building the railroad from East to West as a symbol of national unity.

In its multiple narrative lines (familial, romantic, and moral) and in the selection of its characters, *The Iron Horse* poses a range of potentially divisive and factional elements to create conflicts involving Easterners and Westerners, racial groups and ethnicities (Native Americans, Irish, Italians, and Chinese), workers and obstructive opportunists, and visible distinctions between a rural and a developing industrial society. Furthermore, a motif critical to many Westerns (including Ford's *Stagecoach*) concerns the aftermath of the Civil War and its divisive effects on national unity that embodies antagonism between the "defeated" South and the "victorious" North. In Ford's Western, the Union Pacific Railroad becomes the sign of unity between North and South and their regional surrogates West and East, (visualized by the images of Abraham Lincoln expressing his dual priority of winning the war and of creating the railroad in the interests of a peaceful Union.)

Further mediating elements involve the family celebrated at the end in the marriage of Miriam Marsh (Madge Bellamy) to the film's protagonist, Davy Brandon (George O'Brien). The couple is identified with Lincoln's adopted home of Springfield, Illinois. Davy overcomes earlier obstacles to their union and links the epic narrative to their romance and to the wedding of nature and technology, labor and industry. Their wedding promises not merely the integrity and continuity of the family, but also national union and industrial productivity. The differences between workers and bosses, scouts and entrepreneurs, politicians and lawmakers, are subsumed within the overarching union of the rails and the romantic couple.

The awesome spectacle of a panoramic landscape, the choreography of individual characters in relation to their groups, and the laborious advance of the building of the railroad are in the vein of Deleuze's description of the affection-image. Through the perception of space, the movement (alluded to in the very title of the film), the drive toward progress is animated through affection-images generated through the overcoming of large internal and external, natural and social, organic and mechanical obstacles to inspire heroic action.

The Romance of the West: Versions of *The Virginian* from Novel to Screen

The numerous filmic adaptations of Owen Wister's popular novel, *The Virginian* (1914, 1923, 1929, and 1946), afford an opportunity to map the evolution of the Western from the silent years to the heyday of the studio era.[17] The classic events from the novel are present in their various cinematic adaptations from the early silent era to 1929, relatively unaltered by transformations in American culture and in the history of cinema. In fact, *The Virginian* remains one of the most stable of all Western cinematic texts, only disturbed in its final studio-era version.

The familiar mythic elements identified with Wister's novel and codified in his characters and situations involve the struggle of a Southerner from Virginia, resettled as a cowboy in the rugged life of the West. The Virginian's sense of "justice" involves overriding personal ties in the interest of reinforcing the "moral" order in this emergent community. The hero's growth into manhood is complicated by his friendship with a reckless young man, Steve, who is drawn to the lawless Trampas through promises of adventure and individual wealth that run counter to the demands of society and the ranch economy. The Virginian eventually sides with his wealthy boss and is complicit in the lynching of Steve and other cattle-rustlers. Wister renders both this betrayal of masculine friendship and the use of the white Southern institution of lynching in a "free" Western landscape as natural decisions, actions of a true gentleman, and necessary to the growth of the West.[18]

Romance is inherent to the drama in the novel. The Virginian's relationship with Molly Wood, an Eastern schoolteacher whose gentility and social decorum are opposed to frontier codes of honor, establishes a conflict between sentimental traditions of romance and the necessity of action in this new world. The education of Molly (and of the reader) entails an orientation to the ethical values that distinguish the world of the West. The novel culminates in the inevitable duel between the Virginian and Trampas that transforms traditional forms of honor from an individual to a social register through the identification of Trampas with the degenerate forces of greed and lawlessness and unethical individualism.

In its various incarnations, *The Virginian* evolves new ways to balance competing motifs: male bonding and heterosexual romance, contentions over masculinity and femininity, individualism and community, competition and cooperation, the wilderness and domesticity, national and regional space (East versus West, South versus North, West versus South). These oppositions highlight the primacy of masculine force and athleticism in a rugged and untamed landscape. The romance of Wister's "country . . . was made visible to future Americans" by their quotation in the films.[19] Furthermore, both D. W. Griffith's early Westerns, and in later film versions of *The Virginian*, "the romantic subplots . . . involve the vindication in a Northern woman's eyes of a white Southerner's commitment to a form of social justice that transcends written law."[20] The affect in the novel is engendered through the familiar fusion of heterosexual romance with the imperative of the foundational motif via the large cinematic form described by Deleuze.

The Virginian (DeMille, 1914)

Following a stage adaptation of the novel (1903–04), Cecil B. DeMille's adaptation for film was his first directorial foray produced by the Jesse L. Lasky Feature Play Company. The film was intended to appeal to middle-class "genteel" audiences.[21] As such, the film focuses largely on a contrast between romance and friendship and, hence, on two colliding conceptions of ethical responsibility. Much more elliptical than later versions (since DeMille assumed familiarity on the part of the audience with the novel), DeMille's film is built up episodically of scenes that draw on the successful stage play of 1904. The film sets up binary distinctions between Eastern gentility and its morality, and the raw exigencies determining life in the rugged world of the West. For this distinction, shots between interior space and exterior are central to develop the moral antinomies of the narrative.

The film begins in the outdoors with a shot of the Virginian (Dustin Farnum) situated against the landscape, reminiscent of Frederic Remington's epic portraits of the cowpuncher. This shot is interrupted by a cut to Molly's life as a music teacher in Vermont. Increasingly, the film alternates between the two geographic spaces—East and West—until her arrival in Wyoming. Also intercut are the Virginian's relationships with his Western cohorts, Steve and Trampas. DeMille's film focuses on the personal drama of love, friendship, and honor. In these three instances, the audience is privy to the differences and conflicts between two perceptions of the frontier world: as individual and as collective history. In the case of Steve's transgression of the law of frontier property, the Virginian must place duty above friendship, and punish Steve for his alignment with Trampas, the "tin-horn" gambler and bully. However, despite the Virginian's "rescue" of Molly from a drunken stagecoach driver, she chastises him for his violation of social decorum, involving his prank of swapping babies.

Throughout the narrative, the crosscutting distinguishes Molly and the Virginian's ethical values before the final confrontation with Trampas legitimizes the Virginian's actions. The reconciliation with Molly—given her opposition to the hanging of Steve and, later, to the duel with Trampas—is a testimony to the emotional appeal of the Virginian's character. Played by Farnum, who had starred in the stage play, he embodies the image of a "boy who hasn't grown up" and who expresses "a cruel form of masculine energy" that reinforces his rugged frontier persona.[22] Once again, the movement-image's reliance on affect legitimizes the protagonist's behavior and actions.

The Virginian (Tom Forman, 1923)

In 1923, a version of *The Virginian*, based on the novel but not on the stage play (1904), was independently produced. Directed by Tom Forman, and featuring Kenneth Harlan in the role of the Virginian, the film appeared, along with *The Covered Wagon* and *The Iron Horse*, to offer another vision of the Western protagonist and his milieu, particularly focusing the affective dimensions of the protagonists. Hutson affirms that the film "was as much a character study as an action narrative,"[23] characteristic of the studios' concerns to reach a broader audience: women and urban dwellers. Instead of beginning the film with the panoramic image of the expansive Western land-scape and with the protagonist filmed against the landscape, the film begins with the card game that produces the familiar quotation on the part of the Virginian, "When you call me that, smile." His portrait as a man sensitive to slights to his honor is augmented by his role as a defender of threatened femininity. This is dramatized in his initial rescue of Molly from the stagecoach, where her life is threatened by the driver's reckless handling of the horses. In terms of Deleuze's movement-image, the film is generated around the affective components in the Virginian's antagonistic relation to the lawless Trampas (Russell Simpson) and in his determined wooing of the capricious Molly (Florence Vidor).

In this version, the Virginian's evolution as an agent of social redemption is central to his initiation into gentility. Before this role can be legitimated, the film draws on the comic mixing up of babies (also present in the DeMille film) that causes Molly to reprimand the Virginian for his childish behavior. The uneven development of their romance is given greater prominence than in the DeMille version. Competition for Molly's affection between Steve, an old friend, and the Virginian further enhances the emotional vectors of the narrative. Despite the Virginian's friendship with the young man, he must finally punish him for transgressing the sanctity of Western rules of property (and of friendship). However, Molly's objections to the lynching of Steve and to the duel are integral, not ancillary, to the larger ethical conflict between legitimate and illegitimate conceptions of property and self-defense to which she must succumb. The emotional character of romance enters "into singular combinations or conjunctions with other affects", in this case with the imperatives of action.[24]

The legitimacy of the Virginian's character lies in this version of an organic view of the "just" struggle to establish a lawful society, evident in the film's stressing the Virginian's conflict over loyalty to his friend and adherence to duty, and resolved in the Virginian's action to bring Steve to justice along with the other rustlers. The final duel with Trampas underscores the necessity of punishing those outsiders who transgress against the wellbeing of the community, threatening life and property as well as the integrity of the agent who ensures stability and continuity. Molly, as the incarnation of decorous Eastern life, recoils in horror at what she regards as savage behavior before succumbing to the argument that the culture of the West is different from Eastern culture. As in the novel, she submits to the Virginian and his mastery over his environment.[25] But her submission in the context of the overarching imperative to establish law must appear as the personal sacrifice of an individual "caught in a psychological rather than a social situation."[26]

The Virginian (Victor Fleming, 1929)

With the coming of sound to film, the Western realizes the potential of sound to complicate the character of the male protagonist. For those growing up in the 1930s and 1940s, the names of Gene Autry and, later, Roy Rogers were among the most popular stars (as well as other singing cowboys who emulated their personas) and contributed to the rejuvenation of the Western.[27] The songs identified with these figures involve folk music, romantic ballads, work songs, and celebrations of the landscape. The singing cowboy further contributed to the figure of the Western, lending legitimacy to his persona as agent of the community through a populist, folksy, and commonsensical approach that combines "New World sophistication with Old World values."[28] The monumental form of The Virginian incorporates musical elements of the singing cowboy film to enhance the sensory and affective appeal of the protagonist and his milieu. The impact of sound on film was to enhance the form through music and dialogue. Furthermore, while still relying on the foundational epic, the sound versions gave greater prominence to melodrama, and more elaboration on the conflicts among the major figures, including conflicts between duty and romance.

At stake from the first silent version of The Virginian to the 1929 version was the industry's ongoing attempt to expand the composition of its audience by appealing to a wider base of spectators. Thanks in part to the Fleming version, the 1930s was to witness the further evolution of the "A-Western" that was to boost the profile, prestige, and profitability of the genre, while retaining and also innovating many characteristics of the earlier versions. This form of production brought the genre in line with more expensive productions that solicited the expertise of technicians (camera, sound, scriptwriters, lighting, later of Technicolor). Transformations in the genre involved increasing narrative length, development of multiple plots, greater attention to costume, and forms of acting, but, above all, emphasis on acting.

The Fleming version modernized *The Virginian*, particularly in its affective focus on "the struggle of youth" and its "impulse toward modernity" in this "first version of conflicts of the generation gap."[29] If the Virginian's sidekick, Steve, remains blocked in adolescence, the Virginian is transformed into an adult, personified in his decision to hang Steve and to duel with the older and ethnically "other" Trampas (Walter Huston with an out-sized black mustache). The lynching and duel are further naturalized as the Southerner/Westerner's necessary taming of "foreign" elements in the frontier. Furthermore, the Virginian's conversion is connected to his growing romance with Molly, a nod to the Western's growing female audience and to the power of romance that this version develops more fully than the others. But the success of the film also relies on the uses of sound, in witty dialogue and in the dramatic tension created through the verbal badinage between the Virginian and Molly that lends her role greater prominence.[30]

The casting appears also to reinforce the changing iconography of the Western. The selection by Victor Fleming of a young Gary Cooper transformed the cowboy into a sexual icon and also prefigured, if not established, dominant star qualities of the Western hero that merged the seemingly familiar with the extraordinary world of desire.[31] Cooper's casual movement, his near inarticulateness replete with pauses and stammers, situates Cooper as a "natural" action hero, yet also as one that evokes mythic transcendent qualities, contributing to an "aura of authenticity."[32] Furthermore, the Virginian's relationship with Steve portrays both his playfulness and also his conflict between loyalty and justice, thus endowing his character with humor and pathos for dramatic affect.

The film also incorporates interactions with the community as agents more extensively than in the previous versions, particularly as participants and vulnerable observers to the comic drama of the horseplay of Steve and the Virginian in the baby-swapping episode.

The more fateful interactions are the tense choreography of the chase to find the rustlers, and finally the showdown between Trampas and the Virginian, as the community waits for the outcome of the duel. The melodrama invokes the increasingly familiar conflict between romance and commitment to law to be resolved in the union of the couple with different backgrounds and social values. The romance involves the playful but often aggressive interactions between the Virginian and Molly during the course of their courtship. The wounding of the Virginian and Molly's subsequent nursing of him creates a tension between his dependence on the woman for his life and his public mission of vengeance. To succumb to her appeals to abandon the duel would render him "less than a man." Thus, while the film has stressed the vicissitudes of their romance, it finally elevates the motif of honor. His mastery over her is fused to his mastery over her Eastern values, heightening the affective dimension that leads to the epic action prescribed by Deleuze's large form.

Stagecoach: From Romance to Myth

The year 1939 was a watershed year for the Western, marked by the appearance of *Stagecoach*. The Western epic had come into its own as a serious form after a period of waning interest in the early 1930s, but with noteworthy revisions (*Cimarron*, 1931; *The Plainsman*, 1936; *Robin Hood of El Dorado*, 1936). The last half of the decade can be taken as exemplary of a graduation to the classical form prefigured by the 1929 *Virginian*. *Stagecoach* was responsible for the changed status of the genre and for the rise of John Wayne as star figure.[33] *Stagecoach* was to establish the careers of both John Ford and John Wayne as embodying the enduring vision of the Westerner and his landscape.[34] The film's focus is not only on the male protagonist, but also on a distinctive cast of diverse characters played by recognizable actors: Claire Trevor (identified with melodramas and romance), John Carradine (a versatile character actor identified with a wide range of genre roles), Andy Devine (a prominent comic character actor), Thomas Mitchell, and Donald Meek (also familiar actors). Their performances highlighted the differentiated forces inherent in the frontier community and, according to historians like Frederick Jackson Turner, its inherently "democratic" foundations.

According to Deleuze, the film creates a portrait of the West that affirms action by a different version of the national epic, veering toward a "small form in which it is not the situation that triggers the action," but action that "discloses the situation."[35] The action "advances blindly and the situation is disclosed in darkness or ambiguity," suggesting signs of history growling at the periphery.[36] *Stagecoach* links the epic to a commonplace world in its focus on institutionalized morality and conceptions of justice to characterize the cramped and ungenerous world of the town against the expansiveness of the social outcasts and of the Western landscape. The landscape is a vital element, signifying openness of space against its closure in the settled towns. Thus, the film is not a celebration of the national community so much as a drama of the encroachments of the national community on free spirits. In contrast to *The Covered Wagon*, and versions of *The Virginian*, *Stagecoach* reveals a shift in emphasis from traditional frontier/nation-making Westerns, revealing a crisis of the "movement-image" that will intensify with the coming of the Second World War.

Allegory seems a suitable form for describing this film's uses of the past. *Stagecoach's* history is not a sequential narration of the winning of the West and the establishment of civilization in the untamed world of the frontier. The town of Lordsburg is integral to an allegory of the changing frontier world. The film, a fiction, is addressed to a 1939 audience, and its portrait of an earlier moment in time is not archival or antiquarian, not intended to reproduce how it "actually was," but to evoke a world poised between the circumscribed modern world and the breathing spaces of a West that is closing up.[37] Thus, the film evokes the difficulties of contemporary urban economic and social life in the 1930s.

The major trope of the film is a journey that is both material and figurative. The travelers include Ringo, Dallas, Doc, and Peacock who are exiled from the town of Tonto to find themselves in the company of those who are leaving the town of Tonto for other reasons, some highly questionable as in the case of the unscrupulous Southerner, Hatfield, and the dishonest banker, Gatewood. The film reiterates class, sex, and regional antagonisms that rely on internal and external distinctions between conflicting social values identified by the opposition between claustrophobic Western town and the open spaces of the frontier, as well as open and closed portraits of social distinctions.

The prostitute, Dallas, and the genteel Southern lady, Lucy Mallory, embody two different conceptions of femininity in relation to class, sexuality, and maternal behavior in which the prostitute emerges with the qualities of a lady. Dallas is a residue of an earlier vital frontier (if not also an allusion to the censorious judgment of moral "reprobates" in the Hollywood of the late 1920s and 1930s).

The careful tending by Dallas of Lucy Mallory and her baby born in this natural environment highlights the vitality of an organic, rather than automatic moral response to contingency, or predetermined views of social position. The opposition between the two women is further linked to that of North and South (figured in the faux but snobbish Southern chivalry exhibited by Hatfield, killed not by Ringo or Marshall Curly but by the Indians. In contrast to *The Iron Horse* and *The Virginian* with their reconciliation of North and South, Hatfield, as an embodiment of the racist and class-bound Southerner, is portrayed as unworthy of belonging to the morally responsible and nurturing community exemplified by these exiles from the now ambiguous "blessings of civilization." The alcoholic and penniless but genial Doc Boone is contrasted to both Hatfield and to the dishonest and cowardly banker, Gatewood, redeemed by a sense of ethical responsibility through his delivery of Lucy's baby.

Ringo, the outlaw, is the film's agent in affirming a democratic and humane form of respect for the beleaguered (white) outcasts of a world that has lost its ethical moorings. He incarnates Deleuze's notion of the hero as an "Encompasser" who "is larger than life and . . . He is the only one who is capable of rivaling the situation in its entirety."[38] Himself a victim and outlaw, his grievances are not such as to deter him from pursuing justice, though he does not function as in the epic form as the agent for re-establishing the larger social order.[39]

The history embedded in the film encompasses several moments in time: the nineteenth century; the aftermath of the Civil War; the earlier open and spacious world dramatized in epics of the westward movement; and the morally and physically reduced contemporary world of the settled town, if not of contemporary America. The allegorical struggle involves the Ringo Kid's defiance of existing law to pursue his ethical quest of vengeance. Through his actions in conjunction with the other outcasts, Ford breathes new affective life into the Western cult of individualism, masculine honor, and freedom through mobility in space against the constraining letter of the law and the prejudiced frontier community. Ringo's treatment of Dallas invokes an ethics that reinforces an idealized conception of the frontier (if not of the nation) guided by an unwavering sense of social justice in which all (whites) are treated equally.[40]

Wayne's portrayal of Ringo was to solidify his star identification with the myth of the Western hero as it changes in the genre over time. Ringo is the hinge of the narrative, a figure who, like the Virginian, lacks formal education, but one who has preserved the frontier spirit and a morality tied to the Eastern code of male honor and a form of law that transcends constraining and corrupt practices that have come to be identified with the narrow institutional (including sexual) morality characterized by the "civilized" inhabitants of Tonto. John Wayne in his persona as Ringo is a free spirit, less committed to action in the interests of "saving society," than to personal mobility and freedom. With Doc and Marshall Curly's sanction, he and Dallas eventually escape the "blessings" of the American frontier for the free landscape of Mexico. Despite Ford's reconstruction of the Western hero in *Stagecoach*, Ringo's departure signals that America's epic frontier vision is no longer sustainable within its own borders.[41]

Destry Rides Again: Deleuze's Small Form and the Burlesque, a Different Action Hero and Redemption

Burlesque relies on the action-image inherent to the Western, but can be more definitively described as a "small form" that presents a different version of affect and action. It pokes fun at the large and epic form, lending prominence to characters that are no longer greater than life but who appear weak, if not foolish, and reveal disparities between modes of action. In the case of the small form, it is the action, not the situation of the large form that "triggers off a new action."[42] Also appearing in 1939, *Destry Rides Again*, with its burlesque qualities, has been described as "a 'different' Western." This difference "made the dyed-in-the-wool Western devotees shudder, especially those who recalled with pleasure the Old Tom Mix version."[43]

Destry was a success, in large part, because of the performance of Marlene Dietrich in the role of Frenchy and of James Stewart in the starring role of Destry. *Destry's* Frenchy belongs to another, peripheral, and alien burlesque world. In contrast to other Western heroines—for example, Molly in the various versions of *The Virginian*—Frenchy is a disruptive force working against the domesticated portraits of femininity that work against her in the restoration of respectability. While Molly Wood puts on a convincing performance as a foil to *The Virginian* in the 1923 and 1929 films, Dietrich's role creates differences in the action that leads to a situation that becomes equivocal, as in the transformations and inversions in character and action that ultimately become ethical.[44]

Both Dietrich as Frenchy and Stewart as Destry seem to invert, if not undermine, expectations of the Western hero, as well as of familiar forms of femininity that deform gender through a functional reversal or permutation of opposites.[45] Frenchy is initially less abject than Dallas in *Stagecoach*, her sister from the margins, though she will finally pay the price for her feistiness and arrogance with her death. Her foreign persona is significant for genre production in the 1930s, as well as for Hollywood history and its response to national and social changes in this decade. Dietrich's Frenchy was one of several women to transgress Western genre boundaries in the years around the Second World War (Jean Arthur, *Arizona*, 1940; Gene Tierney, *Belle Starr*, 1941; Jennifer Jones, *Duel in the Sun*, 1946).

Destry follows the trajectory of the Western in its emphasis on the "attempts by the White frontier community to impose and establish a law-abiding settlement through the agency of a male protagonist."[46] In order to maintain this position, the film must eject Frenchy in behalf of restoring femininity to a proper role as a defender of civil society. Dietrich's persona and her character in the film both bring out the decadent aura of her other films, the siren and the *femme fatale*, but also dramatize feminine vulnerability in her encounters with Destry. The burlesque portrait of an imperious, amoral, gender-bending, and disruptive Dietrich is converted to an abject and sacrificial figure of femininity.

A related burlesque feature centers on the initially "gun-less," indeterminate masculinity of Destry. In his sermonizing and resistance to violence (based, as he recounts it, on the traumatic memory of his father's being shot in the back), he becomes an object of ridicule by the frequenters of the Last Chance Saloon. In contrast to Frenchy, Destry initially refuses to answer violence with violence. However, following the death of another father figure, Wash (Charles Winninger), Destry is finally moved to duel with the unscrupulous Kent (Brian Donlevy), whose character bears the burden of the community's ills: greed, gold, and violence. The film is riven by unresolved cleavages in the conversion of the pacifist Destry to the gunman in his killing of Kent, and in the elimination of Frenchy, who although converted by Destry's moral guidance, nonetheless, must yield to the domestic power of the town's wives.

The film reveals its divided strategies, its designs on the box office through soliciting mixed generational and class audiences, and on confronting the changing times in its address of sexuality, morality, violence, and xenophobia by both permitting the pleasures of looking at the excessive physical vitality and eroticism of Frenchy, while killing off the source of feminine pleasure, a renegade from domesticity and conventional morality.[47] Her role places her uneasily in the position of the woman between different conceptions of gendered and sexual performance. In its contradictory cinematic evocation of the American nation and changing national identity, the film gives further

evidence of an emerging crisis of the movement-image in relation
to clear-cut moral imperatives identified with the former world of
the West. The burlesque form, in its revelation of "slight differences
in the action which bring out slight differences in the situation,"
produces laughter but also pathos and incongruity.[48]

The Ox-Bow Incident: The Crisis of the Western and the Movement-Image

In keeping with the evolution of the Western into the 1940s, The
Ox-Bow Incident (1943) offers insight into the transformations of
the genre in the war years, focusing on "the inability of the hero to
right the wrongs of the West . . . [introducing] a new social realism
and overt political liberalism to the genre" that undermines, if not
dismantles, Western foundational narratives like The Virginian.[49] The
Ox-Bow Incident is removed from Stagecoach, Destry, and The Virginian
in that it transforms the protagonist from a romantic conception
of the outlaw to a tired cynic who is morally paralyzed, though
his bitterness is ascribed to his being jilted by a woman. Instead of
being a man with a mission, he is, as Dana Polan writes, a wanderer,
"occupying a place outside history."[50] This portrait is reminiscent of
Deleuze's discussion of the "crisis of the movement-image" in which
"sensory-motor action or situation has been replaced by the stroll . . .
[in which] the situation in which the character finds himself outstrips
his motor capacities on all sides and makes him see and hear what
is no longer subject to the rules of a response or an action . . . He is
prey to a vision, pursued by it or pursuing it, rather than engaged
in an action."[51] Like a sleepwalker, he views indifferently the hysterical men (and one woman) who organize a posse to bring presumed
cattle-rustlers and murderers to judgment without the sanction of a
trial. In contrast to early versions of The Virginian which rendered the
lynching of the cattle-rustlers as natural to preserving the frontier's
social and economic order, The Ox-Bow Incident presents the behavior
of the posse as a nightmare of egregious vigilante justice and indicts
the community for the murder of three innocent men. Gone is the
monumental version of frontier life. However, the film, identified with
the emergent social problem films of the 1940s,[52] is still at pains to
explore the motif of law, specifically in relation to failed conceptions
of masculinity and of community.

Carter (Henry Fonda) is bitter about being jilted by a woman who
is first seen as a reclining erotic object in a bar painting. She appears
later, briefly, wed to a wealthy upstart who warns Carter to treat her

properly as his wife. The film's portraits of failed masculinity do not
end with Carter. Major Tetley, another of the legion of Southerners
with questionable pasts, is obsessed with a son whom he is determined
to "make a man." The men who form the posse to catch the rustlers
are determined to get immediate justice, displaying indifference to
trial by jury and the need of evidence to justify their own murderous actions. The issue of race is introduced through the character
of Sparks, a Black minister whose little brother was a similar victim of
lynching, and thus the film prefigures other 1940s war films that
slowly include African American characters and situations.[53] The film
(shot in the studio and not on location) eschews any scenes that might
contribute to the mitigation of the posse, devoting a large portion of
the narrative to the helpless portraits of the three innocent men who
are summarily hanged.

The ultimate irony of the film is the arrival of the sheriff after the
hanging. He reveals that the man presumed dead by the posse is still living
and that the actual rustlers have been caught. The posse is unambiguously
identified as a bunch of murderers. Thus, the final confrontation between
the posse and the unjustly accused three men, a Mexican (Anthony
Quinn), a young rancher Martin (Dana Andrews), and "Dad," a senile
old man, is an unmitigated travesty of "civilized" Western society. The
film seeks to moderate its harsh parable in Fonda's gradual realization
of this miscarriage of justice and his determination to make amends by
supporting Martin's wife and children. He and his sidekick Art (Henry
Morgan) ride off into an uncertain future.

The film is proleptic of the failure of belief in the "American Dream,"
despite (or because of) wartime propaganda to solidify the national
community.[54] Visually and dramatically different from the earlier
versions of *The Virginian*, the film joins other films during the war era,
especially with film noir, to dramatize the uncertainty surrounding
the nation, its past and its future. Fonda's performance resonates with
other roles that would increasingly cast him as a hard-working champion of justice in a world of "angry men" (*Young Mr. Lincoln*, 1939;
My Darling Clementine, 1946; *Twelve Angry Men*, 1957; *The Tin Star*,
1957; *Fail-Safe*, 1964). By 1943, the movement-image is moribund,
and the epic has entered its decline. Hollywood has, despite itself
and its imposed moralistic endings, also entered a new regime of the
cinematic image by entering into "real time" and a critical view of the
frontier past. The film heralds the advent of a form, Deleuze's "time-
image," to challenge the historical and stylistic clichés of the prewar era.[55]
The Ox-Bow Incident challenges the world of *The Virginian* through its
reconfiguration of character and space by foregrounding the unsettling

central presence of race and ethnicity via the "lynching," presenting
a diminished photography of landscape, undermining heterosexual
romance, and substituting cynicism for heroic commitment. Even in
the attempts to vitalize the form, as in the postwar version of *The
Virginian*, the signs of the changing times are evident.

The Virginian (Stuart Gilmore, 1946)

If earlier adaptations of *The Virginian* chart the changing fortunes of
the Western, the 1946 film, made in the immediate postwar milieu,
offered another treatment in Technicolor with meticulous emphasis
on costumes and interiors, more akin to the *mise-en-scène* of Minnelli's
Meet Me in St. Louis (1944). The 1946 version was justly described
by the *Variety* reviewer as having the charm of a daguerreotype . . .
with nostalgic flavor."[56] The film starred familiar actors: Joel McCrea
as the Virginian, Barbara Britton as Molly, Sonny Tufts as Steve, and
Brian Donlevy as Trampas. Unlike the social realism of *The Ox-Bow
Incident*, the film is dependent on extreme stylization, particularly in
its treatment of character, setting, costuming, lighting, and choreography, creating the effect of a self-conscious media event. The film's
focus on surfaces clashes with both the monumental large and small
forms through its foregrounding of style. However, changes in the
performance and behavior of the characters afford telltale clues to this
film's differences from earlier adaptations, appearing more clichéd and
coercive, suggesting control over conflict.

A significant difference in this 1946 version of *The Virginian* can be
seen in the treatment of femininity. While Molly shares the Virginian's
discontent with conformity in her desire to escape (she from Vermont,
he from Virginia), the struggle between the two entails his insistence
on subduing her imperious spirit that he likens to the "taming of a
horse." Further, the complex series of scenes involving the containment
of the rustlers, the hanging of Steve, and the duel with Trampas
reinforce the film's unswerving affirmation of the values of respectability, law, and property that override earlier versions of the Virginian's
desire to escape conformity.

Instead of Cooper's vibrant and youthful playfulness, sensitivity, and
gradual transformation to responsibility in the 1929 version, McCrea's
heavier physical appearance, dialogue, and bodily movement reinforce a
virile conception of his character that seems more assertive and domi-
neering, more alert to injury to his self-esteem, than earlier versions of
the Virginian. McCrea's image of the cowboy evokes later 1940s films
in their concern over the dangers that can occur when "women try to

move beyond the limits of place," in their dramatization of masculine anxieties over the feminization of culture and the increasing presence of strong women in Westerns (*Cimarron*, 1931; *The Plainsman*, 1936; *Arizona*, 1940; *Belle Starr*, 1941; *Duel in the Sun*, 1946).[57] Gone in this version of *The Virginian* are both the playful baby-swapping scene and the Virginian's rescue of Molly from the drunken stagecoach driver. Instead, there are several rescue scenes that create misunderstandings between the hero and heroine. Finally, the film's abrupt, clichéd ending as the couple rides off into the sunset attempts to reinforce the film's nostalgia in delivering them to a place outside time, or, in the film's words, as seeking to live "closer to nature." In short, the film appears a throwback to a legendary world as a response to an uncertain future that it has attempted to escape.

Conclusion

The movement-image is identified with the "idea of the West and westward expansion as a formative feature of American national identity,"[58] characterized by open space, mobility and agency, generating affect and corresponding action to transform the nation. The large, epic form of *The Covered Wagon* and *The Iron Horse* enacts a monumental form of that transformation. The small form too, through romance and burlesque, in *Stagecoach*, early versions of *The Virginian*, and *Destry Rides Again*, remains within this affective regime of the image, albeit with recognition of increasing constraints on space and mobility, but still maintaining the vitality of a belief in movement and in ethical action. Signs of a "crisis" of the movement-image truly emerge in *The Ox-Bow Incident* and the 1946 version of *The Virginian*. As Deleuze points out, the crisis depended on many factors: "The war and its consequences, the new consciousness of minorities, the unsteadiness of the American Dream in all its aspects, the rise and inflation of images both in the external world and in people's minds."[59]

The cinema responded to these events by "undoing the system of actions, affections, and perceptions on which the cinema had been fed up to this point."[60] While the 1946 version of *The Virginian* reiterates the form and formulas of the foundational narrative characteristic of the action-image, it was acknowledged as "a little dated," "a mite slow," and "plodding," a sign of its regression to the past, if not refusal to confront the changing times.[61] By contrast, *The Ox-Bow Incident* thrusts the viewer into a world of uncertainty about the rule of law and of national, gendered, sexual, and racial identity, themes which

earlier versions of *The Virginian* had always suppressed. The film is
closer to confronting the new challenges to cinematic culture by
injecting the permanent effects of time, age, and racial conflict to
the genre. The postwar Western, produced in Hollywood and internationally, would continue to bear the signs of these changes, taking
Hollywood increasingly away from its mythic comfort zone.

Notes

1. For more on the Western's connections with mainstream frontier
   historiography, see Richard Slotkin, *Gunfighter Nation: The Myth of the
   Frontier in Twentieth-Century America* (New York: Atheneum, 1992).
2. Gilles Deleuze, *Cinema 1: The Movement Image*, trans. Hugh Tomlinson
   and Barbara Habberjam (Minneapolis: University of Minnesota Press,
   2001): xiv, ix. See also David Martin-Jones, *Deleuze, Cinema and National
   Identity: Narrative Time in National Contexts* (Edinburgh: Edinburgh
   University Press, 2008).
3. Friedrich Nietzsche,"On the Uses and Disadvantages of History for Life,"
   Untimely Meditations, trans. R.J. Hollingdale (Cambridge: Cambridge
   University Press, 1991): 57–125, 67–8); Deleuze: 150.
4. Deleuze: 148, 151.
5. More obviously, the assessment evokes classic structuralist genre studies
   of the Western which situate the films in a timeless milieu determined
   by classic binary conflicts within a well-organized national order.
6. Joy Kasson, *Buffalo Bill's Wild West: Celebrity, Memory, and Popular History*
   (New York: Hill & Wang, 2001).
7. Deleuze: 64.
8. *Ibid.*: 96, 97.
9. *Ibid.*: 146.
10. *Ibid.*: 18.
11. Kevin Brownlow, *The War, the West, and the Wilderness* (London: Martin
    Secker & Warburg, 1979): 334.
12. *Ibid.*: 295.
13. *Covered Wagon*, A James Cruze Production, Publicity Booklet
    (Hollywood: Paramount Pictures, 1923).
14. Slotkin: 56.
15. Deleuze: 163.
16. David Lusted, *The Western* (Harlow, England: Longman Publishing,
    2003): 136.
17. Owen Wister, *The Virginian: A Horseman of the Plains with Paintings
    by Fredric Remington and Drawings by Charles M. Russell* (New York:
    Macmillan Publishing Co. Inc., 1902).
18. Jane Kuenz, "The Cowboy Businessman and 'The Course of
    Empire': Owen Wister's *Virginian*," *Cultural Critique* 48 (spring, 2001):
    98–128.

19. Nixon Orwin Rush, *The Diversions of a Westerner: With Emphasis Upon Owen Wister and Frederic Remington Books and Libraries* (Amarillo, TX: South Pass Press, 1979): 146–7.

20. Patrick McGee, *From Shane to Kill Bill: Rethinking the Western* (Oxford: Blackwell Publishing, 2007): 27.

21. Richard Hutson, "Early Film Versions of *The Virginian*," in Melody Graulich and Stephen Tatum (eds.), *Reading the Virginian in the New West* (Lincoln: University of Nebraska Press, 2003): 126–47, 130.

22. Hutson: 132.

23. *Ibid.*: 134.

24. Deleuze: 98.

25. Jane Tomkins, *West of Everything: The Inner Life of Westerns* (Oxford: Oxford University Press, 1992): 141.

26. Deleuze: 163.

27. Peter Stanfield, *Hollywood Westerns and the 1930s: The Lost Trail* (Exeter: University of Exeter Press, 2001): 56–77.

28. *Ibid.*: 77.

29. Hutson: 137.

30. Stanfield: 49–55.

31. Michael Sragow, *Victor Fleming: An American Movie Master* (New York: Pantheon Books, 2008): 119.

32. Stanfield: 52.

33. Lusted: 15.

34. Sickels: 153.

35. Deleuze: 164.

36. *Ibid.*

37. See Kevin L. Stoehr and Michael C. Connolly (eds.), *John Ford in Focus: Essays on the Filmmaker's Life and Work* (Jefferson, NC: McFarland & Co. Inc., 2008): *passim*. The impact of the Depression on America's frontier image was considerable. In 1934, Franklin Delano Roosevelt finally closed the Public Domain, a region that had animated debates about Turner's Frontier Thesis.

38. Deleuze: 184.

39. *Ibid.*: 147.

40. Sickel: 142–3.

41. Deleuze: 148.

42. *Ibid.*

43. George Fenin and William K. Everson, *The Western: From Silents to Cinema* (New York: Bonanza Books, 1962): 253.

44. Deleuze: 160, 182.

45. *Ibid.*: 166.

46. Florence Jacobowitz, "The Dietrich Westerns: *Destry Rides Again* and *Rancho Notorious*," in Ian Cameron and Douglas Pye (eds.), *The Movie Book of the Western* (London: Studio Vista, 1996): 88–98, 88.

47. Stanfield: 172

48. Deleuze: 170.

49. Lusted: 177.
50. Dana Polan, *Power and Paranoia: History, Narrative, and the American Cinema 1940–1950* (New York: Columbia University Press, 1986): 264–5.
51. Gilles Deleuze, *Cinema 2: The Time-Image*, trans. Hugh Tomlinson and Robert Galeta (Minneapolis: University of Minnesota Press, 1989): 3.
52. Marcia Landy, "Movies and the Fate of Genre," in Wheeler Winston Dixon (ed.), *American Cinema of the 1940s: Themes and Variations*, (New Brunswick, NJ: Rutgers University Press, 2005): 222–45, 238.
53. Landy: 239.
54. Mary Beth Crain, "The *Ox-Bow Incident* Revisited," *Literature Film Quarterly* (summer, 1976), 4(3): 240–8, 247.
55. Deleuze (2001): 206.
56. *Variety*, January 30, 1946.
57. Lusted: 64–5, 94. J.E. Smyth, *Reconstructing American Historical Cinema From* Cimarron *to* Citizen Kane (Lexington: University Press of Kentucky, 2006): 46-9, 91-6.
58. Lusted: 19.
59. Deleuze (2001): 206.
60. *Ibid*.
61. *Variety*, January 30, 1946.

4

Ripping the Portieres at the Seams: Lessons from *Streetcar* on *Gone with the Wind*

Susan Courtney

In the course of researching Hollywood's re-imagining of national and regional U.S. identities in the mid-twentieth century, I spent considerable time with the run of popular films throughout the 1950s and into the 1960s adapted from the work of Tennessee Williams, a run that effectively began with *A Streetcar Named Desire* (1951).[1] My primary project with the Williams films was to confront what I've come to call the "leaky" forms of white subjectivity and cinematic space that riddle them, in order to understand how those forms fuse together a then re-imagined screen South and a range of "slightly queer" identities, and the implications of their having done so precisely during the Civil Rights era.[2] In the course of that work I made an unanticipated discovery, the subject of the present chapter, also relevant to the complex representational histories of identity embedded in the history of popular moving image culture. What I also learned from *Streetcar* came when I next taught *Gone with the Wind* (1939), upon watching it again with my students. For I then recognized, with a level of awareness and precision I had acquired through its deconstruction in *Streetcar*, a familiar cinematic syntax for conjuring white subjects in "Southern" space and the tremendous work it does in the 1939 film—a national and international blockbuster in its day that still ranks domestically as the best-selling film of all time (including multiple theatrical re-releases over multiple decades), in addition to its history of popularity in the home video market with multiple editions (e.g., "Collector's," "Anniversary," "Deluxe Box Set") in every key format from Betamax to Blu-ray.[3]

That *Streetcar* directly engages *Gone with the Wind* is most obvious, of course, in the casting of Vivien Leigh as Blanche DuBois. For with it,

49

the 1951 film renders the profound damage and ultimate destruction of conventional white femininity so central to Williams's play and the film alike all the more palpable, and consequential, for being performed by, and upon, the very same body—through the very face, voice, and gestures—with which *Gone with the Wind*, only a little more than a decade earlier, had produced Hollywood's iconic Southern belle as, above all else, the image of a *sustainable* feminine ideal, come what may.[4] That Hollywood's *Streetcar* wrenchingly exposes and unravels this myth upon that very body, thus expressly extends Williams's destabilizing gender project to a history of popular film, and a history of filmically imagining the South in particular, that was thoroughly implicated in the mass production and dissemination of such conventions. Any viewer of *Streetcar* who has ever seen *Gone With the Wind* can hardly avoid, at some level, registering the undoing of its monumental screen heroine. And in light of the enormous, international fandom of Leigh's Scarlett—due in part to the structure of that melodramatic epic that aligns the spectator with her for the better part of nearly four hours of her loves, labors, and losses—*Streetcar*'s deconstruction pinpoints precisely the character in whom one is likely to have been most deeply invested.[5]

But the ways in which *Streetcar* engages the history of cinematic representation is by no means limited to Vivien Leigh's remarkable performance. In addition, as I hope to show here, Blanche DuBois's repeated undoing in and through disastrously permeable Southern space has the further potential to expose a structuring set of forms within which Scarlett O'Hara and her idealized white Southern kind were routinely cinematically conjured, and also put at risk, and through which *Gone with the Wind*'s national and international viewers have been invited to find themselves quite precisely positioned as filmic spectators ever since. For reasons elaborated below, I will call this amalgam of forms "the plantation suture."

In what follows, I will briefly introduce key features of the leaky forms of space and subjectivity that structure Hollywood's *Streetcar* (and, in fact, mark a wide range of the nonetheless varied Hollywood adaptations of Tennessee Williams in its wake), before following the invitation I find in these forms to reconsider the earlier, more routinely sealed forms of identity and filmic representation, that, by turns, pervade and haunt *Gone with the Wind*.

Leaky Subjects in Leaky Space

Despite Hollywood's routine softening of the tragic and otherwise unsettling tendencies of plays like *Streetcar* and *Cat on a Hot Tin Roof*, the radical instability that so marks Williams's dramatic characters and relationships on stage continues in the feature films adapted from them not only in the psychic ruptures conjured through performance and dialogue, but also in the filmic rendering of space, and the selves and relations that unfold and unravel within it.[6] This is so frequently and excessively the case as to lead me to suggest that the considerable cinematic legacy that attaches to the name "Tennessee Williams" resides largely in the co-existence, and co-production, of leaky white Southern space and subjectivity. This tradition begins most vividly with Hollywood's *Streetcar*.[7]

Most of the film takes place in the small New Orleans apartment of Stanley and Stella Kowalski (Marlon Brando and Kim Hunter), a set the film production team took considerable care to render not only confining, but permeable, from without and within.[8] Upon arriving at her younger sister's run-down flat, Blanche DuBois immediately remarks on the lack of a door between its two small rooms, separated only (when at all) by a curtain—or "portieres," as the play indicates.[9] Also from the play, the upstairs neighbor pours boiling water through the cracks in her floor when she wants to break up Stanley's late night poker parties. What is more, the film's use of the set, blocking, cinematography, lighting, and the like all build on these inherited thematics to render cinematic the routine transgression of the fragile boundaries centrally in question: namely, Kowalski vs. DuBois; male vs. female; immigrant working class vs. white Southern aristocracy; sanity vs. insanity.

As a self-described "ruin" whose unstable mental health and transgressive sexual history preoccupy the film, Blanche is clearly the leakiest of subjects in *Streetcar*, and this takes explicit cinematic form in the ongoing depiction of her in and through noticeably unsealed space. She famously enters the film emerging from the steam of the train that has brought her to New Orleans, and is further set apart from the modern crowd by her apprehensive demeanor, gauzy dress and the netted veil of her hat (Illustration 4.1). The visual motifs that begin here, permeable fabrics and atmospherics that work to underscore the permeability of Blanche's psychic borders, will continue throughout the film as she is perpetually represented through, and associated with, vapors (steam, perfume, smoke), liquids (habitual hot baths, habitual drinking), light (her continual avoidance of it, and ultimate exposure in it), and a long list of windows, doors, shutters, and curtains that appear throughout the film visibly (and often dangerously) open, broken, and transparent (Illustration 4.2).

The relationship between the radical fragility of Blanche's psychic boundaries and the noticeably leaky space that is the Kowalski apartment is vivid upon her arrival there, and central to her filmic demise. This is apparent throughout the film's final scenes—including her brutal rejection by Mitch (Karl Malden) upon his learning of her sexual past; her assault and (offscreen) rape by Stanley; and finally a terrifying nervous breakdown—each of which maps her psychic collapse within and through spaces with increasingly unreliable borders and boundaries. This comes to a disastrous climax with her nervous breakdown at film's end, rendered through an attack of convulsions that find her, and the camera, momentarily caught in the liminal space between curtains and sheers of a closed window she cannot escape out of, thumping and moaning against it like an injured bird. For the current chapter, however, the most elucidating example of the film's co-production of leaky space and subjectivity—the one that helps us link *this* Southern screen space to the one Leigh also starred in as a Southern belle of much heartier stock—comes earlier, when we first see, and hear, a clear confirmation of Blanche slipping into madness, also dramatically staged at one of the apartment's unusually precarious windows.

The moment in question comes soon after Mitch's rejection. After Blanche's initial self-respecting anger at his sexual double standard has melted to desperation (Mitch has been her last hope, emotionally and economically), her fragility seems to open her up still further to haunting by past trauma at her family's lost plantation, Belle Reve. This is sparked when, having tried to explain that her meetings with "strangers" were desperate attempts to fill her emptiness upon the death of her husband, Blanche hears a woman's voice outside and opens the front door. As the woman approaches, selling "*flores para los muertos*," death itself threatens to cross the threshold. Terrified, Blanche quickly closes the door and leans back against it as if to seal it up. But it's too late: her demeanor has changed dramatically, as if whatever she was trying to shut out has seeped inside to profoundly alter her state of mind. Speaking now in a deeper, monological voice, she is overtaken by memories of having "lived in a house where dying old women remembered their dead men." Her speech becomes strikingly fragmented, and its pieces, Leigh's performance, and Alexander North's suddenly haunted score render an intense collage of trauma and loss: "Crumble and fade. Regrets, recriminations. 'If you'd done this, it wouldn't have cost me that.' Legacies. And other things. Such as blood-stained pillow slips." After these perforated glimpses into Blanche's ruptured psychic history, some narrative coherence gradually returns, but in telling the story that unfolds she appears disturbingly relocated, in time and space, at one of the large windows that open onto the street. Following a reaction shot of Mitch just after the fragmented lines cited above, a cut to Blanche finds her seated, and a narrative begins with the suggestion of an imagined return to the space of her haunted memories: "I used to sit here, and she used to sit there. And death was as close as you are." Blanche then proposes that death's "opposite is desire," and her story suddenly turns to recall her relief at Belle Reve.

While the sudden, disjunctive pivots here—from present to past, from death to desire, from the apartment in the French Quarter to the mansion at Belle Reve—signal the ruptured state of the psychic space Blanche now seems to inhabit, the staging and performance of these recollections also subtly, yet quite remarkably, expand the origin story of her deviant desire for younger men, here relayed through the speech adapted from the play. She tells how "young soldiers" from a nearby base used to "stagger onto my lawn" on Saturday nights and call out her name. As she mimics them—slowly singing out "Blaa-anche, Bla-anche"—her eyes and ears lead her to the window behind her, and she rises and drifts around to it as if drawn there by the young men's call. She pulls back the sheers to peek out through the shutters, and as she does so an eerily dissociative but distinctly girlish giggle erupts (Illustration 4.3). The disturbing difference of the giggling sounds at the window from the troubled adult voice we have been listening to confirms that Blanche is slipping into madness before our eyes. What is more, erupting at the window as she peeks out in response to the boys' call, this very slip is located in a space that here suddenly seems to open onto not only the street outside (where a stranger on the street is visible with his back to her—in a pose suggestive of urinating, no less), but also that plantation lawn that she could see from her window at Belle Reve; where those boys looked up to her, framed within that Big House, and she could look back to see them there, wanting her. The scene thus exposes not only the early history of her desire for younger men, but also its structure having been utterly shaped by "the place within them columns," as Stanley earlier describes Belle Reve and, with these, a very specific fantasy of a younger, desired, and desiring white feminine self framed within that Big House window. Painfully exposed here too, of course, is Blanche's derangement by the intractable hold of that no longer tenable fantasy.

Representing the Big House

After recognizing the excess with which *Streetcar* and the Williams films that follow it deploy leaky windows, curtains, doors, and the like in their perpetual unhinging of white Southern identity, what becomes evident upon revisiting *Gone with the Wind*'s epic melodrama of whiteness idealized, at risk, and renewed (in seeming perpetuity) is that that film, too, maps its white Southern subjects in precise, continual relation to threshold spaces at the perimeter of its Southern homes—namely the façade, front door, windows, balconies, and porches of the plantation mansion. But there the articulation of characters, and the spectator, in relation to such threshold spaces at the Big House repeatedly functions—from the opening sequence to the film's final shot, and at most every key juncture in between—carefully to seal together, and at times threaten to split apart, the psychic lives that unfold (mostly) within (the white house, the white self) and the social structures routinely figured to extend without (in the fields where slaves work the land; on the grounds where parties gather and troops depart for war). Insofar as the Williams films radically undermine such cinematic routines, they have the critical potential to disrupt, and invite us to recognize more precisely, classical Hollywood's plantation suture.[10]

Before elaborating this history of filmic representation evidenced throughout *Gone with the Wind*, it pays to situate it within a larger history of critique of popular representations of the plantation home. Of particular note is the work of Melvin B. Tolson, whose contributions to the history of film criticism have been recently brought to light by Anna Everett in her extensive recovery of African American writing about film in the black press. Tolson, who authored a weekly column from Washington, DC, wrote two different articles on *Gone with the Wind* in 1940, one of which he titled "The Philosophy of the Big House." As Everett puts it, "Tolson recognized the political economy symbolized by the big house" in *Gone with the Wind* and related Hollywood "antebellum films," the ways it "traded on America's nostalgia for an imagined past of economic stability and white aristocratic splendor [and] helped ensure that the racial chasm dividing the black and white masses would remain intact during th[e] volatile period of national crisis" that was the pre-Civil Rights 1940s.[11] In Tolson's own words, "everything in *Gone with the Wind* could've been left out of both the novel and the picture but one thing. The movie could've had other characters, other settings, other happenings . . . [even] another plot." The one and only thing essential "to create *Gone with the Wind*," Tolson continued, was "the Big House." Critically re-enacting the house's pervasive presence in order to call it into question, Tolson makes the point again and again: "This novelist had to put into the book the Big House. The director of the movie had to use the Big House. Southern aristocracy could not be pictured without the Big House. The Big House is the most significant thing in the history of Dixie."[12]

If the ideological work of the Big House in *Gone with the Wind* was thus obvious to some as early as 1940, Tara McPherson has recently helped us understand the longevity of this representational legacy.[13] Linking contemporary images of white-columned Big House façades from brochures advertising plantation tourist sites to Margaret Mitchell's novel and the film, McPherson analyzes their invitations to fantasize history and identity, offered as much through space and the movement of the tourist through it as through any tour guide's narration: "the visiting tourist is powerfully positioned within a Southern *mise-en-scène* of imagined hospitality, an immersive experience underwritten both by the mansions' high ceilings, ornate furnishings, and lush garden settings and by the erasure of slavery . . . Strolling down Oak Alley's magnificent tree-lined path toward the veranda, the unsuspecting visitor is swept into a stage set ripe for fantasy."[14] McPherson thus invokes Cora Kaplan as she invokes that strain of psychoanalysis that stresses that "identification 'may shift in the course of a fantasy scenario' and that 'scenario thus takes precedence over any fixed identification of the subject with any one character in the scene.'"[15] Such thinking leads McPherson effectively to expand Tolson's insight by stressing the powerfully psychological dimensions of white investments and identities secured through conventional representation of the plantation home:

> Scenario is key . . . the plantation home surfaces as the primary environment of memory and desire. This genteel landscape enables a powerful *fixing of white identity within a very particular mise-en-scène*, a setting that structures the possibility for the novel's racial performances. Late-twentieth-century tourism will whitewash this Old South landscape while still celebrating grandeur and elegance.[16]

While McPherson's keen analysis of *Gone with the Wind* will go on to plumb relations between the white mistress and her black mammy that unfold within this fantasmatic scene in the novel especially, she also makes clear that scene's centrality to the continued national habit of splitting apart such powerful invitations to white nostalgia from any signs of the history of racial violence and black trauma that necessarily underwrite it.

What Hollywood's *Streetcar* can add to this history of critique, I suggest, is the recognition of a precise, by turns robust and fragile set of cinematic routines with which popular filmic representation shaped and expanded the fantasy of the Big House from Mitchell's novel; cinematically conjuring an alluring position of white privilege Hollywood spectators were invited to imagine themselves within, even as they were also then clearly invited to feel that position to be at risk. From our own historical vantage point, this history of film form can perhaps shed further light on the resilience of the fantasmatic scene in question, and *Gone with the Wind*'s continued popularity since its release over seventy years ago, despite so much effort since to disrupt and reject the racial–political economy that scene and the film openly celebrate. In addition, considering the Williams films in their own historical moment, they become all the more intriguing in this context for the ways they can be said to contain the possibility of a mid-century encounter with a by no means straightforward decon-struction of *Gone with the Wind*: one that could radically dismantle that film's enormous cinematic efforts to position the spectator within its imagined racial economy, even while nonetheless facilitating the disavowal of the racial history that marks Blanche DuBois's mental illness by figuring that illness as, above all, a feminine condition.[17] While elsewhere I confront the ways in which the Tennessee Williams films routinely swerve away from race to cast the perversity of their white Southern subjects as, ultimately, sexual, here I want to open up the structuring seams of the plantation suture before *Streetcar* nonetheless rips them apart.

The Plantation Suture

The example that most neatly crystallizes the plantation suture occurs early in the 1939 epic (before the dream is "Gone . . . ") at the enor-mous "barbeque" at Twelve Oaks, the plantation home of John Wilkes and his son, Ashley. It occurs across two short sequences, the second of which can be read to answer, and complete, the first, inserting the spectator into the place, and subject position, it more explicitly reveals.[18]

After a posted sign in close-up names the plantation, its owner, and the exclusive nature of the territory we are about to enter ("Anyone disturbing the peace on this plantation will be prosecuted"), the first sequence effectively begins with an establishing shot of Twelve Oaks (Illustration 4.4). What is established is the distinctly social and prop-ertied context of the fantasmatic scene emerging, delivered as an invitation to the spectator to enter it via a distinct route. We pause in a long shot before the front gate through which a line of carriages travel down the long, oak-lined path that holds out the plantation home as its desirable endpoint. A cut pulls us in to arrive with carriages at the home's grand entrance, and another draws us up onto the porch, in the more human scale of a full shot, to be welcomed by the host just before the next onscreen arrival appears. With Scarlett's arrival soon after, we move with her through the porch and front door into the mansion's vast entry hall. Reiterating the syntax introduced in the film's opening sequence (as we'll see below), the barbeque's opening shots thus map the spectator's entry into this world in distinct relation to the façade of the plantation home. We are situated not only to take in the impressive scale and grandeur of the estate, but also to do so within the familiar perspectival geometry that organizes space on screen and off around the center point of the mansion's façade, our place and course thus plotted in relation thereto before we are drawn inside, with Scarlett, where the melodramatic action unfolds.[19]

The second pivotal moment comes a short while later, after we've been oriented to the space within, additional characters, and the romantic couples and triangles forming among them. After Scarlett has seen Rhett Butler (Clark Gable) for the first time (staring at her), the camera fades out on her as she walks off with a gossip to whisper about him. In the near black of the fade-out, we dissolve into a private moment with Ashley and Melanie (Leslie Howard and Olivia de Havilland), his new fiancée, as they, at first remaining in near darkness, walk towards the light of sheer-draped French doors. Initially visible as mere silhouettes of a "lady" and "gentleman" (through outlines of hoopskirt, bonnet, and formal suit) in whose places we can all the more readily insert ourselves, the pair is dramatically lit by the glow from outside as they pause for a moment before the doors' large windows, to be framed precisely here (Illustration 4.5). After declarations of happiness, Ashley (with the help of invisible labor on the left) opens both doors in one grand gesture to reveal in a spectacular expanse of light and Technicolor a verdant, manicured landscape teeming with brightly-dressed guests strolling and being served about the grounds of his estate. As the couple and the camera move onto the balcony fully to take in the dazzling view of property and leisure, Ashley makes even more explicit the invitation to take residence in the position of white privilege being choreographed from the balcony for Melanie and the spectator alike: "You seem to belong here, as if it had all been imagined for you." Accepting the position thus offered, Melanie confirms the fantasy of the larger scene upon which it depends: "I love it as more than a house; it's a whole world that wants only to be graceful and beautiful." Continuing this curious projection of the subject and desire in question onto the "world that wants" (as if it exists without them, or they without it), but also thereby underscoring the centrality of the larger fantasmatic scene to the subject position on offer, no sooner have these shots inserted the spectator here, on the balcony, sharing the proprietary, surveying gaze, than Ashley invites us to begin nostalgically to mourn the loss of it all: "It's so unaware that it may not last, forever." Very quickly, then, the film's primary fantasmatic/ideological scene (the Big House), subject positions (the white master and mistress), and affect (intense pleasure in these positions coupled with intense grief at the threat of their disappearance) are distinctly mapped together to encourage us to find ourselves here. This is the work of the plantation suture (Illustration 4.6).

Despite its obviousness (one of those Hollywood forms that is perhaps striking for having worked so well despite its transparency), the potential power of this cinematic structure is obviously tremendous, fusing together and intensifying a range of meanings, feelings, and investments in economies of heterosexual romance, property, and race. In the novel there is no such scene—at the barbeque, on the balcony, or otherwise—and invitations to the reader to imagine herself within the multiple economies in question are routinely more distinct, dispersed over many pages (and chapters), and without such a singular, iconic moment. In the novel, too, Scarlett will pine for Ashley, money, and the good old days when these are gone (although more often she is annoyed by others' nostalgia for life before the war), but such yearnings do not routinely collapse together so neatly there as they do here early in the film. What is more, the film will go on perpetually to recall this moment in so many variations that revise, refuse, and partially restore it. Indeed, what is perhaps most surprising about the plantation suture upon recognizing it, if so many familiar Hollywood forms of continuity and identity at work in it are not, is how systematically its variants shape the film's structure. For it is modified throughout to form not only the initial "world" and the privileged identities conjured through it, but also the pivotal conflicts that perpetually put these at risk, as well as the film's key scene of Scarlett's reconstruction. My analysis of key examples of this structuring presence of the plantation suture thus aims to highlight further contributions it makes to *Gone with the Wind*'s considerable representational legacy.

Like a far more elaborate version of the establishing shots of the Twelve Oaks barbeque (a few scenes later), the film's opening credit sequence is a compendium of establishing long shots that map the extensive territory that surrounds the plantation home (well before we see it, in this case) before inviting us to enter into "the Old South" (so named in scrolling text over the image) at the threshold space of the porch, where the diegesis begins. And the rendering of this map is crucial to the meanings and sentiments that subsequent articulations of the plantation suture will both carry with them and elide.

With a glowing Technicolor palette and the unforgettable swells of Max Steiner's score, the mode of feeling on offer is unabashedly nostalgic and that sentiment is here fused to a very specific filmic geography. After production credits (including the studio's white-columned mansion headquarters/logo with "Selznick International Studios" written atop its colonnade), romantic travelogue shots catalogue the plantation's vast holdings: slaves picking cotton under a purple sky; wide tracking shots of fenced land under a painterly sunset (with huge letters of the film's title sweeping across it, amplifying the reach of land and loss); grazing horses; a river; flowering pink blossoms; a mill; more picturesque imagery of slaves at work; images of the film's two main plantation homes as backdrops to the scroll of players at each; and, ultimately, more glowing images of slaves working at sunset. These last initially form the background for the scrolling text that takes us back to "a land of Cavaliers and cotton fields," a "pretty world" where "the last ever [was] to be seen of Knights and their Maidens Fair, of Master and of Slave." After such words roll away, the image that remains closes this sequence with a now unobstructed view of silhouetted slaves tending cattle against a towering, stunningly radiant sky. Although we are told here to "Look for it only in books, for it is no more than a dream remembered," the film not only delights in bringing it before our eyes, but maps it as a particular space—the glowing expanse of the plantation's vast holdings—we are invited to survey and then enter for the shared dream/memory that follows.

With a fade to black and a quick fade-in, the nostalgic silhouette of slave labor is immediately fused to the fantasmatic center of the landscape just mapped, and we are delivered there through the portal of the Big House façade: first, we see it in long shot, with a slave chasing a turkey down the dirt path that leads our eye to it; we then dissolve into a tightly framed side view of the porch, with an initially obscured but distinctively hoop-skirted lady attended by two gentlemen. When the camera tracks in to reveal (ultimately) the star in a close-up as one of the grown twins she toys with steps aside, she delivers her famous opening lines: "Fiddle-dee-dee. War, war, war. This war talk is spoiling all of the fun at every party this spring. I get so bored I could scream." But despite Scarlett's verbal protest, as if the politics of war and party pleasures are mutually exclusive in this film, the architectural space of the porch that literally brings such spheres together is also here aesthetically bound to the images and sentiments of the opening credits that immediately precede it. This occurs not simply through the juxtaposition of the sequences and obvious continuity between them (slaves working in the fields and here chasing down dinner by the house; spring blossoms featured in the opening tour and here initially framing the porch), but also through the intensely luminous glow that continues here as well, albeit in daylight, as if its source were that "world" just viewed that surrounds the home and now dramatically lights it up. For instead of the shade we might expect under the porch's deep roof, a flood of warm, bright light initially bathes the mansion's façade (until the news of Ashley's engagement to Melanie kills Scarlett's happy demeanor and with it this light), such that the glowing Big House remains visible for most of the scene, as crucial as the white woman in her voluminous white dress (if not more so) to setting the larger fantasmatic scenario we are here invited to enter.

After the opening scene on the porch, the expanse of property surrounding the home is reiterated further, with more scenic views of slaves at work in multiple locations and Scarlett's father, Gerald O'Hara (Thomas Mitchell), loping and leaping through it on horseback before a creek-side stroll with his daughter that culminates with his famous speech about the value of "the land" to their "Irish" identity (read immigrants who have become white).[20] What is more, his speech is delivered as the film builds to one of its most (if not *the* most) iconic images, wherein the celebrated identity is visually and spatially rendered through the O'Haras' placement as the land's proud owner-occupants; a placement articulated here too, albeit in variation, in distinct relation to the façade of the plantation home, and in ways that will indelibly mark the film as a whole. For this scene builds to and closes with the iconic shot—repeated in variation at key moments at the film's middle and end. In it we see the O'Haras, with their backs to us, silhouetted at sunset under an enormous oak as they look out over their land that spreads deep into the horizon. Anchored by the oak that roots them in the foreground, the reach of the landowners' claim is measured and secured in relation to the façade of the plantation home that serves as the focal point of their gaze in the far distance. While our view in this shot begins just behind (and below) them, as the Steiner refrain again swells the camera pulls dramatically back (and up) such that the distance between their gaze and ours expands, modeling our view after theirs, but adding our own distinctly spectatorial position as the ultimate eye/witness confirming this masterful viewing position (Illustration 4.7).

More remarkable in this shot is its revision of the visual motif with which the opening credits culminated, of silhouetted figures against a blazing sunset. For here, that imagery distinctly returns—clouds and sky glow and almost burn with orange behind the cut-outs of hoopskirt and coattails romantically blowing in the wind (yes, the wind)—but without any sign of the original slave content of the silhouettes-at-sunset motif. As a result, this extreme long shot variation of the plantation suture, that will become a key structuring element of the film as a whole, effectively siphons off the aesthetic and the nostalgic sentiment that was explicitly conjured for the slave economy in the opening sequence, but disavows the ownership of slave bodies and slave labor *also* central to the celebrated identity on the "land" Gerald here espouses. For all this shot does, and how affectively saturated is its invitation to the spectator (cue again the swelling score as well as the eye-popping visuals) to enter and nostalgically hold onto the privileged position thus mapped, it is not surprising that its key features return when they do, at two pivotal moments when the future of its onscreen subject is most in question. In the first, when all seems lost with the war and Scarlett's view from the house is anything but pretty, after she gags on a raw carrot and vows never to be hungry again, the power of forces to remake her and/through Tara are registered not only by the famously determined, fist-shaking speech and performance ("As God is my witness . . . "), but also by the filmic rendering that begins with a nearly silhouetted close-up, only to cut to a full shot that sweeps epically back to relocate her within another vast, glowing sunset reminiscent of the iconic father–daughter shot under the oak (Illustration 4.8). The tree she now stands next to has been burned, the earth is barren, and the house is not yet visible (or repaired), and we look *at* Scarlett (frontally), not with her from behind (we must wait until after Reconstruction for *this* shot's reverse shot). But the promise of the enormous, radiant sky in the picture she is here relocated within offers a very specific promise of hope (that will be delivered). And the same promise returns at film's end. After Melanie has died, and with her Scarlett's fantasy of Ashley, and Rhett has walked out for seemingly the last time, Scarlett's decision to return to Tara closes the film with the near restoration of the original silhouetted shot under the oak with Scarlett (albeit alone) gazing at Tara in the distance (Illustration 4.9). While her final lines in the film, spoken at the foot of the Butler staircase just before this last shot, admit the uncertainty of her plan for winning Rhett back ("Home, I'll go home. And I'll think of some way to get him back"), the final fiery shot that once again tracks epically back to put her, and us, into the spot from which to nostalgically survey and reclaim this view clearly has begun to map the solution.

As this reading has been suggesting, and as the borrowing of the by now academically retro language of "suture" implies, the forms I

have been describing routinely suggest powerful, consolidating cinematic forces of ideological cohesion and restoration, especially at the
film's beginning, middle, and end. At the same time, as its title insists,
Gone with the Wind is of course preoccupied with profound loss, both
personal (Scarlett's unrequited love for Ashley; the deaths of her mother,
father, child, and so on) and social (the loss of the Cause, the "dream,"
the "world"). While the overwhelming nostalgia evoked through both
kinds of losses (affectively fused in the film in large part through the
forms in question) renders this melodrama deeply conservative in its
perpetual yearning for what was, it is nonetheless structured perpetually to face the dream's disruption. And this process, which becomes so
relentless as to make any restoration come to feel increasingly fleeting,
is routinely enacted in part through set-ups that recall, even as they
threaten and refuse them, forms of the plantation suture.

Throughout, the film's waves of loss briefly overcome only to
be set in motion again, examples of the plantation suture at risk are
ample. In the first half, they register Scarlett's loss of both Ashley and
the world he offers to Melanie instead. For later at the Twelve Oaks
barbeque, after we have shared the young couple's proprietary view
from the balcony, Scarlett's disappointment upon learning of their
engagement is staged, with Ashley, before another window; but here,
after the two have confessed their mutual love, when he delivers the
bad news that he's "going to marry Melanie," they stand in a two-shot
just in front of closed shutters that block anything like the view and
position he has just offered his fiancée. Similarly, when news of the
war's outbreak arrives soon after and the men at the party race off to
enlist, Scarlett's loss is again figured at a window, this time with a clear
view to the oak-lined entry where Ashley says good-bye to Melanie.
Here, Scarlett initially stands in a full shot alongside Charles Hamilton
(who she will here agree to marry to spite Ashley), looking out of
the paned window that effectively bars her, and marks her distance,
from the romantic scene in which she longs to be (Illustration 4.10);
a reverse shot isolates her still further in close-up, framed behind a
single pane, as she watches the other couple's parting kiss.

Ashley similarly disappoints Scarlett before a window at the end of
his brief furlough, and this time her romantic loss is explicitly layered
with what he here laments as "the end of our world." What is more,
these losses now are staged in a virtual undoing of the suture initially
offered from Ashley's balcony. After a brief moment of romantic hope,
registered before the window as Ashley warmly accepts Scarlett's gift
of a new sash, the mood turns somber when he bemoans: "Now the
end is coming . . . the end of the war . . . and the end of our world,

Scarlett." As he speaks his despair, the gap between them widens as she sits down and he moves to the window to look out at a dark, rainy scene while relaying tormented visions: "I see the Yankees always coming and coming, always more and more." The visual and spatial "end" of anything like the promise originally held out at the balcony is underscored by the camera's placement, angled away from Ashley's sightline such that our glimpse of even the wintry view is shallow and largely obscured. In desperation, Scarlett throws her arms around him and declares her love, only to have him return her kiss but walk out in silence. And Scarlett's loss, too, is again registered at the window (Illustration 4.11), her look at him disappearing into the grey now doubly coded as not only personal (Ashley), but social ("our world" with him). In short, even before the Yankees arrive, the cinematic articulation of the original fantasmatic scenario, the carefully crafted invitations to imagine ourselves within it, are already in jeopardy.

When the war does reach Tara and Twelve Oaks, its most devastating blows are also registered through articulations of desperate white Southerners in threshold spaces that no longer guarantee anything like the luminous, well-tended seams between their former social and psychic positions. When Scarlett has fled a burning Atlanta to get Melanie and her newborn baby safely back to Tara, she races in near darkness through its haunted grounds and the musical crescendo of reunion swells as she approaches the filthy façade and pounds on the darkened front door which will reveal her devastated father. Inside she'll learn of her mother's death, and when it seems things couldn't possibly be worse, she finds Pa sitting in the dark with his back to another window with only a shallow view of bare branches, and here soon discovers that the surviving parent with whom she has reunited has also been lost, to madness. In another overlay of social and personal loss at a darkened Big House window, a conversation that begins about Gerald's (worthless) Confederate bonds and their need for money changes suddenly when Scarlett first witnesses his delusion that his wife is still alive (Illustration 4.12).

For all the cumulative power of these examples, nowhere is the film's investment in the plantation suture, and the psycho-social seams it once sealed, more dramatically revealed than in the famous scene of a despondent Scarlett suddenly inspired to remake herself with the green velvet drapes, or "po'teers," as Mammy (Hattie McDaniel) calls them, that still hang at Tara when most everything else is gone. In the moment leading to this inspiration, Scarlett's losses are rendered at yet another of Tara's large windows. This time panes of glass are broken and boarded up, and as she leans against them in despair, any remaining view is blocked still further by the hand in which she buries her eyes (Illustration 4.13). And it is precisely *this* low moment, staged so as completely to refuse the plantation suture, that gives rise to her sudden inspiration to repurpose the green portieres that formerly helped to frame the critical space and its view in order to remake her own image and position as the proud, secure owner of Tara. Drifting away from the window in worry about taxes, she absent-mindedly fingers the drapery fringe and thinks aloud, "Rhett," as she heads to the mirror to imagine how to attract him and his money. Disheartened by what she sees, she notices the drapes now behind her in the mirror's reflection, and a rush of hope returns. Drafting a reluctant Mammy into the project, she soon stands before the mirror, wrapped in her favorite color with a returning smile; and when we next see her she will appear to have pulled off the scheme, much to Rhett's liking. And all of this is done, we can now appreciate more fully, with material whose original function was to mark, protect, and adorn the crucial seam of the Big House window.

Scarlett's subsequent rebuilding projects continue to be punctuated by variations on the plantation suture. And as loss hits, again and again, so do more by now familiar framings. After their marriage, Rhett, upon realizing Scarlett's continued love of Ashley, leaves her for several months. He returns to knock her down their giant staircase accidentally, and his despair at possibly losing her for good—and the baby she carries—is staged first with a shot of his open bedroom window through which rain pours inside, until Melanie comes to close it shut before offering comforting words before another viewless window (Illustration 4.14). Years later, their daughter Bonnie's tragic death by pony accident is rendered as a spectacular scene of parental horror staged at the threshold viewing space of the elevated porch of the Butler mansion, when their proud gaze at her trotting amidst manicured grounds becomes a help-less witnessing of her accidental death. (If Ashley and Melanie's marriage virtually begins on his balcony, Rhett and Scarlett's is decidedly over here, losing the one thing they shared.) And with the film's final tragedy, when Scarlett realizes too late that she does love Rhett, the fog that descends entirely obscures any possible view outside the window that forms the initial backdrop of their final conversation, before she watches Rhett walk out the front door and into it in his final exit

Gone with the Wind ends, as noted above, by returning Scarlett in silhouette once more to take in a radiant view of the Big House at Tara—a view that anchors her and the spectator one last time with its promise of reclaiming a place of strength from within that space. In keeping with the above catalogue of tragically *failed* views, however,

that transpire along with the 1939 film's obviously restorative ones, I want to return in my own ending to *Streetcar*.

Amidst so many unravelings of Blanche DuBois within the dangerously leaky space of the Kowalski apartment, twice—in staging not indicated by the play in either case—we witness her psychic dissolution at leaky windows explicitly linked to the loss of her former life, and self, at the plantation. One of these scenes, as we have seen, explicitly conflates and contrasts the threshold space of the window that opens onto the noisy street in the Quarter with the (memory) window that once secured her at Belle Reve. What becomes clearer now, I hope, is that that scene, combined with so many others that spatially map the psychic ruptures performed by Vivien Leigh, makes a strong case for reading *Streetcar* as relentlessly dismantling the plantation suture canonized by *Gone with the Wind*, and potentially exposing in the process some of the 1939 blockbuster's precise, *cinematic*, efforts to conjure and support—even as they also register the dreaded end of—foundational structures of the white South and the film's most privileged identities.

That said, there is no doubt that *Streetcar* is more concerned with the psychic dimensions of socially constituted identities than with the social structures of power that underwrite them. Even so, a second crucial scene in the film gestures more explicitly towards the ways in which the loss of Blanche's younger, eroticized self image is also intertwined with the loss of a distinctly racialized economy. And here, again, the exposure occurs at one of the apartment's large windows, presented in this scene so as neither fully to shut out nor clearly open onto the world outside. For after Stanley threatens to expose Blanche's sexual past, worried and anxious she explains to her sister: "I haven't been so awfully good the last year or so since Belle Reve started to slip through my fingers." The sounds of a downpour outside are audible, and as she moves towards the window Blanche speaks of having never been "hard or self sufficient enough," explaining that "soft people have got to court the favor of hard ones. They've got to shimmer and glow." With this formulation of her Southern belle options for success in our ears, we cut to a medium shot of Blanche before the window that does glow from without, but with light so grey and diffused by the gauzy sheers on one side and the water sheeting down on the other as to keep her largely in shadow. With no point to looking out (there is nothing and no one to see or be seen by) Blanche is planted in profile, gripping the sheers as her desperation escalates: "I don't know how much longer I can turn the trick. It isn't enough to be soft. You've got to be soft . . . and attractive. And I . . . I'm fading now." Duly depressed, she stands a while longer at the wet, grey

window as Stella walks away; but suddenly Blanche breaks away from
it with panicky excitement to ask, "Oh, is that Coke for me?" In the
cut to a long shot we see her framed by the window behind her with
the lines of its plantation-style fanlight pattern suddenly visible at the
top, as Stella confirms that the Coke is for her, lifting Blanche's spirits
dramatically (Illustration 4.17). She is buoyed in part by the thought
of "a shot" to fortify it, but the ensuing exchange also confirms her
overwhelming relief in the act of being served. Stella offers, "I like
to wait on you Blanche. It makes it seem more like home." But even
as Blanche confesses her (mildly) guilty pleasure ("I have to admit . . .
I love to be waited on."), the redoubled sense of loss thus marked, of
the "fading" security not only of her youthful femininity but also of its
whiteness, throws Blanche back into despair. First rushing away from
Stella to cry alone before another filtered window (Illustration 4.18),
she then falls into Stella's lap, promising through her tears not to be a

Illustrations 4.1–4.18 Spatial distributions in *Gone with the Wind* (1939) and *A Streetcar
Named Desire* (1951) (See p. ix for full captions and credits.)

burden with a delivery that sounds more like Scarlett O'Hara (in one of her rare moments of remorse) than most others in *Streetcar*. Thus, it is precisely before this wet window without a view that the film most distinctly articulates the inevitably dismal fate of an identity that only survives by "turn[ing] the trick" of feminine allure (with velvet curtains if need be), *and* links that by now (in this film) frighteningly untenable conception of self to an economy that also enjoyed the pleasures of being served.

Such are the textual details that lead me to argue that *Streetcar* has considerable potential to disrupt and expose a very particular cinematic history of "the South" and its cinematic modes of inviting viewers (in any geographic location) to imagine, idealize, and identify with—for better and for worse—its most privileged subjects. Indeed, insofar as *Streetcar* systematically unravels not only Vivien Leigh's character, but also some of the most structuring cinematic

Illustrations 4.1–4.18   Continued

forms (of editing, *mise-en-scène*, figure placement, and so on) that
had also profoundly shaped the spectator's experience of the earlier
film, we can appreciate more fully the layered resonance of *Streetcar*'s
deconstruction of those forms in 1951, when viewers' memories of
the 1939 film would have been by no means exceedingly distant.
Indeed, having so relentlessly dismantled such an unusually popular
and structuring cinematic architecture of whiteness, I would argue,
Streetcar's deconstructive potential put into question not just one
monumental film, but what clearly had become, and has remained,
a set of exceptionally seductive Hollywood conventions.

Notes

I am grateful to Dan Streible and the students in his film historiography course at
NYU, with whom I first shared this material, for their enthusiastic engagement.

1. While *The Glass Menagerie* (1950) was the first Williams property
   adapted to the Hollywood screen and *Streetcar* was the second, the latter
   was not only a greater critical and box office success but initiated what I
   argue would become cinematically distinctive about the Williams films.
2. David Savran describes "Williams's project as a playwright" as "recolo-
   nizing an old-fashioned theater and turning it into an enigmatic, if
   slightly queer, site of resistance," (*Communists, Cowboys, and Queers: The
   Politics of Masculinity in the Work of Arthur Miller and Tennessee Williams*
   (Minneapolis and London: University of Minnesota Press, 1992): 78).
3. Cobbett S. Steinberg, *Film Facts* (New York: Facts on File, 1980): 3, 15,
   19; and Box Office Mojo, "*Gone with the Wind* (1939)," http://boxof-
   ficemojo.com/movies/?id=gonewiththewind.htm
4. Tara McPherson, *Reconstructing Dixie: Race, Gender, and Nostalgia in the
   Imagined South* (Durham and London: Duke University Press, 2003):
   152–3; and, more generally, chs. 1 and 3.
5. The pivotal reception study is Helen Taylor, *Scarlett's Women:* Gone with
   the Wind *and Its Female Fans* (New Brunswick, NJ: Rutgers University
   Press, 1989). More recently (January 28, 2008) on NPR, Karen Grigsby
   Bates considered having been, in the summer of 1966 at age 15, a "black
   girl who was mesmerized by Scarlett." See "Shrewd, Selfish Scarlett:
   A Complicated Heroine," http://www.npr.org/templates/story/story.
   php?storyId=18482709
6. R. Barton Palmer and William Robert Bray have written the first
   book, *Hollywood's Tennessee* (Austin: University of Texas Press, 2009), to
   consider the films well beyond such familiar limits of studies of adaptation. Also suggestive is Leonard J. Leff, "And Transfer to Cemetery: The
   Streetcars Named Desire," *Film Quarterly* 55(3) (2002): 29–37.
7. I make this argument more fully, considering the larger body of films
   in the context of Williams's tremendous popularity at mid-century, in

a work in progress on negotiations of regional and national identity in postwar U.S. moving image culture.

8. In one striking example, the film sets were designed so that walls could be moved from scene to scene. While Kazan explains such design as a means to intensify Blanche's confinement, his (self-) reported instructions to the art director that "the walls [should] perspire! . . . I want the walls to be crumbling. I want the walls themselves to be rotten" also suggest production investments in eroding the very notion of "wall." Eliza Kazan, *A Life* (New York: Knopf, 1988): 384; interview with Elia Kazan in Michel Ciment, *Kazan on Kazan* (London: BFI, 1973): 67–8.

9. Tennessee Williams, *A Streetcar Named Desire* (New York: Signet, 1980): 45, 50, 52, 57, 78, 82, 97, 105, 131, 137, 138, 141.

10. If the film theoretical concept of suture, most simply, designates how the editing of shots (including shot-reverse-shot formations, most obviously) works to fold the spectator into filmic space thus created, and thereby also to locate/produce the spectator as a subject positioned precisely within the filmic world imagined, then the plantation suture I diagnose enacts this process in the particular imagined location of the antebellum plantation, inserting the spectator in distinct relation to, and alignment with, the privileged white subjects who own it. For a related discussion of *The Birth of a Nation*, see Courtney, *Hollywood Fantasies of Miscegenation: Spectacular Fantasies of Gender and Race, 1903–1967* (Princeton: Princeton University Press, 2005): ch. 2.

11. Anna Everett, *Returning the Gaze: A Genealogy of Black Film Criticism, 1909–1949* (Durham and London: Duke University Press, 2001): 296.

12. Tolson, cited in Everett: 296.

13. Tolson's critique of Big House mythology explicitly confronts it with history, calling out the dependence of the plantation home upon "the poverty of the cabins, the half-fed and ragged slaves and serfs." In doing so, and with particular resonance for my analysis, Tolson rewrites the mansion's picture windows as thresholds not only of vision and space, but of smell (something cinema enables the myth to avoid entirely): "The Big House is built on corpses. Through the wide windows of the Big House floats the stench of the cabins." Tolson, "The Philosophy of the Big House," reprinted in Robert M. Farnsworth (ed.), *Caviar and Cabbage: Selected Columns by Melvin B. Tolson from the Washington Tribune, 1937–1944* (Columbia, MO and London: University of Missouri Press, 1982): 222. More recently, Thavolia Glymph offers historical evidence to move us beyond "the ideological and historical screens that obscure the plantation household as a . . . world of violence . . . and the threat of it"; violence, she documents, routinely and brutally perpetrated by white women (as well as white men) inside the home (as well as beyond it) (*Out of the House of Bondage: The Transformation of the Plantation Household* (Cambridge and New York: Cambridge University Press, 2008): 31). Glymph vividly documents entirely different maps of race, caste, gender, and space than the psycho-spatial fantasies of the plantation

suture: "when slave women and mistresses came to blows indoors or when masters dragged slave women out of their homes, the plantation household comes into clearer focus as an embattled workplace that extended to its outbuildings, lawns, and gardens" (41). Not surprisingly, then, "often slaves' first act after the departure of slaveholders [during the war] was the physical destruction of planter homes. Slaves did not torch or destroy fields or store houses as they did in other slave societies, but they burned and destroyed plantation houses and the material accoutrements of planter power that graced them" (111). So underwritten by violence was life at the Big House, according to Glymph, that "ultimately, [even] mistresses found no shelter behind the curtains of the great house, not from slaves [white women's violence did not breed loyalty], not from the larger white public" that condoned patriarchal violence, too (59).

14. McPherson: 43–4.
15. McPherson: 54; citing Kaplan (who is, in turn, citing J. Laplanche and J.-B. Pontalis), "*The Thorn Birds*: Fiction, Fantasy, Femininity," in *Formations of Fantasy*, Victor Burgin, James Donald and Cora Kaplan (eds.) (London and New York: Methuen, 1986): 150.
16. McPherson, 54; my emphasis.
17. A telling excision in this regard comes in Blanche's fragmented "legacies" speech just before she slips into madness at the apartment window that, as per my reading, opens onto the lawn at Belle Reve. In the play, the speech includes: "'Her linen needs changing'—'Yes Mother. But couldn't we get a colored girl to do it?' 'No, we couldn't of course. Everything gone but the—'." That the film cuts these lines clearly contributes to its muffling of whiteness, and amplification of femininity, as the domain of Blanche's illness (Williams, *Streetcar*: 119–20).
18. Kaja Silverman, "Suture," in *The Subject of Semiotics* (New York and Oxford: Oxford University Press, 1983): 194–236.
19. Jean-Louis Baudry, "Ideological Effects of the Basic Cinematographic Apparatus," in *Narrative, Apparatus, Ideology: A Film Theory Reader*, Philip Rosen (ed.) (New York: Columbia University Press, 1986): 286–98.
20. This invocation of Noel Ignatiev, *How the Irish Became White* (London: Routledge, 1995), does not dismiss the rich body of critical work that considers the instability of racial boundaries in Mitchell's novel. On relations between ethnicity and race in the book, see Eliza Russi Lowen McGraw, "A 'Southern Belle With Her Irish Up': Scarlett O'Hara and Ethnic Identity," *South Atlantic Review* 65(1) (winter, 2000): 123–31. See also Elizabeth Young's reading of Rhett and Scarlett as "symbolically . . . an interracial couple": "The Rhett and the Black," in *Disarming the Nation: Women's Writing and the American Civil War* (Chicago: University of Chicago Press, 1999): 256; and Alice Randall's powerful novel that makes such couples literal, and central, *The Wind Done Gone* (New York: Houghton Mifflin, 2001)). I would suggest, however, that the representational work I am attempting to expose here contributes to the ways in which the film works to constrain and resist such readings.

5

Hollywood about Hollywood: Genre as Historiography

Robert Sklar

> It's very difficult in Hollywood to make a picture about Hollywood. Because they really scrutinize you.
>
> Billy Wilder[1]

For much of its existence, Hollywood's indifference toward its own past could be summed up in two words: old product. Old product, save for the rare re-release and the occasional silent comedy compilation, could only be an impediment to new product's screentime. It sat in vaults and was mined for remakes. If you really wanted to see old product, there was the Silent Movie Theatre on Fairfax Avenue, and not much else.

The movie-making community was, of course, deeply narcissistic about itself, but almost solely in present and future tenses. In the scores of films that Hollywood made about Hollywood, with few exceptions, the past hardly plays a role, in any historical sense. Characters, of course, experience change—nobodies become somebodies, and vice versa—but institutions and social relations appear fixed and immutable. The same was true of Hollywood biopics, where the passage of time affects individuals, not the structures in which their lives were led. In whatever temporal setting, Hollywood presented itself in synchronic rather than diachronic form.

Even the changing circumstances brought about by World War II and the early postwar labor and political turmoil in the industry initially made little impact on Hollywood's disregard for its past—or, for that matter, on similar attitudes in the culture at large. Popular books about movies continued predictably to focus on personal stories told through memoirs and biographies, while an emerging scholarly interest in the medium—in social science works like Hortense Powdermaker's *Hollywood: The Dream Factory* and *Movies: A Psychological Study*, by Martha Wolfenstein and Nathan Leites—was present-minded and accepting of the status quo.[2] Siegfried Kracauer's controversial 1947 study, *From Caligari to Hitler*, viewing German silent cinema as a precursor to Nazism, was a special case of film history with no—or, at least, hardly thinkable—Hollywood counterpart, yet U.S. publishing also lacked basic histories such as Paul Rotha's regularly updated *The Film Till Now*, in Britain.[3]

But Hollywood's faith in "now," not to speak of the future, was beginning to be shaken. Its self-protective consensus had been shattered by union strife and the right-wing attacks on Communists that established an industry blacklist. These ruptures were swiftly followed by others—the Paramount anti-trust decision, leading to movie companies divesting their theater holdings; declining motion picture attendance, rapidly accelerated as television sets became prevalent in the home—that pointed toward imminent decline for the motion picture industry. Faith in the formulas of the "Hollywood about Hollywood" genre, however, remained steadfast. The early 1950s offered familiar biopics such as *Valentino* (1951), *The Story of Will Rogers* (1952), and *The Eddie Cantor Story* (1953), and typical fiction films such as *The Star* (1952).[4]

Nevertheless, for several filmmakers contemplating projects concerning Hollywood, the crisis could not be ignored. They broke through the standard norms of Hollywood's self-representation, in a manner hardly (if ever) seen before. They introduced temporality into the Hollywood story, not just for individuals but also for the industry as a whole. They viewed their subject in multiple time frames, the present actively regarding the past, the past in turn shedding light on the present. Within their narratives they posed questions about all of their time periods and allowed sufficient openness for spectators to raise questions of their own. These films, in chronological order, were *Sunset Boulevard* (1950), *The Bad and the Beautiful* (1952), and *A Star Is Born* (1954), the latter not least for its status as a remake of the prior 1937 title.

Because they offer up the Hollywood industry not as an entity unaltered in form throughout time, but as a malleable subject amenable to critical analysis and evaluation, they are rare instances of their genre: works that inscribe as well as foster a historiographical approach to U.S. motion picture history.

Sunset Boulevard

Sunset Boulevard is notorious among others things for the legendary verbal attack on its director, Billy Wilder, by the head of M-G-M studio, Louis B. Mayer. After a screening, Mayer is said to have shouted at Wilder, "You bastard, you have disgraced the industry that made you and fed you. You should be tarred and feathered and run out of Hollywood." Wilder's response was, "Fuck you."[5] That the film went on to gain eleven Academy Award nominations suggests that historiography can be as divided and contentious a subject among moviemakers as among professional historians.

In the years since, the ample scholarly writings on the film have not been particularly interested in exploring what made Louis B. Mayer so angry. They have focused, instead, on the appearance and behavior of the former silent film star, Norma Desmond (Gloria Swanson), the décor of her decaying mansion at 10086 Sunset Boulevard, and the melodramatic events that take place there. They have emphasized its gothic sensibility, its affinities with the horror genre, and its visual linkages of Norma Desmond to classic vampire figures in cinema history (an early image of Norma, with the fingers of her right hand grotesquely curled, will inevitably call to mind the vampire played by Max Schreck in F.W. Murnau's 1922 German silent film *Nosferatu*). The vampire thematic has been linked by critics to the voiceover narration by a man who has been fatally shot when the movie begins, so that the movie in multiple ways appears to represent the realm of the dead (Illustration 5.1).[6]

Illustration 5.1   Sunset Boulevard (1950): Hollywood's vampire (Gloria Swanson) projects her version of the silent film past © Paramount Pictures Corporation

The no-longer-living played an even more expansive role in the original conception of the film by Wilder and his producer and co-screenwriter, Charles Brackett.[7] The presence of multiple talking corpses created a "fiasco" even more notorious than Mayer's insult when the film was first publicly screened in September 1949, at a sneak preview in Evanston, Illinois.[8] The version presented that night opened with shots of a hearse arriving at the Los Angeles County morgue. The sequence continues with the delivery of a corpse into a room filled with dead bodies, with nametags attached to a toe. "Don't be scared," one of them addresses the newcomer, and a general conversation ensues among the corpses about their deaths and lives, until the new man, Joe Gillis (William Holden), takes over with a voiceover narration recounting the circumstances leading to his demise.[9]

"We got some bad laughter," Brackett noted in his diary after the Evanston preview. "Odd laughs—the taking of the socks from the dead boy's feet and the tying of a tag to his toe and the wheeling of his body into the morgue. No laughs whatever on the dialogue in the morgue." The next night, in Joliet, "the same bad laugh on the tag attached to Holden's toe." The reaction a few days later in Peekskill, New York, "was singularly like the other previews." Back in Hollywood, Brackett heard Cecil B. DeMille's opinion—the picture was "bad," but not because of the morgue scene, which he urged the filmmakers to retain.[10] Nevertheless, along with various rewrites and retakes prompted by preview cards and their own ruminations, the filmmakers cut the opening sequence (long thought lost or hidden beyond reach, segments of the morgue material can be viewed, without sound, as a special feature with Paramount's DVD release of the film). Holden's Gillis remains as the singular dead man speaking, a phenomenon sufficiently unique in Hollywood, and rare in film history, as to skew further the film's interpretation, among critics and theorists, toward its most macabre aspects.

Although the gothic and the ghoulish have predominantly drawn scholars to *Sunset Boulevard*, these elements tend to obscure the film's central concern with "the industry that made you and fed you"—not just, retrospectively, the industry as represented by Norma Desmond's career in silent pictures, but the industry of the postwar present. To shift emphasis toward the film's historiographical approach to Hollywood inevitably draws attention away from its more bizarre features, and perhaps may serve to counter some common assumptions about the work, even as it provides an opportunity to open up new perspectives.

One may tend, for example, to ignore or minimize Joe Gillis's circumstances as a screenwriter as mere "Hollywood about Hollywood" genre background, to set up his fateful chance arrival, around twelve minutes into the picture, at Norma Desmond's mansion. From another angle, it portrays the world of moviemaking in the film's own present. In Holden's sardonic tones, following the details of his murder, Joe presents himself as "nobody important, really—just a movie writer with a couple of B pictures to his credit." Nothing's selling, he's broke, and a couple of guys want to repossess his car. He goes to the Paramount lot where he knows a producer, Sheldrake (Fred Clark). "He was a smart producer," Joe says. "With a set of ulcers to prove it."

Paramount, the film's production company, was vigilant about its image in the work. Luigi Luraschi of the studio's front office wrote to Brackett and Wilder in April 1949 about a line they gave to Sheldrake in an early script draft. "Is . . . 'Not even if you were a relative,' necessary? You're talking about the Paramount studio, don't forget, and you must admit, there is no nepotism here."[11] The line came out, but it represents the impertinent tone the writers were striving for and otherwise retained. Joe pitches a story about a baseball player threatened by gamblers, not bothering to mask his insincerity and self-disdain. During the course of the meeting Sheldrake belches, plays with a cigar, leaves his desk to lie prone on a leather couch. "Do you see it as a Betty Hutton?" he asks. "If we made it a girls' softball team. Put in a few numbers. Might make a cute musical. 'It Happened in the Bullpen: The Story of a Woman.'" Brackett, for one, had a strongly negative reaction when this scene was shot. "Fred Clark . . . translated the lines of what was not meant to be a heavy-handed scene . . . into a scene of such nasty cruelty that I hate it violently," he wrote in his diary. "It isn't bad for our story but it makes our attitude towards Hollywood snide and unworthy of the treatment Hollywood has given us."[12]

Joe lies to Sheldrake that Twentieth Century-Fox is interested in his outline. In Paramount's production files for the film, a memo from April 1949 notes that the studio had been refused permission to use the names "Twentieth Century-Fox," "Tyrone Power," and "Zanuck" in the picture.[13] Since all three names appear in this scene, either permission was later granted (without a record having survived) or Brackett and Wilder simply ignored the prohibition. Joe rises from his chair, turns his back to Sheldrake, faces the camera and says "They're pretty hot about it over at 20th—except I think that Zanuck's all wet. Can you see Ty Power as a shortstop?" The phrase "Zanuck's all wet" is rushed and somewhat swallowed by the next sentence. Colloquial as it may be, it's a surprising critique, especially if the Fox studio head never gave permission for his name to be used.

A third studio's name is invoked later in this opening segment when Joe goes to Schwab's Drugstore. Over a shot of him using a payphone, the voiceover remarks, "Then I talked to a couple of yes men at Metro. To me they said no." Joe finds his agent on a golf course. "Don't you know the finest things in the world have been written on an empty stomach?" says the agent, refusing to give Joe a loan. The cumulative effect of this sequence and its jokey lines is to mock not only Joe's futility, but also a certain fatuity in the movie industry itself. We're so accustomed to put-downs of Hollywood historically in other media, and later in movies as well, that it's easy to overlook the fact that little or nothing as caustic and direct, naming names and companies, had appeared in a feature film before.

As Norma Desmond enters the picture, one should bear in mind that what we learn of her—along with the visual evidence of her person and environment—is couched in the language of a man whose caustic wit about his own life situation has been considerably sharpened by his death at her hands. Is it possible to perceive Norma in ways different from Joe Gillis's "commentary" about her, as Charles Brackett named the voiceover?[14] This is not to deny that Norma is ghoulish, self-deceived, and, eventually, plain crazy. Consider her handwritten screenplay for a film about Salome. Enlisted to help her complete it, Joe's voice tells us that it's "tripe," a "silly hodgepodge of melodramatic plots." But would not a person of Joe Gillis's temperament be likely to say the same thing about DeMille's *Samson and Delilah* (1949), which features briefly in *Sunset Boulevard* when Norma visits DeMille on the set? Brackett, who can be quite as acerbic in his diary as Gillis in his voiceover, opined there, on viewing DeMille's film: "It's an alive two miles of celluloid, but the characters are so wooden, the dialogue so stereotyped that I dozed a lot. The fight with the lion, the jawbone-of-an-ass battle, and the collapse of the temple are wonderful, however, and the blinding of Samson effective."[15] He's right, DeMille could collapse a temple like few others.

Norma's visit with DeMille is particularly significant in this context because it's one of the few scenes in the film where Gillis is not present, or controlling the perspective through voiceover. He declines to enter the set with her and remains outside in her touring car, the Isotta-Fraschini with 1932 license plates. Does this sequence tell us anything that we haven't heard from Joe, or give us clues that might lead to questioning his judgment? DeMille has been forewarned before she arrives on the set, and he's already alluded to "that awful script of hers" (he should talk). He's delicately cordial, but busy setting up a shot (*Sunset Boulevard*'s black-and-white can't even give a hint of

Samson and Delilah's Technicolor glories, with it blazing red costumes and the golden stewpot helmets of the Philistine soldiers). Norma experiences an iconic moment when a boom microphone grazes the feather on her hat. Hog-Eye, an electrician on the catwalks, recognizes her and bathes her in a bright spotlight. Extras and crew surround her. "Why I thought she was dead," one says. Tearfully, Norma asks DeMille, "Did you see them? Did you see how they came?" About the script, DeMille tells a polite lie: "It's got some good things in it." But he cautions her, "Pictures have changed quite a bit."

Pictures have changed quite a bit: that, of course, is a central theme of *Sunset Boulevard*'s historiography. But it's a historiography skewed in a schematic way, hung on a framework of fundamental rupture between silent cinema and talkies. On one level, this represents the overwhelming and obvious pathos—and demented desperation—of Norma's narrative trajectory, seeking to reclaim what she lost with the coming of sound. Yet, it may also be seen as a tactic, to make a point and simultaneously allow a canceling of its effect, by having it spoken in a self-aggrandizing, self-deluded way. "They're dead, they're finished," Norma rants against the current movie world. "There was a time in this business when they had the eyes of the whole wide world. But that wasn't good enough for them. Oh, no. They had to have the ears, too. So they opened their big mouths and out came talk, talk, talk." This sounds patently absurd, but its residue is a certain assertion of unease that goes beyond Norma's version of history. Earlier, she proclaimed to Joe the classic, often quoted line, "I am big. It's the pictures that got small." Less remembered is Joe's reply, "I knew there was something wrong with them," which, beyond his immediate sarcasm, he does indeed.

Beyond Norma's private struggles, the film's viewpoint on Hollywood history is simultaneously conventional and revelatory. Who was talking about silent cinema in 1950, other than Fairfax Avenue habitués and the film curators at New York's Museum of Modern Art? James Agee's essay on silent screen comedians, "Comedy's Greatest Era," appearing in *Life* magazine in September 1949, drew, according to an editor's note in a posthumous collection of his criticism, "one of the greatest responses in the magazine's history," making "it possible for everyone to be nostalgic for something that perhaps they have never known."[16] This anonymous, off-the-cuff remark perhaps invites more speculative interpretation than its weight will bear—does it suggest a longing for an unknown and unattainable past, simulta-neously more innocent and more sophisticated than the present, a different type of being in the world, expressed through the body, not the voice? Brackett and Wilder, writing their screenplay well before Agee's essay appeared, may have anticipated this latent desire. But they responded to it largely by evoking names, rather than screen images and performances.

This was the conventional part of their historiography, for the notion of rupture between silent and sound cinema depended on the sad fate of a few prominent performers who could not make the leap, rather than the predominant continuities in most other aspects of Hollywood filmmaking practices and personnel. "They took the idols and smashed them," Norma concludes her declamation against talkies. "The Fairbanks, the Gilberts, the Valentinos." She's right that the careers of Douglas Fairbanks and John Gilbert ended in the early sound years, though the causes are debatable (it was also the depths of the Great Depression, and stars of the silent era with mammoth salaries were particularly vulnerable, voice problems notwithstanding). Rudolph Valentino, who died in 1926, may be on the list as a way of sowing doubt about her reliability.

Additional names crop up as the film goes along. In April 1949, Paramount sought consent for the use of eight names invoked in the original screenplay, only four of which appear in the picture; Olivia de Havilland and Samuel Goldwyn are on record as refusing. Joe's voiceover mentions several other silent stars, including Vilma Banky, whose career also ended in the early 1930s, allegedly the victim of her Hungarian accent; Rod La Rocque, Banky's husband, who continued working until his final role in *Meet John Doe* (1941); and Mabel Normand, who died in 1930.

The most significant invocation of past personalities—and surprisingly, the most contradictory—comes with Norma's bridge game with three other silent film performers, Buster Keaton, Anna Q. Nilsson, and H.B. Warner. Joe's voiceover calls them "dim figures you may still remember from the silent days," and collectively names them the "Waxworks" (Illustration 5.2). Spectators familiar with film history, however many existed in 1950, would have recognized a reference to Paul Leni's 1924 German horror film, *Das Wachsfigurenkabinett* (*Waxworks*), in which wax museum figures are imagined as coming to life. As cinematographer John F. Seitz presents each of the aging or prematurely aged trio in brief medium close-up, the allusion seems inescapable (less so for Nilsson, at around age sixty, a swift glimpse of allure; "the ghost of a beauty," Brackett called her, a term explicable only by Hollywood's obsession with youth).[17]

The contradiction lies in the fact that all three were, at the time, steadily working actors. Spectators would have been more likely to

Illustration 5.2   Two from the "Waxworks": Harry B. Warner and Buster Keaton in *Sunset Boulevard* © Paramount Pictures Corporation

recognize Warner not from silent days, but from his role as the pharmacist Gower in *It's a Wonderful Life* (1946); his final film was DeMille's *The Ten Commandments* in 1956, perhaps a fitting conclusion for the actor who performed as "Jesus, the Christ" in DeMille's 1927 *The King of Kings*. Nilsson, whose career began in 1911, several years before Gloria Swanson's, regularly played small roles, often uncredited, up through *Seven Brides for Seven Brothers* (1954). And Keaton, though a much-reduced figure from the silent era's comic legend, performed in films and on television until his death in 1966. The irony may be that working actors were more suitable to play these parts than has-beens.

Actual screen images and performance from silent days make short appearances before and after the bridge game. In the first instance, Norma and Joe watch at home a screening of a silent film: here, the conflation of Norma Desmond and Gloria Swanson, of fiction and film history, becomes most complete. For the film is *Queen Kelly* (1929), once a legendary "lost" film of the silent era, starring Swanson, produced by her independent company, and directed by Erich von Stroheim, who, to be sure, portrays the fictional formerly great silent director Max von Mayerling, one of Norma's ex-husbands, now her butler and factotum, and on this occasion the projectionist. Hardly thirty seconds of the film appear in *Sunset Boulevard*, source unacknowledged, possibly their first public appearance in the United States. Stroheim's extravagance during shooting caused the production to be shut down; versions of the completed footage played overseas in the early 1930s; a restoration running 96 minutes finally was released in the U.S. during the 1980s. In several short shots, we see Norma/Gloria's character at prayer, in side and full-face close-ups. It prompts her exclamation—"We didn't need dialogue. We had faces."—followed by another harangue about producers.

The second instance occurs just before the trip to Paramount, when Norma is seeking to entertain a bored and jaundiced-looking Joe, lying prone and smoking on a couch. First, she appears as a "Mack Sennett Bathing Beauty," twirling an umbrella and wearing the figure-hiding costume of an earlier day. Then, she returns in a tramp outfit performing a Charlie Chaplin imitation. These acts serve to link her with the far-distant time of early cinema, accentuating her atavism, but they also show her as agile, buoyant, and comic, a Gloria Swanson, as Stroheim thought (according to Brackett), "too young and desirable for the role of Norma."[18]

Thinking about Gloria/Norma in this way links *Sunset Boulevard* to one of the strongest and most persistent tropes of the "Hollywood about Hollywood" genre, the need to control and regulate the behavior of female stars. In most films of the genre that treat this theme, a male authority figure—producer, director, husband, lover—guides the errant star figure to her senses, an understanding of her limits, her debt to holders of power, who are ultimately figured to be her audience, sitting in judgment. What is significant in *Sunset Boulevard* is that no male can exercise that authority—not DeMille, not Max, not Joe—which may be equally a symptom of her craziness or a lack that drives her crazy.

What makes the film different from nearly all others in the genre is its capacity, as we have seen, to engage the motion picture industry as a historical entity, changing through time, with more than hints of a problematic present. Louis B. Mayer had reason to be angry with Billy Wilder. Joe Gillis was not the only person to whom the yes men at Metro were saying no; the nay-sayers were reaching right up to their own top boss. In mid-1951, Mayer, whose movie industry career dated back to 1907, was ousted from Metro-Goldwyn-Mayer, the studio that bore his name.

The Bad and the Beautiful

The project that eventually became *The Bad and the Beautiful*, which received approval at M-G-M from Mayer's heir-apparent, Dore Schary, a few months before Mayer himself was deposed, was concerned, appropriately, with the subject of motion picture studio management. This was an aspect of moviemaking rarely treated in the "Hollywood about Hollywood" genre, which focused on the problems of stars and regarded bosses as benevolent figures, sticking to the background, emerging in crises to offer sage career-enhancing counsel to their celebrity employees.

The catalyst was a short story, "Memorial to a Bad Man," by a magazine writer, George Bradshaw, published in the February 1951 *Ladies Home Journal*.[19] It concerns a tyrant Broadway producer who, after his death—shades of *Sunset Boulevard*—in a posthumously opened letter justifies his cruel behavior toward collaborators on the grounds that it pushed them to develop their artistry. Broadway bullies were familiar types, however, while Hollywood's—well-known to fiction and the press—had previously been taboo as screen subjects.[20] The film's producer, John Houseman, neglected to mention *Sunset Boulevard* when he recalled, in his autobiography, the rationale that it had been many years since the 1937 *A Star Is Born*, and, with "the industry . . . in its decline," it was "the right time to make a picture about the Great Days."[21]

The writer Charles Schnee was hired to shift Bradshaw's story into a Hollywood framework, Vincente Minnelli brought on to direct, and major names, headed by Lana Turner and Kirk Douglas, cast for the principal roles. It seems to have been a trouble-free production; the only disputes concerned whether to shoot in color rather than black-and-white, an idea that was rejected; and what to do about a title. The working title was "Tribute to a Bad Man" right up to the early sneak previews, but there was concern that moviegoers might think it was a Western; *Return of the Bad Men* had been a recent RKO offering in that genre. Houseman hoped to keep the word "Tribute" and find some synonym for "Bad Man" that would retain "the irony of our original title," but that proved impossible.[22] *The Bad and the Beautiful* became the title of record, ironic or not.

No Hollywood personalities appear in the film as themselves, as with DeMille and the "Waxworks" in *Sunset Boulevard*, but parallels with actual persons are apparent, and some seem to have been discretely promoted by the studio. The Hollywood trade press and gossip columnists speculated even before the film's release on whether Douglas's character, the producer Jonathan Shields, resembled David O. Selznick.[23] Even as the studio warned Minnelli to avoid obvious references to John and Diana Barrymore in depicting the relationship between Lana Turner's character, Georgia Lorrison, and her late actor father, the connection was clear.[24] Actors who played the roles of film directors were cast and made up so as obviously to resemble caricatures of Alfred Hitchcock and Fritz Lang. An early sequence depicting low-budget B-picture filmmaking was meant to evoke the RKO horror thrillers produced by Val Lewton.[25]

The film's structure, drawn from Bradshaw's original story, owes an obvious debt to *Citizen Kane*—personified in actor Paul Stewart's performance as Jonathan Shields's punctilious, cold-eyed factotum, similar in nature to his film debut as Charles Foster Kane's valet.[26] After an opening sequence in which a movie director, a female star, and a writer are shown dismissively rejecting overseas calls from Shields in Paris, a Shields company executive (Walter Pidgeon) gathers all three for a late-night meeting. Then commence flashback sequences in which each, in turn, narrates in voiceover their career experience with Shields, culminating for all three in the producer's unforgivable betrayal. After each one, the executive reminds them that their careers didn't exactly suffer after Jonathan's cruelty, leaving the implication that what he did, however painful at the time, was in their own best interests. (For example, he tells the director, identified as a winner subsequently of two Academy Awards, "[Jonathan] brushed you off his coattails so you had to stand on your own two feet.") Throughout the film—different from *Citizen Kane*—we never see the main character on screen except through the filter of the other's stories.[27]

Minnelli's files for the project contain a chronological outline keyed to Jonathan's age, perhaps for make-up purposes, but this historical specificity was only partly communicated to spectators. The first flashback, narrated by director Fred Amiel (Barry Sullivan), begins in 1934, when Jonathan is listed as twenty-eight years old. He's thirty-nine when Turner's movie star character Georgia Lorrison begins her segment, dated 1945, and forty-three in 1949 for the final episode told by writer James Lee Bartlow (Dick Powell).[28] The film's present coincides with the time of its release, and finds Shields, as we've seen, in Paris, apparently in exile and disgrace, but seeking to persuade the trio to make a picture with him.

Considering that the outcome of each character's account is an act of deceit and disloyalty by Jonathan Shields, the film's tone is unusually light-hearted, with many scenes accentuating comic elements, accompanied by upbeat or romantic renditions of the theme music by David Raksin. It's true that the nature of each treachery darkens over the three stories. In the case of Fred Amiel, his creative partner in their B-movie apprenticeship, Shields breaks a promise and takes over an Amiel project as his own, launching himself as a major producer.

With Georgia, he nurtures her acting career with a private intimacy that turns, on her part, into love, and then brutally rejects her at the moment she achieves stardom. Lastly, in order to get a screenplay out of James Lee, Shields isolates the writer, until the shocking news that the latter's fun-loving wife was killed with a Latin lover when their small airplane crashes on a flight to Mexico. Later, Shields inadvertently reveals that he arranged the tryst; Bartlow slugs him, but the producer, unfazed, responds, "Whether you like it or not, you're better off. She was a fool. She got in your way. She interfered with your work. She wasted your time. She wasted you. You're better off without her."

(Jonathan's shocking callousness notwithstanding, Gloria Grahame's brief performance in the role of Rosemary Bartow, as an effervescent, slyly sexual Southern belle, was one of the film's particular delights; Grahame won an Oscar as supporting actress, one of five Academy Awards for the work.)

The severity of Shields's insults darkens—as does Robert Surtees's black-and-white cinematography—following the trajectory of his career. With Fred (1930s) he's a struggling apprentice, with Georgia (1945) he's on top of the industry, with James Lee (1949) he's facing a crisis. His last two pictures have flopped. The bankers are stirring. Putting Bartlow's screenplay—a Civil War epic—into production, he clashes with the director, and takes over directing himself. Of the resulting picture, he's the most severe critic: "I botched it . . . I have no tension, no timing, no pace, nothing. I took a beautiful, sensitive story and turned it into a turgid, boring movie." He shelves the picture, and he's out of the movie-making game.

In a film in which time and change play so central a role, the question about its historiographic import comes down to this: can the Jonathan Shields story be read as a metonym for the movie industry itself, or is it limited to an individual moral tale in which the larger structure of the business is not implicated? In the film's present-day frame, Fred, Georgia, and James Lee appear to be thriving, making movies, and gaining box-office success. The Shields company executive tells them that on Jonathan's name he couldn't raise five cents, but on theirs together, "I can raise two million dollars by noon tomorrow." So, the problem appears to be of Jonathan's making, not affecting the industry itself.

What is Jonathan's problem? In Kirk Douglas's dynamic, complex performance—like so many of his screen characters, he's charming and compelling, devious and dislikable, all at once—several factors stand out. On the professional side, what's remarkable about Shields seems to be his overblown activism as a producer. He's omnipresent on the set, overshadows his directors, and gives advice and direction to actors; even the all-time meddler Selznick stuck his nose in via memo rather than in person. Finally, a director calls him on it, telling Jonathan, after their disagreement on the Civil War picture, "It will be done your way—but not by me. And not by any other director who respects himself."

On the personal side, Jonathan's behavior also calls attention to itself by what one might describe as its departure from the normal and expected. In the Amiel episode, there's a curious nighttime scene at a beach in which Jonathan tells Fred and his girlfriend that "It's time you two made it legal" and produces a wedding ring that he gives to them. With Georgia, even if his romancing her is instrumentally a sham, the climax of that sequence seems excessive in his rejection of her: he doesn't attend their picture's celebration party, holes up at his mansion with a calculating bit player, and when Georgia seeks him out, he berates her at a screaming pitch, yet one which seems to hide strong feelings for her overridden by an aversion to dependence. This latter emotion seems borne out by his tirade to James Lee about the deceased Rosemary. He has gone from fostering a relationship to destroying several, but the motive in each case seems to distance himself from his and others' private attachments, the better to foster his work.

There is, however, one attachment that supersedes all others—to his dead father. After the M-G-M logo opens the picture, appearing under the film's title and opening credits is a bas-relief sculpture of a knight's armor helmet, with Shields Pictures Inc. above it, and below the words "*Non Sans Droit*"—Not Without Right. This, we soon learn, before it was Jonathan's company's symbol, belonged to his father. Fred Amiel's flashback opens on Hugo Shields's funeral, in which the deceased is eulogized as "one of the pioneers who built our great motion picture industry," until it turns out that all of the "mourners" have been lured by Jonathan's cash. Fred, a skeptic, infuriates Jonathan by muttering that the father was a "madman" and a "butcher." Later, when the two men meet again, Jonathan's circumstances are described—his father once made "great pictures," but now the money is gone, the name reviled. "And you're going to ram the name of Shields down their throats?" Fred inquires.

Would spectators—and the Hollywood community—link this tale to Selznick family history? The patriarch, Lewis J. Selznick, was indeed a movie industry pioneer, a competitor of M-G-M and Paramount, with his own name on a production company, but his business had crashed in 1923, and his son David was well-established as an executive at his father's death in 1933. And there was also another child-movie industry pioneer connection in the film, as noted earlier, that of Georgia with her dead actor father George Lorrison, which was seen to echo the relationship of Diana Barrymore to her famous actor father, John. George Lorrison also played an important role almost as a substitute father figure for Jonathan. "He gave me my first drink when I was thirteen, my first cigar at fourteen, and when I was fifteen, he taught me the facts of life," Shields tells Fred, leaving to our imagination how the latter was accomplished.

Jonathan seeks to rescue Georgia from the inhibiting legacy of her father, but he has no intention of challenging his own father's heritage for himself. Rather, it seems, he seeks to restore it and carry it forward. Photographs and images of Hugo Shields are omnipresent in his son's work and living spaces, even in Jonathan's bathroom. A persistent but inchoate theme of *The Bad and the Beautiful* is how much the sins of the father are passed on to, or inherited or willingly absorbed by the son—whether Jonathan's character traits, his triumphs and his fall, recapitulate the parent's successes and failure. In this sense, although much less centrally articulated than in *Sunset Boulevard*, the movie industry's past haunts its present in this film, as well.

Although Norma Desmond's "return" ends in madness while Jonathan Shield's "return" is at least hinted at by the beguiled looks of Fred, Georgia, and James Lee as they listen on the telephone to his pitch from Paris, the shadow of the father's lost fortune and reputation hovers over the film. Only Jonathan Shields may be directly affected in the narrative of *The Bad and the Beautiful*, but the cumulative effect of his inheritance from the past, and present-day uncertainties, casts an aura of anxiety outward, toward the movie industry writ large.

A Star Is Born

The 1954 *A Star Is Born* was developed and went into production in the precise moment when Hollywood began to respond—at least, technologically—to the crisis that was becoming overwhelmingly apparent. In 1952, the first three-dimensional feature was released, and the major studios quickly produced several dozen titles in the 3D format the following year. The first widescreen picture using the anamorphic CinemaScope lens, owned by Twentieth Century-Fox, also appeared in 1953. In addition, new single-strip color processes that were less expensive than three-strip Technicolor were becoming available. The 1937 *A Star Is Born* had quintessentially represented the synchronic standards of the "Hollywood about Hollywood" genre: people are transformed, while institutions appear immutable.

The 1954 remake was inevitably diachronic: it bore a temporal relationship to its source, and its production circumstances altered in confusing confluence with the changing tactics of its studio. People are transformed, indeed; but so, too, definitively, are institutions, in the picture's narrative and in the midst of its coming into being.

If the previous two films were concerned with the hoped-for "return" of fictional characters, Norma Desmond and Jonathan Shields, the idea of remaking the 1937 *A Star Is Born* was motivated by a strategy for the "return" of an actual performer. Judy Garland had last appeared in a film in 1950, after which she had been dropped by M-G-M, the studio that had employed her since her 1930s debut as a child star. Her husband and manager, Sidney Luft, acquired rights to the 1937 film and set out as a first-time producer to re-fashion the story as a musical for his wife. Warner Bros. signed on to finance and distribute the picture, the New York playwright Moss Hart was hired to write a new screenplay, and George Cukor was brought on to direct. James Mason was cast in the role of Norman Maine, played by Fredric March in 1937, while Garland, of course, would be Esther Blodgett/Vicki Lester, the role earlier performed by Janet Gaynor.[29]

The project was conceived as a big-budget color musical. How would all the technological innovations affect it? The conundrum was exacerbated by Jack Warner's machinations, as the studio's production head, to develop proprietary technology bearing the company's name. At the beginning of production, scenes were shot in traditional "flat" two-dimensional, three-strip Technicolor. But Warner wanted to try out a widescreen process that they named WarnerScope, so scenes were shot in that format, only to be evaluated as inadequate. Eventually Warner gave in and leased CinemaScope equipment from Fox, and scenes previously shot were performed again for the anamorphic camera. Multiple sequences in the film were staged repeatedly over and over again to accommodate the different technological formats.

Under the circumstances, as fresh specialists were called in to operate the new technologies, delays mounted, budgets soared. Ultimately, production costs came in at slightly over $5 million, making it the second most expensive picture in Hollywood studio history up to that time. (A 1961 Warner Bros. document states that the studio lost $3 million on the picture.)[30] The original print ran 182 minutes, even after Jack Warner, without consulting the filmmakers, took it upon himself to cut a few minutes out. Plans to release the film in two parts, with an intermission, were considered and abandoned.

The release was as chaotic as the production. Not long after the October 1954 opening, the Warner Bros. New York office ordered further cuts. As prints were called in and altered, the dropped footage was destroyed, and no full-length print survived. The original release version of *A Star Is Born* became, fundamentally, a lost film. Nevertheless, three decades later, a film curator, Ronald Haver, obtained film industry support for a quest to restore the film. He found a complete original soundtrack and snippets of cut footage. In 1983, also utilizing still photographs in the continuing absence of original footage, he put together a 176-minute version. Eventually, this version became available on DVD, in CinemaScope ratio (an enhanced restoration of the Haver print, with additional moving image and audio material as special features, was released by Warner Bros. on Blu-ray in 2010).

A Star Is Born told a familiar story—the genealogy of which, the studio asserted in several memos, went back beyond the 1937 film to such titles as *Broken Hearts of Hollywood* (1926) and *Show Girl in Hollywood* (1930). The purpose of these documents was to build a defense against possible litigation from rights holders to *What Price Hollywood?* (1932); they argued that multiple examples of similar plots had "placed such ideas and formulas in the public domain, unprotectable by copyright."[31] The basic "ideas and formulas" involved a successful older Hollywood male taking under his wing a younger female movie aspirant, only to see his career founder because of his all too apparent flaws—predominantly, being an irresponsible, misbehaving drunk—while hers soars. The film-makers of 1954 were aware, however, that historical change constrained them from telling the story in the old formulaic way. In the 1937 version, Esther Blodgett was one in a long line of "movie-struck" girls whose aim in life, almost from the very origins of the film industry, had been to make it on the silver screen. In the screenplay for the remake, the heroine, a singer, aspired to be a recording artist.

"I think we have lost one element of the original picture," Moss Hart noted, in the run-up to production, mingling names of actors and a character. "Janet Gaynor had a dream to go to Hollywood—that was working for us. In our case, Judy has a different dream, and it is Norman who tells her to go after bigger things. Somehow, I would like to indicate that after this she has an ideal and a dream. It will be more moving when she gives all this up."[32] What was missing, in other words, was the woman's implacable drive for success in motion pictures. Her lover/mentor/husband tutors her in this ambition, and she gains what he wants for her, yet, it seems clear that the remake never convincingly imparts this "ideal and a dream" as the female star's own.

As the filmmakers struggled to maintain the obsolescent formulas they had inherited, they repeatedly inserted into the work signs of their own contemporary travails. The producer Oliver Niles

(Charles Bickford) speaks to a director on location (these words, from a scene cut from the original picture, appear on the recovered complete soundtrack over stills and clips in the 1983 restoration: "Cut some corners, Bob. You've got to bring it in on time. You know how tough things are right now. They're on my neck from New York every day." Later, Norman Maine remarks, "things being so tough the way they are." And then Norman and Oliver have the following exchange, after further reference to "the New York boys":

Norman: My last two pictures haven't grossed as much as they used to, but neither has anybody else's.
Oliver: Those big fat plush days when a star could get drunk and disappear and hold up production for two weeks are over . . . no one can afford it any more. Things are too tough.

Could it have been made any more clear, that things were tough and getting tougher?[33]

How tough things were was perhaps inadvertently revealed in one of the film's major scenes, the Academy Awards ceremony at which Vicki Lester—Esther Blodgett incarnated with her studio-bestowed name—wins the Oscar as best actress. According to Haver's account, Hart placed this scene in the Cocoanut Grove nightclub of the Ambassador Hotel, perhaps unaware as a New Yorker that the awards had been presented in a theater, rather than as a dinner event, since the early 1940s. Cukor, who knew better, allowed this inaccuracy to remain, with the studio's acquiescence, perhaps for the convenience of setting up and shooting the sequence in an open space.[34] After several preliminary shots, a long shot introduces the interior of the nightclub, with a pan from left to right revealing three motion picture cameras and then, finally, a television camera recording the scene. Further long shots in the sequence show a stage occupying the left two-thirds of the CinemaScope frame and, in the right third, a large screen displaying a black-and-white image of the speakers on stage. It seems as if the TV camera we have previously seen, far from the stage, is producing this image, because the figures on the TV screen are similar in size to the individuals who occupy the stage in the panoramic long shot.

Vicki is then announced as a winner, and she takes the stage for her acceptance speech. Suddenly a linked movie camera/TV camera unit dollies in from the left of the frame right up to the front of the stage and, as it moves forward, the black-and-white image of Vicki on the television screen grows into a close-up, while the "actual" Vicki on the left remains a small, distant figure in the film's long shot set-up (Illustration 5.3). In the shot, the attendees at the dinner

Illustration 5.3 Vicki Lester's (Judy Garland) small image at the Academy Awards now competes with television's larger picture: *A Star Is Born* (1954)
© Warner Bros.

tables have their eyes turned toward the stage, but from the spectator's viewpoint, that which draws one's attention is the television screen and the movement into close-up of Vicki's face. A highly effective CinemaScope *mise-en-scène* for this sequence also functions as a sign of television's emerging dominance.

Vicki's speech is interrupted by Norman's appearance at the back of the room and, as he drunkenly approaches the stage, the cameras that had taken position there are nowhere to be seen. Norman's remarks, leading up to the moment when he inadvertently strikes Vicki in the face, are filmed in a conventional medium shot/close-up montage, and we are returned to the private drama of the formulaic narrative, the man's fall and the woman's rise. As in *Sunset Boulevard* and *The Bad and the Beautiful*, we are invited to focus our attention on the fate of individuals rather than institutions, but all three films succeed in inscribing their unusual historiographic perspective on Hollywood's contemporary crisis through their various means of integrating, or comparing, present and past.

Notes

I thank Barbara Hall and Jenny Romero of the Margaret Herrick Library— Department of Special Collections, Academy of Motion Picture Arts and Sciences, Los Angeles (hereafter cited as AMPAS) and Jonathon Auxier of the USC Warner Bros. Archives (hereafter WBA) for invaluable research assistance. Thanks to Adrienne Harris and J.E. Smyth for their editorial suggestions.

1. Cameron Crowe, *Conversations with Wilder* (New York: Knopf, 1999): 27.
2. Hortense Powdermaker, *Hollywood: The Dream Factory* (Boston: Grosset & Dunlap, 1950); Martha Wolfenstein and Nathan Leites, *Movies: A Psychological Study* (Glencoe, IL: Free Press, 1950).
3. Siegfried Kracauer, *From Caligari to Hitler: A Psychological History of the German Film* (Princeton, NJ: Princeton University Press, 1947); Paul Rotha, *The Film Till Now: A Survey of the Cinema* (London: Jonathan Cape, 1930), was reissued in a revised and updated edition as *The Film Till Now: A Survey of World Cinema* (London: Vision, 1949), with a U.S. edition published by Funk & Wagnalls.
4. A number of works broadly survey the "Hollywood about Hollywood" genre, including Patrick Donald Anderson, *In Its Own Image: The Cinematic Vision of Hollywood* (New York: Arno Press, 1978); Alex Barris, *Hollywood According to Hollywood* (South Brunswick, N.J.: A.S. Barnes, 1978); Rudy Behlmer and Tony Thomas, *Hollywood's Hollywood: The Movies about the Movies* (Secaucus, NJ: Citadel, 1975); Richard Meyers, *Movies on Movies: How Hollywood Sees Itself* (New York: Drake Publishers, 1978); James Robert Parrish and Michael R. Pitts, with Gregory W. Mank, *Hollywood*

on Hollywood (Metuchen, NJ: Scarecrow Press, 1978); and Anthony Slide, *Films on Film History* (Metuchen, NJ, and London: Scarecrow Press, 1979).

5. Maurice Zolotow, *Billy Wilder in Hollywood* (New York: Putnam's, 1977): 167–8.

6. Articles that develop these themes include: Morris Dickstein, "*Sunset Boulevard*," *Grand Street* 7(3) (spring, 1988): 176–84; Lucy Fischer, "*Sunset Boulevard: Fading Stars*," in *Women and Film* (*Women in Literature*, New Series, vol. 4), Janet Todd (ed.) (New York: Holmes & Meier, 1988): 97–113; Andrew Gibson, "'And the Wind Wheezing Through That Organ Once in a While': Voice, Narrative, Film," *New Literary History* 32(3) (summer, 2001): 639–57; and Julian Wolfreys, "Uncanny Temporalities, Haunting Occasions: *Sunset Boulevard*," *Occasional Deconstructions* (Albany: State University of New York Press, 2004): 35–60, 306–10.

7. Brackett and Wilder enlisted D.M. Marshman, Jr. to work with them on the screenplay; all three received screen credit.

8. "Fiasco" is the title for the chapter recounting these events in Sam Staggs' *Close-Up on* Sunset Boulevard: *Billy Wilder, Norma Desmond, and the Dark Hollywood Dream* (New York: St. Martin's, 2002).

9. All quotations from films in this essay are transcribed from spoken dialogue; punctuation is the author's responsibility.

10. Charles Brackett Diary (1949): September 21, 22, 26, and October 11, 1949, box 27, folder 7, Charles Brackett Papers, AMPAS.

11. Luigi Luraschi to Brackett and Wilder, April 27, 1949, *Sunset Boulevard*— Production File, box 199, folder 11, Paramount Pictures Production Records, AMPAS.

12. Brackett Diary, May 9, 1949.

13. Luraschi to Brackett and Wilder, April 12, 1949, *Sunset Boulevard*— Production File, AMPAS.

14. Brackett Diary, November 1–3, 1949.

15. Brackett Diary, June 14, 1949.

16. These words, author unknown, preface "Comedy's Greatest Era" in James Agee, *Agee on Film: Reviews and Comments* (Boston: Beacon Press, 1958): 2.

17. Brackett Diary, May 3, 1949. In his May 2 entry, Brackett notes that Theda Bara and Jetta Goudal rejected offers to appear in the bridge scene.

18. Brackett Diary, May 4, 1949.

19. George Bradshaw, "Memorial to a Bad Man," *Ladies Home Journal*, February 1951: 37, 134–5, 137, 139; The producers also purchased a second Bradshaw story with a similar theme, "Of Good and Evil," *Cosmopolitan*, February 1948: 34–5, 154–6, 159–62, *The Bad and the Beautiful* Story File, Metro-Goldwyn-Mayer Script Collection, AMPAS.

20. Perhaps the most unscrupulous Hollywood figure in fiction was the writer-producer Sammy Glick in Budd Schulberg's *What Makes Sammy Run?* (New York: Random House, 1941). Although the novel has not been adapted for a feature film, Paddy Chayefsky's dramatization for early

postwar television was broadcast live on the Philco Television Playhouse, on the NBC network, April 10, 1949. A second television production, written by Schulberg and his brother Stuart, was broadcast in two parts on NBC Sunday Showcase, September 27, and October 4, 1959, and is available on DVD.

21. John Houseman, *Front and Center* (New York: Simon & Schuster, 1979): 372.

22. John Houseman to Dore Schary, July 9, 1952, *The Bad and the Beautiful*— Post-production File, box 1, folder 6, Vincente Minnelli Papers, AMPAS. *Tribute to a Bad Man* was eventually used by M-G-M as the title for a 1956 Western starring James Cagney.

23. R. Monta to Vincente Minnelli, March 31, 1952, *The Bad and the Beautiful*—Production File, box 1, folder 7, Minnelli Papers, AMPAS.

24. See, for example, *The Hollywood Reporter*, October 24, 1952.

25. Houseman: 374.

26. Orson Welles is another possible model for Jonathan Shields, as J.E. Smyth has suggested in editorial correspondence.

27. A sequence showing Jonathan in Paris was shot and appeared in the film during previews. The screenplay material for the sequence is appendix A in Charles Schnee, *The Bad and the Beautiful: A Screenplay*, Matthew J. Bruccoli (ed.) (Carbondale: Southern Illinois University Press, 1998): 119–21; see also "The Customer Is the Boss," *Life*, February 2, 1953, for a report on a preview of the film and scenes that were cut afterward, including this one.

28. *The Bad and the Beautiful*—Production File, box 1, folder 7, Minnelli Papers, AMPAS.

29. Details about the production of *A Star Is Born* are drawn from Ronald Haver's comprehensive book, A Star Is Born: *The Making of the 1954 Movie and its 1983 Restoration* (New York: Knopf, 1988).

30. Unsigned memo to R.J. Obringer, February 8, 1961, Transcona Enterprises, Inc. file, *A Star Is Born* Files, Warner Bros. Archives, University of Southern California.

31. Stephen Karnot, "Comparative Analysis Report," December 1953, and "Comparison Notes," December 29, 1953, *A Star Is Born* Files, WBA; an extensive scholarly analysis of *What Price Hollywood?* and the 1937 *A Star Is Born* in the context of the "Hollywood about Hollywood" genre is J.E. Smyth, "Hollywood 'Takes One More Look': Early Histories of Silent Hollywood and the Fallen Star Biography, 1932–1937," *Historical Journal of Film, Radio and Television* 26(2) (June 2006): 179–201.

32. Moss Hart, September 17, 1953, in *A Star Is Born*—Script File, box 22, folder 230, George Cukor Papers, AMPAS.

33. There are two references to movie business matters in the 1937 *A Star Is Born*. At a party early in the film, Norman Maine remarks to Oliver Niles, "Costs are going up, grosses are going down." Later, in the garden scene, Norman asks, "Oliver, how's the dividend situation?"

and the producer replies, "Very pleasant. I think we'll show two million in the next quarter." In context, however, both these moments reflect personal stardom issues that drive the narrative: in the first, Norman obliquely acknowledging his fading appeal, in the second, Niles stating the favorable results of Vicki Lester's popularity (there's also a shot of a brochure, presumably intended for investors, with the title "Get Rich with Oliver Niles Productions").

34. Haver: 102, 146.

6

Some Like It Hot and the Virtues of Not Taking History Too Seriously

David Eldridge

> The locations worked for us, the period worked for us, the situation of the gangsters that was also correct. You know, it was not taking itself too seriously . . . Everything we attempted in that picture came out in spades.
> Billy Wilder[1]

From the very start of *Some Like It Hot* (1959), writer, producer, and director Billy Wilder took the conventional apparatus of the historical film and used it for a gag. Sirens suddenly wail as a police car gives incongruous pursuit to a vintage hearse. Both vehicles careen through wintry streets, skidding around sharp corners. Thuggish "undertakers" pull out concealed sawn-off shotguns, smash the back windows and fire at the cops, who hang off the side of their vehicle shooting back. As the police car crashes into a fence, the hearse escapes; but geysers of liquid now spurt from bullet holes in the coffin in back. This is explained when the hoodlums lift the lid to reveal not a body, but shattered bottles of whiskey. Only then do the words "CHICAGO, 1929" flash up on the screen—the "text signifier" of place and time so traditional in Hollywood's history films, now rendered wryly comical by coming *after* this chase, as if a cinema audience could possibly mistake such a scene for anyplace, anytime else (Illustration 6.1). As the film's star, Tony Curtis, says: "like it could be Orlando in 1974! I thought that was a wonderful set-up for a joke."[2]

This sardonic attitude is underscored again a few minutes into the film. Just before the speakeasy in which he plays is about to be raided by police and Prohibition agents, saxophonist Joe (Curtis) scolds his friend, bass-player Jerry (Jack Lemmon), for being pessimistic:

> *Joe:* Jerry-boy—why do you have to paint everything so black? Suppose you get hit by a truck? Suppose the stock market crashes? Suppose

Illustration 6.1   Wilder's playful "intertitle": *Some Like It Hot* (1959) © Ashton Productions

> Mary Pickford divorces Douglas Fairbanks? Suppose the Dodgers
> leave Brooklyn? Suppose Lake Michigan overflows?

Of course, Wall Street suffered its disastrous crash in October 1929;
Pickford divorced Fairbanks in 1936; the Brooklyn Dodgers played
their last game at Ebbets Field in 1957 and moved to Los Angeles;
and Chicago was subject to some of the worst flooding in its history
in 1957. When actors in historical films like *Titanic* (1953) declare
the ship to be unsinkable, the audience's privileged position of being
informed by hindsight helps to make poignant the character's lack
of foresight. However, often such overtly portentous dialogue could
also provoke derisive sniggers; so Wilder exploited the convention to
generate a deliberate laugh instead.

In short, *Some Like It Hot* makes no pretence of being serious about
history. Contemporaries commended it for having "great sport with
some of the lunatic aspects of the twenties," catching "the fun" of the
"celebrated era of bathtub gin, flappers and stock market millionaires."[3]
It was rightly seen as a "wacky and wonderful spoof" that turned
"satiric handsprings with all the obvious cultural institutions of the 20s,"
including "bootlegging, gangland rub-outs, cloche hats and musical
memories"—all material considered "good for laughs."[4] And first and
foremost, everyone knows it as a classic comedy about two musicians
whose only escape from gangsters is to slip on high heels and join an
all-girl jazz band headed for Florida. Thus, it can be the American Film
Institute's "Funniest American Movie of all time."[5] It can be the "most

entertaining cultural spectacle of the last hundred years."[6] But surely not an American historical film?

Scholarship concerned with cinema's depictions of the past has often attempted to define what counts as a "historical film." To challenge the prejudice among academic historians that Hollywood's accounts of history were unremittingly inaccurate, isolated examples of films have been identified and feted as being comparable to written historiography in "communicating a thoughtful picture of the past."[7] However, almost all of those adjudged to be "good" historical films are ones made *after* the fall of the studio system, which underscores the fact that demarcating a canon always entails excluding as well as including. When Leger Grindon, for example, sought to characterize the "historical fiction film" as a genre, he consciously "set aside" any film that "adopts a period setting but fails to engage historical issues."[8] On such grounds, Pierre Sorlin decreed that "the expression 'historical film' should be restricted to movies which purposefully aim at depicting, as accurately as possible, a past period"—and explicitly excluded "those pictures which are basically costume comedies," thereby putting a film like *Some Like It Hot* completely beyond the pale.[9] Robert Brent Toplin even once suggested consigning to "the waste heap" any movie that would "simplify history, trivialize it, or bend it to shape the needs of the artist."[10] Yet, such a waste heap would include thousands of melodramas, comedies, Westerns, musicals, swashbuckling adventures, and other period-set films, especially those made in the "classical" Hollywood studio era. It is, I would argue, both ludicrous and counter productive to dismiss such productions, since such a huge volume of material actually reveals much about the historical understanding (for good or bad) of the people who made these films, and of the cultural value of history itself.[11] To ignore most historically-set movies made before the 1960s just because they do not seem to be asking the "right" questions or respect the "integrity" of the past contributes nothing to our understanding of the position of film in America's historical consciousness. Recent work does suggest a growing recognition of this: "that all kinds of films, and not just biopics or films based on historical events, put history to use."[12] However, the very simple fact that the majority of "classical" films do not take history seriously has, in itself, still not really been probed. One question that comes immediately to mind is that if the factual realities and issues of a particular moment in history did not actually matter much to filmmakers, why did they choose that specific setting in the first place? Why did Wilder set *Some Like It Hot* in "Chicago 1929" (and, indeed, "Florida 1929"), if he were not taking it seriously?

Make It Seem True

One approach would be to entertain the possibility that Wilder was more serious about history than might at first appear. This is difficult to prove because the paper trail is limited. Few of Wilder's documents relating to the production of *Some Like It Hot* have survived to be archived; and identifying the specific historical resources used in developing the screenplay is rendered more problematic because United Artists did not have the sort of in-house research department that major Hollywood studios had operated since the 1930s.[13] We know that during his production of *The Spirit of St Louis* (1957) at Warner Bros., for instance, Wilder consulted copies of *Aerodigest* magazine and contemporary newspapers concerned with Charles Lindbergh's transatlantic flight, and sent researchers to examine artifacts in the Smithsonian Museum. Requests for such materials exist in the extensive files of Warner's research department.[14] At United Artists, however, Wilder and Diamond would have had to undertake their research independently, and therefore no known comparable record of this process exists for *Some Like It Hot*.

However, there is considerable evidence within the film itself to indicate that the writers *had* done their research. Substantial elements of the film's representation of Prohibition-era Chicago draw upon historical facts—with the most notable referent being the St. Valentine's Day Massacre. Invoked in the film when gangster boss Spats Colombo (George Raft) determines to rub-out "Toothpick Charlie," the real massacre at the S.M.C. Cartage garage at 2122 North Clarke Street saw seven men lined up against the wall and killed in a hail of machine-gun fire.[15] A newsboy who shouts out the headlines informs the audience that the film's garage is, indeed, on the "North Side," and later the federal Prohibition agent Mulligan locates it as being on "Clarke Street." The significant date is similarly made evident since Joe and Jerry are trying to get to a "St. Valentine's Day Dance" in upstate Illinois, when they inadvertently witness the atrocity. Yet, one thing that suggests that Wilder and Diamond were familiar with more than just the most basic facts is their inclusion of an unfortunate garage pump-attendant as one of Spats' victims. This appears to derive from R.L. Duffus's contemporary account in the *New York Times* which identified an "obscure" mechanic among the dead men.[16] Moreover, also killed in the massacre was an optometrist, Reinhart Schwimmer, who had "abandoned his practice to associate with the gang and gamble."[17] Wilder clearly knew this, telling Diamond: "You know there was a guy who was killed who shouldn't have been there . . . A thrill seeker, hanging out with these hoodlums. So he got killed." That someone had been in the garage who "shouldn't have been there," thus directly inspired the idea of placing Joe and Jerry in the "wrong place" and the "wrong time" as well.[18]

This kind of content is consistent with J.E. Smyth's demonstration that the makers of early gangster films like *The Public Enemy* (1931) and *Scarface* (1932) drew upon a plethora of historical details about the Prohibition era from the sort of contemporaneous popular histories and newspaper reports that "professional" historians often ignored.[19] Filmmakers in the 1950s continued to privilege such research materials. As press releases for *Pete Kelly's Blues* (1955) would have it, "the best way to learn what the world was like" in the Kansas of 1927, "is not by looking in history books . . . but in reading newspapers of that time." Thus "hoping to make the picture a faithful reproduction of life for that year and place," director Robert Webb was supposed to have "studied headline stories, city hall activities, police reports, entertainment columns and . . . every article that fitted into the setting" of his film.[20] *Some Like It Hot* suggests that Wilder and Diamond consulted similar material.

The opening sequence tapped legends of bootlegging, with Frederick J. Haskin's 1923 history of *The American Government* recording that "Prohibition enforcement agents have found that even coffins are used for illegal transportation of booze . . . Make-believe funerals have been halted and the hearse and casket found to be conveying liquor instead of bodies."[21] Throwaway lines also indicate knowledge of Fred Pasley's *Al Capone: The Biography of a Self-Made Man* (1930). Spats's alibi at the time of the massacre, for example, is that he was attending a performance of *Rigoletto*—an opera mentioned by Pasley as being one of Capone's particular favourites.[22] This historical joke is continued when the gangsters gather for a conference under the "front" of the "Friends of Italian Opera," which corresponds with Walter Burns's accounts of the musical tastes of gangsters like Vito Bascone, Jim Colisimo and Johnny Torrio who "loved to dwell . . . upon the technique of Verdi, Mascagni, Puccini, and point out the faultless rhythm and beauty of notable passages in *La Bohème, Il Trovatore, The Jewels of the Madonna*."[23] Yet, the occasion also draws on the fact that, in May 1929, New York's crime-boss Frank Costello did indeed arrange a conference involving Capone and "some thirty Chicago gangsters, representing all of the important outfits," in an effort to prevent the St. Valentine's Massacre spiraling into open warfare "that would completely disrupt liquor operations and other enterprises."[24] Although the real meeting took place at the President Hotel in Atlantic City, Wilder's relocating of it to the fictional Seminole-Ritz in Florida still possessed historical substance, drawing on Pasley's description of Miami as "the winter Cicero of Chicago's gangdom."[25]

Even the eventual demise of Spats himself, dispatched along with two henchmen at a banquet hosted by Mafia overlord Little Bonaparte, is a blackly comic reworking of the murder of the real killers implicated in the St. Valentine's Day Massacre, John Scalisi and Albert Anselmi who, along with the Unione Siciliana's Joseph Guinta, were assassinated at a "testimonial dinner." Wilder's version seems indebted to Elliot Ness's then-recently published *The Untouchables*, which described Capone (just like Wilder's Little Bonaparte) rising to offer a toast: "Then the smile vanished from his face. Fury blazed in his eyes. 'Guests of honour,' he roared. 'Traitors! Double-crossers!' Guinta, Scalise and Anselmi were rooted to their chairs . . . powerless under the guns of Capone's bodyguards."[26] That Little Bonaparte sanctions the murder because the North Side boss had "grown too big for his spats" correlates with Walter Burns's description of Capone's motives in executing Scalisi who, "having achieved a little power, had grown ambitious for greater power."[27] And while most accounts claimed the men had been bludgeoned to death with baseball bats, Pasley had noted that the post-mortem examination had revealed that the three men had been shot to death while seated at their table, as happens to Spats and his men.[28] Unlikely as it is that their assassin burst out of an over-sized birthday cake, Burns did suggest that some kind of "ruse" must have been used to have taken Capone's "shrewdest killers" by surprise.[29] Wilder and Diamond invented their own "ruse," but the event itself originated in historical sources.

Visual elements of the production suggest an attention to historical detail, as well. Literature about Chicago's gangsters frequently referenced their sartorial extravagance: Dion O'Bannion, for instance, described as "the pioneer and trailblazer of gangland's tuxedo era," or Big Jim Colosimo identifiable by his "flashy clothes, diamond-studded watch, diamond rings and stick-pin and diamond studded garter."[30] Capone himself was always noted as "impeccably attired," but it seems to have been Paul Sann's best-selling *The Lawless Decade*, published in 1957 just as Wilder and Diamond began to write, which inspired the moniker of "Spats Colombo," for it contains a photograph of Capone with the following caption:

> Ever gracious and friendly even when the authorities had occasion to take up his valuable time with questions, Mr. Capone turns on the charm . . . Note Al's spats and Chesterfield collar. He liked to dress according to his station.[31]

As Wilder wrote in the screenplay: "The spats are very important. He always wears spats."[32] Similarly, the particular fedora worn by

Spats suggests that the production designers, at least, had read Elliot
Ness's observation that "pearl gray felt hats with narrow black bands . . .
were the trademark of the Capone mobsters."[33]

Wilder's dictum, he told Cameron Crowe, was: "Make it true, make
it seem true. And don't have something, even in a farce like *Some
Like It Hot* that isn't true."[34] Yet, of course, to suggest that the film is
actually true to history would lose sight of the obvious: *Some Like It
Hot* is a comedy that makes use of the past, but does not recreate it.
Whatever the reviewer for *Time* magazine may have believed, the
film's version of the St. Valentine's Day Massacre was far from "painfully accurate."[35] The real event was far more ingenious than Wilder's
simplistic version, as Capone's men disguised themselves as policemen
so that they could "stroll into the garage in broad daylight without
drawing a challenge."[36] And unlike Spats, who personally finishes
Charlie off, Capone was careful to be far from the scene of the
crime. Presumably, it was the brutality of the sequence that impressed
reviewers as "honest," Wilder succeeding in making it "seem true"
even when it wasn't.

Real history and fictional versions of the past were apparently of
equal merit, if they created the right effect. Take something as basic as
the name of "Little Bonaparte." On one level it actually owes something to historical accounts, invoking one of Capone's oft-repeated
jokes that he had read Emil Ludwig's 1928 biography of Napoleon
and had come to admire the French dictator as "the world's greatest
racketeer."[37] Yet, as most film commentators note, it is also an obvious
nod to Edward G. Robinson's classic gangster film *Little Caesar* (1930).
It clearly did not trouble Wilder's historical consciousness to mix up
the elements—and contemporaries recognized that his movie was a
"double-barreled period piece," parodying the "free-wheeling, gangster-
ridden 20s" in both its historical and its cinematic forms.[38]

The casting made this very evident, in the resurrection of supporting
players indelibly associated with black-and-white gangster movies.[39]
George E. Stone, as "Toothpick Charlie," was "practically synonymous"
with the role of "gangland squealer" since playing "Sewer Rat" in
Seventh Heaven (1927).[40] As Spats himself, George Raft had been
"fixed in the popular imagination as a hood" since *Scarface* (1932) and
films like *Each Dawn I Die* (1939) and *Manpower* (1941).[41] Twice, Raft
had played gangster to Pat O'Brien's Irish-American cop in *Broadway*
(1942) and *A Dangerous Profession* (1949), and Wilder then exploited
this film-history connection by casting O'Brien as agent Mulligan.[42]
Wilder also wanted Edward G. Robinson himself for the role of Little
Bonaparte.[43] When Robinson refused, Wilder instead cast the actor's son

as Johnny Paradise, the young "punk" who insolently flips a half-dollar in the air when talking to Spats—a "cheap trick" that Spats regards with contempt, even though it had been an iconic part of Raft's own performance in *Scarface*.

   Wilder's attitude toward historical materials is similarly apparent in the narrative's main focus on the desperate attempt of Joe and Jerry to escape Spats by hiding in an all-female jazz orchestra. Sweet Sue's Society Syncopators presumably owes a debt to Helen Lewis and Her All-Girl Jazz Syncopators (itself captured on film in 1925), as well as the all-girl band (with "thirty-two of the most attractive legs") that Wilder himself had encountered in Vienna in 1925 when a reporter for *Die Stunde*.[44] The music they play reflects the historical sensibilities of music arranger Matty Malneck, who had composed arrangements for Paul Whiteman's legendary jazz orchestra in the mid-1920s, and was enthusiastically engaged by Wilder to "adapt the right songs for the film" as a way of "legitimizing the period setting."[45] Thus, the soundtrack appropriately includes *Runnin' Wild*, composed in 1922; *Sweet Georgia Brown*, introduced by Chicago-based Ben Bernie and his Orchestra in 1925; and Monroe's standout performance of *I Want To Be Loved By You*, first presented in 1928 by Helen Kane, the original "Boob-Boop-a-Doop Girl." Yet, the "right song" was not always an authentic one, since Monroe's final song, *I'm Through With Love*, had not been published until 1931. However, this was one of Malneck's own compositions and, in underscoring Sugar's heartbreak and vulnerability when she believes her romance with a millionaire is over, the importance of its lyrical content overrode historicity.[46]

   That Sugar would expect to find millionaires in Florida ("flocks of them") certainly had its historical justification. That *Some Like It Hot*'s eccentric millionaire Osgood Fielding III (Joe E. Brown) winters at the hotel Seminole-Ritz is true to the clientele, such as oil tycoon John D. Rockefeller, who frequented the grand resorts built by Henrys Flagler and Plant.[47] The subsequent land-rush and real estate boom of the early 1920s had seen the efforts of developers to attract the "world of international wealth" to Miami and Palm Beach become frenzied.[48] However, Wilder's version of Florida as a "millionaire's playground" contradicts the harsher realities that faced the state in 1929, for the bubble had burst there long before the Wall Street Crash. Severe hurricanes had hit in 1926, and Miami at that time hardly fitted the screenplay's description of a place where "the livin' is easy, fish are jumpin' and the market is high."[49]

   Instead, like *Some Like It Hot*'s gangsters, this image seems to derive as much from other movies as from history, such as the 1941 film, *Moon Over Miami*, in which Betty Grable's efforts to find rich husbands for herself, her sister, and her aunt helped to cement the city's reputation in popular culture "as the place for single women to come to find a millionaire."[50] Wilder exploits this cinematic mythology when Joe himself pretends to be a millionaire in order to deceive and woo Sugar; he even has Sugar first encounter this phony-millionaire (complete with Cary Grant accent) by tripping over his outstretched legs, just as Grable meets Don Ameche's character in *Moon*. But, yet again, there is simultaneously a nugget of real history in a seemingly throwaway line. When asked where his fortune comes from, Joe takes inspiration from a bucket of seashells on the beach and implies that he is the heir to Shell Oil. Although a joke, his seemingly improvised comment to Sugar that his grandfather collected shells and "loved them so much that he named the company after them," has an unexpected basis in fact. The real originator of the company, Marcus Samuel, made his first fortune in importing decorative shells from Asia to London; and when this evolved into the family's lucrative oil import-export business, the scallop shell (which Joe holds up) became the visual manifestation of Shell Oil in 1904.[51] Whether or not Wilder or Diamond knew this fact is impossible to prove, but the notion of historical substance behind the wisecrack certainly fits their style.

The "past world" of 1929 forged in *Some Like It Hot* is one that treats film histories as cultural historical capital on a par with newspaper accounts, populist histories and, indeed, music history, using them all as sources of references points that would be familiar and accessible to viewers. Nostalgia could therefore play a major role in the appeal of the film: the way in which it "harks back to those glorious days" of "old gangster movies," "screwball comedy" and "the old frenetic nonsense of Mack Sennett farces" pleased many reviewers.[52] As in many historical films, this self-conscious referencing of other cinematic representations of the period further works to "legitimize" Wilder's version because it "accords with the understanding" of Chicago and Miami that audiences in 1959 had already acquired through contact with a variety of "modes of historical representation."[53] In fact, as Smyth has argued, there is a case to be made that films like *Public Enemy* and *Little Caesar* were valid sources of Prohibition-era historiography in themselves, effectively documenting the period years before traditional academic historians began to research it, and thereby contributing fundamentally to the public understanding of the history of gangsterdom.[54] At the same time, however, *Some Like It Hot* denies that any of its referents should be treated as "authentic" history, because Wilder repeatedly draws attention to his cinematic pastiche: as in the coin-flipping joke, or the moment when Spats is about to smash half a grapefruit into the face of a stupid henchmen, as James Cagney had famously done to Mae Clarke in *The Public Enemy*. Not taking *any* form of history seriously enabled Wilder to imbue it *all* with a consistently "cartoonish" quality, getting comic mileage out of everything he could.[55] Several commentators did express doubt about his effort to "make funny the St. Valentine's Day massacre," but, to Wilder at least, there had always been "something slightly ridiculous about the gangsters" which he felt justified in utilizing.[56]

Too Hot to Handle?

Some Like It Hot did not, however, originate as "a satire of old gangster pictures." In fact, as first conceived, Joe and Jerry were to be contemporary American musicians, with box-office appeal deriving from a score of hit rock 'n' roll songs of the 1950s. As Wilder often explained, it was only *after* he and Diamond had determined to set the film in 1929 that they realized they could "exploit the period by bringing in George Raft and Pat O'Brien."[57] The actual decision to utilize the period setting was driven principally by anxieties about how American audiences would accept a drag comedy and how censors would respond (Illustration 6.2).

The usual explanation given for the decision to relocate the action to 1929 is that inspiration hit when Wilder was searching for a believable

Illustration 6.2   Daphne (Jack Lemmon) has stopped leading and plays the lady with Osgood (Joe E. Brown): *Some Like It Hot* (1959) © Ashton Productions

reason for Joe and Jerry to don women's clothes. The German film that inspired *Some Like It Hot*, Kurt Hoffmann's *Fanfaren der Liebe* (1951), had its two musicians, Hans and Peter, transform themselves into Hansi and Petra, simply to find work. Wilder and Diamond had already decided that their remake required a more persuasive motivation than poverty, and subsequently claimed that having their heroes on the run from gangsters proved to be "the perfect solution."[58] Yet, they could have achieved this in the present-day setting—indeed, their original intention was for Joe and Jerry to witness a murder at their bookie's office.[59] Having them witness the St. Valentine's Day Massacre instead suggests that the "problem" that needed "solving" went further than simply finding an excuse for Wilder's leading-men to become leading-ladies.

The issue lies in *Some Like It Hot*'s essence as a sex comedy. Even when the men are dressed as men, the comedy is "hot." When Joe poses as millionaire Shell Junior and invites Sugar back to "his" yacht, Wilder turns the expected seduction on its head by having Joe pretend to be impotent—thus prompting Sugar to take the lead. As Wilder put it, "what could be better" than to be "subdued, seduced and screwed by Marilyn Monroe."[60] There is also Sugar's famous innuendo on oral sex, when she expresses dissatisfaction about always getting stuck with the "fuzzy end of the lollipop." But when Curtis and Lemmon are cross-dressing, the double-entendres escalate further. Just the very idea of Joe and Jerry dressing as women generates jokes which flit around the "threat of castration," as when their agent first suggests that they do not fulfil the requirements for the job in Sweet Sue's orchestra:[61]

Joe:	What kind of band is it anyway?
Poliakoff:	You gotta be under 25.
Jerry (insisting):	We could pass for that.
Poliakoff:	You gotta be blonde.
Jerry:	We could dye our hair.
Poliakoff:	And you gotta be girls.
Jerry:	We could . . .
Joe (cutting him off):	No we couldn't!

This joke is used again at the end of the film, once Jerry's disguise as Daphne has won him the affections of Osgood Fielding III. Looking for a way out of the engagement, Jerry/Daphne insists that "I can't get married in your mother's dress," because "she and I, we are not built the same way." He is then greatly alarmed at the implications of Osgood's most nonchalant reply: "We can have it altered."

Such risqué humour was always likely to encounter some form of censorship—and, indeed, censors in both the state of Kansas and the city of Memphis demanded that the love scene on the yacht be cut.[62] Yet, Joe and Jerry's transvestism created even more "difficult" situations in its homosexual implications. As Ed Sikov notes, despite never tackling homosexuality head on, *Some Like It Hot* makes some of its best jokes on the subject.[63] Lesbianism is raised when Joe finally kisses Sugar while still in female dress, telling her, "No guy is worth it." From Sugar's perspective, until realization sinks in, it is Josephine who has kissed her—and the image on screen is of two women kissing. The implications notably become overt when Jerry, pretending to be Daphne, "takes to his feminine persona so thoroughly and, ultimately, so happily, that he even considers the prospect of marrying Osgood."[64] In fact, Jerry refuses to "deny the possibility" of such a marriage even when Joe tries to remind him of the problems:[65]

Joe: Jerry! You can't be serious!
Jerry: Why not? He keeps marrying girls all the time!
Joe: But you're not a girl. You're a guy! And why would a guy want to marry a guy?
Jerry: Security.

And, of course, in the closing moments when Jerry finally admits that he is a man, Osgood is famously neither surprised nor concerned. After all, "Nobody's perfect."

In this unconventional romance in particular, Wilder was directly contravening Article 11.4 of the Production Code, which prohibited even the "inference" of "sex perversion."[66] Empowered by the film industry itself to oversee the "moral content" of all Hollywood movies since the early 1930s, the Production Code Administration had already castigated the makers of one "cross-dressing" film, *Turnabout* (1940), for producing what PCA chief Joseph Breen had called a "pansy comedy," and *Some Like It Hot* was far less circumspect.[67] Cross-dressing, after all, becomes an almost immediate "source of pleasure" for Jerry, as "he boards the Miami-bound train and launches gleefully into a discussion about corsets and seamstresses."[68] Critics used language suggesting they were well aware of what Wilder was about: *Variety* called the film a "gay romp," while the *New York Times* reviewer wrote of "Mr. Lemmon's gay fandango with Mr. Brown."[69] While enjoying the film greatly, John Leonard of the *National Review* speculated that it might well encounter criticism for "tackling so ticklish a subject in this self-conscious age of limp wrists and whither-withered male virility."[70] Unimpressed critics like Ellen Fitzpatrick proved Leonard right, accusing the film of entering realms of "very blue taste," with the kind of dialogue and situations "that titillate sex perverts."[71]

The influence of the Production Code was waning by 1959, but it was not yet "all but dead."[72] Breen had retired, and his successor, Geoffrey Shurlock, had overseen a more liberal revision of the Code in 1956; but Breen's insistence that homosexuality "should not even be hinted at in the movies," remained the one area that the industry held out against "softening."[73] This was apparent in 1958, when M-G-M was required to remove any "taint of homosexuality" from the relationship between Brick and Skipper in their adaptation of Tennessee Williams's *Cat on a Hot Tin Roof.*[74] Wilder therefore knew that his material would be problematic and controversial, and he had had run-ins with the PCA before. *The Seven Year Itch*'s comic subversion of monogamy and marriage had proved difficult to accommodate to the Code's general principle that no film should "lower the moral standards of those who see it," and, ultimately, Wilder had excised all implications that Richard Sherman's character actually committed adultery with Marilyn Monroe's "The Girl."[75] However, with *Some Like It Hot*, Wilder was apparently in no mood to make such compromises.

The usual procedure was that any story idea or draft screenplay that a studio hoped to produce would be submitted to the PCA, to ensure that the final film would conform to the Code and thereby avoid post-production censorship from sources outside the industry. However, the PCA file on *Some Like It Hot* does not record the submission of any script at any stage, and it is documented that Wilder and Diamond were "still polishing" the screenplay during the last weeks of shooting in October 1958.[76] According to Tony Curtis and Mark Vieira, Wilder had decided to stop presenting scripts to the PCA in 1956, after they had refused to countenance his ideas for adapting Maxwell Anderson's play about a murderous young girl, *The Bad Seed*, only to then approve a Warner Bros. production in the following year. He was, however, apparently still "apprehensive" when he submitted the final cut of *Some Like It Hot* to Shurlock on February 9, 1959.[77] The lack of the seal of Code approval could still restrict the number of exhibitors willing to show such a film, representing a significant financial risk to any filmmaker, and the seriousness of the situation was indicated by the presence at the screening of Shurlock and the three most senior members of his team.[78] In the end, however, the PCA decide to take its lead from the reaction of the trade press, noting that no one else who had seen that film had (as of then) "questioned either its morality or its taste."[79] So, on February 10, *Some Like It Hot* was approved for distribution, receiving PCA seal number 1928.

This, however, still left the hurdle of the National Catholic Legion of Decency. The Legion was essentially the watchdog that ensured filmmakers and studios paid attention to the Production Code. If it "condemned" a film as "immoral" or "obscene," the industry risked facing a boycott of over 20 million Catholics who, since 1933, had taken the Legion pledge: "I hereby promise to remain away from all motion pictures except those which do not offend decency and Christian morality."[80] Stoking the anxieties of the studio bosses, Breen had long convinced them that only adherence to Code could keep the Legion (and other external censors) at bay. Wilder had now chosen not to accept this "protection." Like the PCA itself, the Legion in 1959 was less effective than it once had been, and two years earlier had expanded its rating system to include more options for its reviewers to use (A-I—morally unobjectionable for general patronage; A-II—morally unobjectionable for adults and adolescents; and A-III—morally unobjectionable for adults). However, a 1957 papal encyclical, *Miranda Prorsus*, had urged national offices to "continue to classify films using moral standards," and even the threat of a condemnation from the Legion could still have a significant impact.[81] It was the "Legion's chief moral arbiters" that Twentieth Century-Fox had finally caved to in rewriting *The Seven Year Itch*, despite Wilder's "outrage."[82] And in 1959, Stanley Kubrick's adaptation of Nabokov's *Lolita* was stuck in development (and remained so for two years) because no studio or distributor (including United Artists) was prepared to finance production until Kubrick fashioned a screenplay that could receive the approval of both the PCA and the Legion.[83] The Legion was certain not to be happy about *Some Like It Hot*.

Indeed, documents in the Legion's New York archives show that Wilder's film gave the organization "the greatest cause for concern."[84] When columnist Walter Winchell noted that *Some Like It Hot* "had over twenty Legion of Decency people at its screening. They usually only send seven," the Legion's Assistant Executive Secretary felt obliged to offer a correction: "the total number of reviewers was *far in excess* of 20" and included not only "ladies from the Motion Picture Department of the International Federation of Catholic Alumnae," but "more than a dozen members of our Board of Consultors."[85] Comments in the file show that these reviewers regarded Osgood's last line as typical "of the level of cynicism and taste in the whole."[86] The Chair of the Episcopal Committee for Motion Pictures and Television, Bishop James McNulty, contacted the head of the Motion Picture Producers Association, Eric Johnston, to voice his offence at "the most flagrant violation of the spirit and of the letter of the

Production Code."[87] Knowing that a Code seal had been issued, Executive Secretary Monsignor Thomas F. Little wrote angrily to Shurlock in protest. Not only was the film full of "gross suggestiveness" and dialogue that was "outright smut," but what truly breached the Code were the film's "highly questionable moral issues" relating to "the subject matter of transvestism" and the consequent "inferences given to homosexuality and lesbianism."[88] Found to be "seriously offensive to Christian and traditional standards of morality and decency," *Some Like It Hot* was "very close to being condemned."[89]

It was in this context, however, that the St. Valentine's Day Massacre afforded Wilder some protection. David O. Selznick had apparently advised against such a setting: "You want machine guns and dead bodies and gags in the same picture? Forget about it, Billy . . . No comedy can survive that kind of brutal reality."[90] Yet, Wilder knew that the film's transvestite complications were far more likely to give offence than the violence; and it was precisely the "brutal reality" of Chicago's most notorious gangland murders that he needed, to 'make real' the threat hanging over Joe and Jerry. By changing a fictional murder in a 1950s bookies to the St. Valentine's Day Massacre, Wilder could tap into historical and cultural awareness of the atrocity. Audiences would then instinctively associate Spats with Al Capone, thus raising his threat to a literally legendary level. We immediately understand why Joe and Jerry fear Spats so much, because the character borrows Capone's renown as "Public Enemy Number One." Casting George Raft compounded this, exploiting both his tough guy movie persona, as well as public awareness that the actor had his own "underworld" connections with real gangsters.[91] Real history, Hollywood history, and Raft's own history thereby reinforced one another—all directed toward justifying not only why Joe and Jerry disguise themselves as women in the first place, but why they must remain in drag through most of the film. Knowing that censorship—and potentially prudish audiences—would be a problem, Wilder's primary concern, according to producer Walter Mirisch, "was that he required a strong motivation to make two healthy heterosexual men resort to the extreme of dressing as women."[92] As Wilder reasoned, it was the "necessity to be realistic with the massacres" that "made the picture": "The two men were on the spot, and we kept them on the spot until the very end."[93] "Once we had the idea of making it period," he said, the writing "went very, very easy," opening up "a wealth of material to work with—speakeasies bootleggers, Florida millionaires."[94] However, the choice of specific period setting was driven first and foremost by the censorship problem of finding a "heterosexual" motivation for transvestism.

The temporal backdrop also rendered cross-dressing less problematic in another way. The British stage play *Charley's Aunt*, written in 1882 by Brandon Thomas (and filmed several times already) was, as even Shurlock noted, "a classic example of a man masquerading in women's clothing *without offense*."[95] As Diamond understood, this was because *Charley's Aunt* was "always done in period" and when "everybody's dress looks eccentric to us, somebody in drag looks no more peculiar than anyone else."[96] In contrast, a man in contemporary drag had the potential to be "dicey": images of Lemmon and Curtis in the dresses or tight sweaters worn by women in 1959 might have raised disturbing sexual responses among filmgoers.[97] As Curtis said, while the sight of Jack Benny dressing in "old lady" drag in *Charley's Aunt* was "harmless," putting "two young studs" in contemporary women's clothes was potentially "shocking" in the 1950s.[98] In that sense, the setting of 1929 was even more useful in presenting Wilder and Diamond with the design aesthetic of the flapper. The 1920s, after all, was the decade in which "bobbed hair became almost universal among girls" and the androgynous form was the height of sophistication.[99] The "frank use" of cosmetics, and the abandonment of the corset might have epitomized "female daring," but simultaneously "the potential eroticism of [women's] outfits was kept in bounds by the boyish look achieved by binding the breasts to make them appear flat."[100] Designer Orry-Kelly could therefore ensure that Curtis and Lemmon were not "sexualized" while in drag, yet still keep the costuming entirely appropriate to history. Indeed, their very lack of curves could provide its own source of amusement when contrasted with Monroe's "sex bomb" figure. As Sugar herself says to Jerry/Daphne, she envies her "being so flat-chested. Clothes hang so much better on you than they do on me."

Evidently concerned that the "inferences" of transvestism could prove offensive to audiences and censors, Wilder had already cut one brief scene in which a "horn-dog" Jerry had clambered into bed intent on seducing Sugar, only to discover he was coming on to Joe/Josephine. In contrast to the "chaste" romance between Daphne and Osgood, the idea of mistaken identity leading to a sexual encounter between two men was presumably one step too far.[101] The director also once claimed that the reason *Some Like It Hot* was filmed in black-and-white was because Technicolor might have turned it into "a flaming faggot picture."[102] Beyond this, however, practically the only concession made to temper the sexual confusion and innuendo-laden dialogue and situations was the period setting itself. The critic for *The Hollywood Reporter* certainly realized this, observing that

Wilder "cleverly avoids any swish connotation by placing the story in the period of 1929."[103]

And it worked. After lengthy deliberations, the Legion of Decency eventually decided not to condemn the film. Wilder claimed "the censors forgave me because it was funny," but, in fact, the general opinion of the Legion's consultors was that it was an "entirely moronic" and "unappealing farce."[104] However, Little had followed the PCA's example and examined closely what secular film critics were saying. They underlined, for example, *Variety*'s conclusion that Wilder "knows just when to draw back before crossing the line into vulgar."[105] They noted Paul Beckley's assertion in the *New York Herald Tribune* that while "ordinarily I do not find female impersonation a very engaging subject of humor, I did not feel anything offensive in it here, primarily . . . because such skinny-shanked, gawky caricatures as Lemmon and Curtis make themselves into never leave any doubt about their masculinity."[106] Of particular interest was Frank Leyendecker's observation in *Boxoffice* that "Lemmon, *wearing the feminine garb of the Prohibition days*, is truly uproarious without ever being offensive."[107] Not wanting to weaken its own credibility any further by condemning a comedy that looked set to be a box-office smash, the Legion took a step back. *Some Like It Hot* may have remained a "serious menace to morals," yet they classified it only as "B"—"morally objectionable in part for all."[108] Since, by 1959, most Catholics held the opinion that they were "free to see any movie that was not condemned," *Variety* noted that this B rating "generally has very little meaning at the box office." Confrontation and compromise with the Legion was thus avoided—and in this the particular historical setting was crucial.[109] Brandon French once claimed that "comedy is the best camouflage," but, in truth, period-set comedy was even better.[110]

The Period Worked For Us

History provided Wilder with the last laugh, too. In *Some Like It Hot*'s representation of the Prohibition era, almost every character is shown breaking the law. The crimes of Spats and the gangsters are deadly serious, but from the revelers drinking in Mr. Mozarella's speakeasy to Osgood stocking his yacht with champagne, Sugar keeping a flask of bourbon in her garter, or the girls in Sweet Sue's band fixing cocktails in a hot water bottle, everyone is flouting the Eighteenth Amendment. Even the bell-hop at the Seminole-Ritz has "a bottle of gin stashed away." Popular historians in the 1950s, such as Paul Sann, characterized the 1920s as "The Lawless Decade," embracing not only gangsterism but the flaunting of civil, social, and moral laws as well.[111] Capitalizing on that popular image, Wilder and Diamond thus had a setting for *Some Like It Hot* in which all forms of "transgression" were "ostensibly appropriate."[112]

That the 1920s were perceived as a time when "an upheaval in values was taking place," and it was "better to be modern and sophisticated and smart, to smash the conventions and be devastatingly frank" is the source of much of the fun.[113] Wilder was able, for example, to use the flapper image not only to desexualize Josephine and Daphne, but simultaneously to exploit its association with female sexual daring in Sugar's seduction of Shell Junior. That female musicians in all-girl bands were commonly stereotyped as "sexually suspect, either as loose or as lesbian" could serve to explain the kiss between Josephine and Sugar.[114] And that there were eccentric old millionaires like Edward West "Daddy" Browning, who in 1926 "distressed" his fifteen-year-old bride Peaches by "gamboling" naked "around the bedchamber on his hands and knees," helps to put Osgood's dalliances into context.[115] Indeed, Wilder used the whole context of the "licentiously roaring twenties" to support the sexual aspects of his films that might otherwise be regarded as prohibited.[116]

Many commentators have emphasized that the film's central masquerades serve to complicate the notion of fixed gender roles prevalent in postwar America. When the "tough-guy" masculinity of the gangsters represents only "violence and death," Joe and Jerry adopt feminine personas that not only provide protection, but also force them to re-examine "themselves and their view of women" as they experience "unwanted sexual overtures, male voyeurism and the constraints and pleasures of feminine culture."[117] As Daphne, Jerry becomes far more flamboyant and "infinitely more appealing" than the man who is originally "cajoling" and "submissive" in his "regular" friendship with Joe.[118] Joe himself cavorts not only as Josephine but as Shell Junior as well; "allowing Sugar to take the initiative in seducing him" inverts the "aggressive/passive binarism that has previously defined his heterosexual existence."[119] Suppressing his usual sexual aggressiveness and seeing "how the other half lives" from a female perspective ultimately leads Joe to connect with a woman "on the level" for the first time in his life. At the very least, *Some Like It Hot* shows "that despite appearances, the opposite sex is very much like us," and some have even read the film as "an object-lesson in the need for men to abandon their sexual identities in order to survive."[120]

As is true of most historical representations, the issues raised were of particular relevance to contemporary society. The 1950s saw considerable anxiety among sociologists, historians and psychologists over the "decline of the American male" and "the crisis of American masculinity," a concern underscored by the "specter of an expansionist homosexuality" that followed Alfred Kinsey's finding that "at least 37 percent of the male population has some homosexual experience."[121] Moreover, Christine Jorgensen had brought transvestism and trans-sexuality (regarded as much the same thing in the 1950s) to the nation's attention, when the "ex-G.I." George Jorgensen returned to the United States in 1952 having undergone gender-reassignment surgery in Copenhagen. For a time, when news coverage encouraged Americans to believe that Jorgensen had physically and fundamentally "changed sex," the reaction was curious but positive. However, it became much more markedly hostile when medical professionals revealed that Christine was "really" a "castrated man"—as if a hoax had been perpetrated.[122] Yet, while others worried that transvestism, transsexuality, homosexuality and even impotence were part of a threatening "flight from masculinity" at a time when the "burdens of manhood" were too great, Wilder took these issues and encouraged filmgoers to laugh instead at the idea that "nobody's perfect."[123]

And once again, the historical setting facilitates this laughter. Since the Prohibition laws were commonly regarded, by the 1950s, as a defunct and long-discredited product of prewar censoriousness, an audience could readily side with the characters who happily subvert them. Then, when these characters go on to transgress other moral codes—including contemporary sexual boundaries—we are already with them. So, while the period setting "excused" the cross-dressing and tempered censorship, it conversely also enabled *Some Like It Hot* to wear its heart on its sleeve as a provocatively subversive comedy. Thus, it was entirely within the spirit of the film *and* its setting that Wilder took great pleasure in using history to "sneak around" the censors, subverting the moral Puritanism of the Production Code and the Legion of Decency and implicitly suggesting that it, too, was as discredited as Prohibition.[124] On many levels, therefore, the "period worked" for Wilder simply by virtue of "not taking itself too seriously."

Notes

1. Quoted in Alison Castle (ed.), *Billy Wilder's* Some Like It Hot (Berlin: Taschen, 2002): 253.
2. *Ibid.*: 245.
3. *New Yorker* (April 4, 1959): 142; *Hit Parader* (July 1959), quoted in Castle: 19; *Film Bulletin* (March 2, 1959).

4. *Film Bulletin* (March 2, 1959); *New York Herald Tribune* (March 30, 1959); *Boxoffice* (March 2, 1959).
5. Laurence Maslon, Some Like It Hot*: The Official 50th Anniversary Companion* (New York: Pavilion, 2009): 148.
6. Anthony Lane, *Nobody's Perfect: Writings from the* New Yorker (New York: Vintage, 2003): 712.
7. Robert Brent Toplin, *Reel History: In Defense of Hollywood* (Lawrence: University Press of Kansas, 2002): 90.
8. Leger Grindon, *Shadows of the Past: Studies in the Historical Fiction Film* (Philadelphia: Temple University Press, 1994): 2.
9. Pierre Sorlin, "Historical Films as Tools for Historians," in John E. O'Connor (ed.), *Images as Artefacts: The Historical Analysis of Film and Television* (Malabar: Krieger, 1990): 42.
10. Robert Brent Toplin, "The Historian and Film: A Research Agenda," *Journal of American History* (December 1991): 1162.
11. David Eldridge, *Hollywood's History Films* (London: IB Tauris, 2006): 4.
12. Michelle Pierson, "A Production Designer's Cinema: Historical Authenticity in Popular Films Set in the Past," in Marnie Hughes-Warrington (ed.), *The History on Film Reader* (London: Routledge, 2009): 213.
13. A cache of papers was acquired by the Margaret Herrick Library in Los Angeles in 2008 (hereafter AMPAS), but principally the material relating to *Some Like It Hot* is concerned with Marilyn Monroe's performance. Scorch marks on the documents seem to confirm the story that many of Wilder's papers were destroyed in a fire.
14. *The Spirit of St. Louis* Research Record File 1, Warner Bros. Archive, University of Southern California, Los Angeles (hereafter USC). Intriguingly, on July 15, 1955, while making *Spirit*, Wilder asked the research department what was the "date of Valentine shooting in Chicago."
15. See William Helmer and Arthur Bileck, *The St. Valentine's Day Massacre* (Cumberland House, 2006).
16. Quoted in David E. Ruth, *Inventing the Public Enemy: The Gangster in American Culture, 1818–1934* (Chicago: University of Chicago Press, 1996): 142. John May was not actually a member of Moran's gang, but he did accept jobs from them.
17. Herbert Asbury, *The Great Illusion: An Informal History of Prohibition* (Greenwood Press, 1950): 308.
18. Tony Curtis with Mark Vieira, *The Making of* Some Like It Hot*: My Memories of Marilyn Monroe and the Classic American Movie* (New York: John Wiley, 2009): 16.
19. J.E. Smyth, *Reconstructing American Historical Cinema: From* Cimarron *to* Citizen Kane (Lexington: University Press of Kentucky, 2006): 71.
20. *Pete Kelly's Blues* (1955) Press Release, n.d., Warner Bros. Archive, USC.
21. Frederic Jennings Haskin, *The American Government* (Washington DC, 1923): 434. Spats's use of a funeral parlor as a front for his speakeasy is also appropriate to Herbert Asbury's description of the Prohibitionists' celebration of the "death of liquor" being parodied in nightclubs with

"mock funerals" involving coffins "filled with broken bottles and glassware" (Asbury: 151–2). I have yet to find evidence of a funeral parlor being used as a front (although this image is also used in *Pete Kelly's Blues*), but there was a noted association between bootleggers and undertakers, in that "manufacturers of hooch sometimes used embalming fluid to give their whiskey an even greater kick" (Asbury: 273). Wilder evidently knew this, for Mulligan humorously arrests Spats on the charge of "embalming" his customers with "86 proof" drinks.

22. Fred D. Pasley, *Al Capone: The Biography of a Self-Made Man* (New York: Ives, 1930): 8.

23. Walter Burns, *The One-Way Ride: The Red Trail of Chicago Gangland from Prohibition to Jake Lingle* (Garden City: Doubleday, 1931): 22.

24. Asbury: 309.

25. Pasley: 77. It is noteworthy, too, that the "Friends of Italian Opera" in the film are marking their "Tenth Annual Convention" —an anniversary which, in 1929, would have marked their establishment in 1919, the year in which the Volstead Act was passed, instigating Prohibition. Also, 1919 was the year Al Capone arrived in Chicago from New York, at Johnny Torrio's invitation.

26. Eliot Ness (with Oscar Fraley), *The Untouchables* (New York: Buccaneer Books, 1957): 183.

27. Burns: 281.

28. Pasley: 297. Bonaparte's speech in the film fits Pasley's description of the "simulated brotherly love, the unctuous guile of the smiling lip and the lying tongue" which would have put Anselmi and Scalisi at ease, just before their execution (295).

29. Burns: 278.

30. Burns: 86; Pasley: 13.

31. Paul Sann, *The Lawless Decade: A Pictorial History of a Great American Transition* (New York: Bonanza Books, 1957): 208.

32. Castle: 35.

33. Ness: 75.

34. Cameron Crowe, *Conversations With Wilder* (London: Faber & Faber, 1999): 143.

35. *Time*, March 23, 1959.

36. Ness: 40.

37. Burns: 33.

38.. *Time*, March 23, 1959.

39. Wes Gehring, *Joe E. Brown: Film Comedian and Baseball Buffoon* (Jefferson: McFarland, 2006): 179.

40. Maslon: 48.

41. *Ibid.*: 44.

42. *Ibid.*: 48.

43. *Ibid.*: 44.

44. Castle: 355.

45. Maslon: 127.

46. So too, it should be noted, did Monroe's costumes, which were "glamorous, undeniably 1950s outfits and gowns," designed much more around her "star presence" than narrative historicity. (Lorraine Rolston, *Some Like It Hot* (London:York Press, 2000): 50).

47. Susan Braden, *The Architecture of Leisure:The Florida Resort Hotels of Henry Flagler and Henry Plant* (Gainesville: University Press of Florida, 2002).

48. Frederick Lewis Allen, *Only Yesterday: An Informal History of the 1920s in America* [1931] (London: Penguin, 1935): 387.

49. Castle: 123.Wilder had to film on location at the Hotel Del Coronado in San Diego, because Flagler's hotels, the Poinciana and the Royal Palm, had themselves been demolished in the mid-1930s having never recovered from the hurricane damage and the collapse of Florida's tourist boom. Rechristening the Del the "Seminole Ritz" gave a suitable nod toward Plant's Seminole Hotel, which had opened in Winter Park, Florida, in 1886. (See Braden: 222).

50. Gregory Bush, "'Playground of the USA': Miami and the Promotion of Spectacle," *Pacific Historical Review* 68(2) (1999): 168. This image was also perpetuated in Preston Sturges's *Palm Beach Story* (1942). Interestingly, one of the early ideas Wilder and Diamond had for their story was for Sugar (then named "Stella") to get herself inadvisably involved with Spats Colombo when he arrives in Florida—"after all," wrote Wilder, "a beer millionaire is just as good as any other millionaire." (Billy Wilder to Marilyn Monroe, March 17, 1958, Billy Wilder Papers f.78,AMPAS). Indeed, estimates suggest that Capone's beer trafficking, gambling and prostitution rackets in Chicago were generating revenues in excess of $100 million a year, with Capone himself pocketing $30 million of that (Sann: 210–11).

51. See http://www.shell.com/home/content/aboutshell/who_we_are/our_history/dir_our_history_14112006.html (accessed December 2009).

52. *Saturday Review*, March 28, 1959; *New Yorker*, April 4, 1959.

53. Pierson: 215.

54. See Smyth: 60–2.

55. See Rolston: 63.

56. *Films in Review*, April 1959: 241; Crowe: 137.

57. Gene D. Phillips, "Billy Wilder," in Robert Horton (ed.), *Billy Wilder Interviews* (Jackson: University Press of Mississippi, 2001): 107.

58. Barbara Diamond, quoted in Castle: 245.

59. I.A.L. Diamond, "The Day Marilyn Needed 47 Takes to Remember to Say, 'Where's the Bourbon?'" *California* (December, 1985): 132.

60. Crowe: 38.

61. Daniel Lieberfeld and Judith Sanders, "Keeping the Characters Straight: Comedy and Identity in *Some Like It Hot*," *Journal of Popular Film and Television* 26 (1998): 131.

62. Maslon: 141.

63. See Ed Sikov, *Laughing Hysterically: American Screen Comedy of the 1950s* (New York: Columbia University Press, 1996): 128–48.

64. Steven Cohan, *Masked Men: Masculinity and the Movies in the Fifties* (Bloomington: Indiana University Press, 1997): 305.

65. Sikov: 138.

66. Jody Pennington, *The History of Sex in American Film* (Greenwood Publishing, 2007): 6.

67. Thomas Doherty, *Hollywood's Censor: Joseph I. Breen and the Production Code Administration* (New York: Columbia University Press, 2007): 138. *Turnabout's* farcical story involved a mystical "body-swap" between a husband and wife, which was deemed to be "open to the charge of suggesting sexual perversion." The PCA worked to expunge any "pansy flavor" from the sudden "femininity" that ensues when the wife's "soul" inhabits her husband's body. The Legion of Decency was also on the brink of condemning the film for "inferences dangerous to morality" (*Turnabout* Production Code Administration File, AMPAS). Cary Grant's cross-dressing in *I Was a Male War Bride* (1949) was of less concern, since he only appeared in drag for the final ten minutes of the film, and was "depicted as uncomfortable and constantly aware of the ridiculousness of wearing the wrong gender's clothes" (Rolston: 69). However, the PCA was exercised about the motivation behind Grant's character dressing as a woman, warning Howard Hawks that the "element of sex frustration" inherent in the plot was "unacceptable under the provisions of the Production Code." However, since the film was being shot in Germany at the time, the PCA was not able to exercise much control over it. (*I Was A Male War Bride*, Production Code Administration File, AMPAS).

68. Rolston: 68.

69. *Variety* (February 25, 1959); A.H. Weiller, *New York Times* (March 30, 1959).

70. John Leonard, "Marilyn as Marilyn," *National Review* (June 20, 1959).

71. *Films in Review* (April 1959): 240.

72. Ed Sikov, *On Sunset Boulevard: The Life and Times of Billy Wilder* (New York: Hyperion, 1999): 413.

73. Doherty: 94; Gregory Black, *The Catholic Crusade Against the Movies, 1940–1975* (Cambridge: Cambridge University Press, 1998): 184. It was not until 1961, after "the California Supreme Court ruled that Kenneth Anger's *Fireworks*, a film that dealt openly and directly with homosexuality, could not be banned in the state," that the MPAA "quietly changed the Production Code's position on homosexuality" (Black: 191).

74. Black: 185–6.

75. Gregory Black, *Hollywood Censored: Moral Codes, Catholics and the Movies* (Cambridge: Cambridge University Press, 1996): 40; Sikov (1999): 270 and 362.

76. Maslon: 109.

77. Curtis and Vieira: 206.

78. Howard Hughes's *The Outlaw* (1943) had played without a seal in the 1940s, and UA had released Otto Preminger's *The Moon is Blue* without a seal in 1953; but, for the most part, it was only low-budget productions

from independent filmmakers that took the risk (See Black, *Catholic Crusade*: 124–5, 220); "Analysis of Film Content," February 10, 1959, *Some Like It Hot* PCA file, AMPAS.

79. Geoffrey Shurlock to Msgr. Thomas Little, March 18, 1959, *Some Like It Hot* PCA file, AMPAS.
80. Doherty: 321.
81. Black (1998): 179.
82. Sikov (1999): 370.
83. Black (1998): 203.
84. Msgr. Little to Shurlock, March 5, 1959, *Some Like It Hot* file, National Catholic Legion of Decency Archive, Office of Film and Broadcasting, United States Conference of Catholic Bishops, New York (subsequently Legion of Decency).
85. Rev. Patrick J. Sullivan S.J. to Mrs H.M. Burns, the Catholic Parent–Teacher League of the Diocese of Cleveland, March 23, 1959, *Some Like It Hot* file, Legion of Decency.
86. Anonymous Viewer's Report, *Some Like It Hot* file, Legion of Decency.
87. Bishop James McNulty to Eric Johnston, March 5, 1959, *Some Like It Hot* file, PCA, AMPAS.
88. Msgr. Little to Shurlock, March 5, 1959, *Some Like It Hot* file, Legion of Decency.
89. *Ibid.*; Msgr. Little to Lieutenant O'Malley, March 4, 1959, *Some Like It Hot* file, Legion of Decency.
90. Sikov (1999): 415; Horton (ed.): 123.
91. Indeed, the film's publicity emphasized this, noting that Spats was a role Raft "should be able to interpret easily based on first hand observation." (*Some Like It Hot* Pressbook, British Film Institute, London).
92. Castle: 245.
93. Quoted in Colin Young, "The Old Dependables," *Film Quarterly* 13(1) (Fall, 1959): 6; Maslon: 28.
94. Crowe: 137; Sikov (1999): 409.
95. Shurlock to Msgr. Little, March 18, 1959, *Some Like It Hot* PCA file, AMPAS.
96. Diamond, "The Day Marilyn Needed 47 Takes": 132.
97. As it was, one offended viewer did indeed write to the *New York Times* complaining that: "One gets an awfully uncomfortable feeling watching Tony Curtis and Jack Lemmon have too good a time cavorting as female impersonators" (Quoted in Cohan: 306).
98. Curtis and Vieira: 16.
99. Allen: 145.
100. Allen: 147; Lynn Dumenil, *The Modern Temper: American Culture and Society in the 1920s* (New York: Hill & Wang, 1995): 135.
101. The sequence involved Jerry, still believing he is in Sugar's berth, revealing: "In the first place, I'm not a natural blonde—as a matter of fact, there are all sorts of things about me that are not natural." In telling Joe not to scream ("Don't spoil it—it's too beautiful. Just think of it, you and I")

and asking him to "Feel my heart—like a crazy drum," Jerry's seduction of the wrong person would have been comic, but also sexualized in a way that the PCA would not have been able to ignore. (*Some Like It Hot*, Final Screenplay, July 18, 1958, Mike Mazurki Papers, AMPAS).

102. Maurice Zolotow, *Billy Wilder in Hollywood* (New York: Limelight, 1992): 421. The usual explanation given for filming in black and white is that Wilder "felt that it should be done in the medium of its 1920s period," which is undoubtedly true (Walter Mirisch, *I Thought We Were Making Movies, Not History* (Madison: University of Wisconsin Press, 2008). However, this "alternative" explanation helps to illustrate that Wilder *did* perceive homosexuality as a potentially problematic element in the film.

103. The *Hollywood Reporter* (February 25, 1959).

104. Crowe: 156; R.S. Works to Msgr. Little, March 1, 1959, *Some Like It Hot* file; Anonymous Viewer's Report, n.d., *Some Like It Hot* file, Legion of Decency.

105. *Variety*, February 25, 1959, copy in *Some Like It Hot* file, Legion of Decency.

106. Paul Beckley, *New York Herald Tribune*, March 30, 1959, *Some Like It Hot* file, Legion of Decency.

107. Frank Leyendecker, *Boxoffice* (March 2, 1959), section highlighted in *Some Like It Hot* file, Legion of Decency.

108. Memorandum to Bishop McNulty from Msgr. Little, March 4, 1959, *Some Like It Hot* file, Legion of Decency.

109. Black (1998): 182.

110. Brandon French, *On the Verge of Revolt: Women in American Films of the Fifties* (New York: Ungar, 1978): 137.

111. Sann: 7.

112. Lieberfeld: 130.

113. Allen: 152.

114. Sherry Tucker, *Swing Shift: "All Girl" Bands of the 1940s* (Durham: Duke University Press, 2000): 23.

115. Sann: 154; this affair was in the news again in the late 1950s when Peaches (Frances Heenan) died in 1956.

116. Lieberfeld: 130.

117. French: 147; Sikov, *Laughing*: 142; Patrice Petro, "Legacies of Weimar Cinema," in Murray Pomerance (ed.), *Cinema and Modernity* (New Brunswick: Rutgers University Press, 2006): 251.

118. Marjorie Garber, *Vested Interests: Cross-Dressing and Cultural Anxiety* (London: Routledge, 1997): 7.

119. Cohan: 306.

120. Peter Lev, *The Fifties: Transforming the Screen* (Berkeley: University of California Press, 2006): 225; Petro: 251.

121. K.A Cuordileone, "Politics in an Age of Anxiety: Cold War Political Culture and the Crisis in American Masculinity," *Journal of American History* 87(2) (2000): 529; Alfred Kinsey *et al.*, *Sexual Behavior in the Human Male*

(Philadelphia: Saunders, 1948): 623. See also John D'Emilio, *Intimate Matters: A History of Sexuality in America* (New York: Harper, 1988).

122. Joanne Meyerowitz, *How Sex Changed: A History of Transexuality in the United States* (Cambridge: Harvard University Press, 2002), ch. 2; David Serlin, "Christine Jorgensen and the Cold War Closet," *Radical History Review* 62 (1995): 392. Jerry's planned "June wedding" to Osgood must have resonated strongly with the story of Jorgensen to audiences in 1959, since Christine was back in the news that year when New York City officials refused her a license to marry fiancé Howard Knox, because her birth certificate listed her as male.

123. Cuordileone: 530.

124. Crowe: 106.

7

Vico's Age of Heroes and the Age of Men in John Ford's *The Man Who Shot Liberty Valance*[1]

Mark W. Roche and Vittorio Hösle

Vico, the father of historicism, discovered that the nature of man changes: the archaic man feels, think, acts in a way completely different from modern man. In Vico's scheme of the necessary evolution of every culture, three phases are distinguished: the age of gods, the age of heroes, and the age of men. The age of gods is characterized by a theocratic government: it is anterior to any differentiation of the various aspects of culture such as religion, politics, or art. The age of heroes, on the other hand, is dominated by the conflict between classes, the heroes and the plebeians. This age does not yet have a state: therefore, force and violence reign. The right of the stronger is the main ground of legitimacy. Two types of relations are characteristic of this age: the relation between enemies who fight each other, risking their own lives and those of their combatants, and the relation between master and servant. The duel, a fight between two heroes accompanied by their servants, is *the* symbolic action of the heroic age. In it the value of a person is proved, even constituted. Relations toward wives in the age of heroes are clearly asymmetric: women are not yet recognized as having the same human nature as men. "Love of ease, tenderness toward children, love of women, and desire of life" are alien to the heroes, so Vico once sums up his view of the heroic age.[2]

The central characteristic of the age of men is the rule of law based on reason, no longer on force. A monarchical or democratic state replaces the aristocracy of the heroes. The principal equality of all human beings is recognized in the age of men. Not only within the state, but also within the family, relations tend to become more symmetric. The power of the word contributes to this transition: pre-verbal expressions, and later poetry, are replaced by oratory.

Very important in this context is alphabetization. Whereas in the age of heroes only very few persons can write, the age of men is based on almost universal literacy, potentially on general education. The passionate impulses of the heroes weaken more and more and are replaced by calculating intellect. With the process of rationalization a depersonalization takes place: the great individual is no longer necessary; the due procedure of the institutions characteristic of the age of men now guarantees the order without which societies cannot survive.

In Vico's reconstruction of this transition, two aspects are especially noteworthy. First, the absolute necessity he ascribes to it: the speed with which cultures evolve is not everywhere the same, but the progress toward rationalization is unavoidable. It is not special individuals who bring the change about—it is the law of development, which brings individuals forth who then realize the changes. Vico does not believe (as Hegel or Carlyle does) in historic individuals; history is for him an apersonal power that moves in an irreversible way toward rationalization. While the persons who act for the change may view themselves as independent agents, they are in truth driven by the tendency of the development, which transcends their particular aims. The end result of history is something nobody wanted or expected. In this heterogenesis of the ends, Vico sees the expression of what he calls divine providence.

Second, Vico's attitude toward this process is deeply ambivalent. On the one hand, he sees in the process of rationalization something *morally* necessary. The age of heroes is characterized by violence and inequality, and the overcoming of both cannot be praised enough. As a philosopher, Vico is furthermore convinced that the reflexive attitude toward oneself and one's history, as it can be achieved only in the age of men, has a higher intrinsic value than the pre-reflexive mind of the age of heroes. On the other hand, in an era dominated by the belief in progress and enlightenment, Vico was one of the first to see how much is lost in this transition. The age of rationalization is also an age of dis-enchantment (to use Max Weber's term). The unity of the archaic mind breaks, the different subsystems of culture become autonomous, it is no longer possible to be a universal person. The necessity to risk and to sacrifice one's life—so characteristic of the age of heroes—disappearing, a great source of morality vanishes. By fighting for his life, the hero acquired a depth that is missed in representatives of the age of men. Rationalization also destroys the powers of fantasy and creativity. The age of men necessarily culminates in what Vico calls the "barbarism of reflection," (1106) and empty reasoning that has lost any contact to substantial contents, a strategic attitude toward fellow human beings, a lack of roots and traditions and therefore of emotional richness. One aspect of the barbarism of reflection is the spreading of lying. Whereas the hero is constitutionally unable to say something different from what he thinks, the age of men is—at least, in its late phase—characterized by a schism between the internal and the external. According to Vico, the barbarism of reason destroys a culture, and thus the cycle of the three ages begins again.

Vico's theory of culture is one of the richest models for understanding human history, although Vico ignores several aspects. He neglects, for example, the differences between the cycles; in particular, he could not yet grasp the importance of the Industrial Revolution in changing the mind and soul of modern man. These changes in the United States have been more incisive than elsewhere for two reasons. First, the new continent allowed for a fresh beginning; modern capitalism and modern industry could develop more quickly than in Europe, where certain feudal bonds limited the changes. Second, America experienced something that in Europe had become impossible centuries ago: the state of nature which existed at the Great Frontier. The struggle against nature as well as against the archaic cultures of the Indians constitutes the "wilderness" that forms the background of almost all Westerns. Whereas the wars in Europe since the late Middle Ages had been between civilized powers, the Indians represented something radically different, and the necessity of defending oneself against them held alive in the soul of the Westerners moments that are themselves archaic. The frontier situation is characterized by an intrinsic tension: it represented a mentality more archaic than in Europe and at the same time worked toward a process of modernization much more radically than in Europe. The transition between the age of heroes and the age of men, which in Europe lasted several centuries, was concentrated in the United States in a few decades: one generation has been able to witness this transition.

John Ford's *The Man Who Shot Liberty Valance* (1962) is the greatest film about this transition. In a sense, the film consummates the Western: in it a central aspect, perhaps *the* central aspect, of the genre has been fulfilled; after it, another Western is scarcely conceivable. Like Sophocles's *Oedipus at Colonus* or Shakespeare's *The Tempest, The Man Who Shot Liberty Valance* is a work manifestly written by an old man. The film is rich with allusions to Ford's earlier work, which effectively renders the film a summary of the Western tradition.[3]

Ford was one of Hollywood's most eminent directors, having developed a reputation for his striking use of visual images, his masterful stories, and his explorations of the American spirit. A recipient of four Academy Awards for direction, Ford is most famous for his portrayals of moral conflict on the American frontier, including such works as *Stagecoach* (1939), *The Grapes of Wrath* (1940), *My Darling Clementine* (1946), *Fort Apache* (1948), *She Wore a Yellow Ribbon* (1949), *Wagonmaster* (1950), *Rio Grande* (1950), *The Searchers* (1956), and *Cheyenne Autumn* (1964). *The Man Who Shot Liberty Valance* was one of Ford's later films. Not insignificantly, the two main actors were also nearing the end of their careers. The films deals with the death of a man, which represents at the same time the death of a culture; and it contains implicit reflections on the role of art in a world that has been radically transformed.

The narrative structure of the film consists of a short frame story. Senator Ransom Stoddard and his wife, Hallie, arrive in Shinbone for the funeral of a virtually forgotten man, Tom Doniphon. The inner narrative and greater part of the film consists of the Senator's confession, a flashback that commences with young Ranse's stagecoach journey to Shinbone. Liberty Valance and his henchmen rob the stagecoach; teaching the idealistic Ranse a lesson in "Western law," Valance brutally flogs Ranse and rips apart his law books. Tom Doniphon finds Ranse and brings him into town, where he is cared for by Hallie, Tom's "girl." When Ranse announces his intention to bring justice to the territories, Tom, "the toughest man south of the picket wire," instructs him that the only way to challenge Valance is with force. Because Ranse has no money, he pays for his meals and lodging by washing dishes, but he also starts a school, teaching reading and writing as well as civics to the townsfolk, including Hallie and Tom's black servant, Pompey.

Hired by cattle interests, Liberty Valance uses violence in his efforts to keep the territory an open range. Dutton Peabody, founder and editor of the *Shinbone Star*, writes a story about Valance's murderous deeds and is later beaten for doing so. After Ranse is elected, along with Peabody, as one of the local delegates to the territorial convention for statehood, Valance orders him to leave town or face him in a shoot-out. Ranse meets Valance on the street, is shot in the arm, and with the gun in his left hand fires at Valance, who drops dead. After the duel, Tom sees Hallie embrace Ranse and grasps that Hallie, who had been torn between Tom and Ranse, has chosen Ranse. Tom gets drunk and burns down the house he had been building for her. When Ranse doubts his future as a politician because he has qualms over his having "killed a man," Tom informs him—in a flashback within a flashback—of the truth. Hiding in the shadows, Tom fired the shot that killed Valance (Illustration 7:1).

Illustration 7.1   The unacknowledged view of the legend: *The Man Who Shot Liberty Valance*
(1962) © Paramount Pictures Corporation/John Ford Productions

A renewed Ranse helps win statehood and moves on to greatness as a
politician. The newspaper editor, who elicited the story by relentlessly
asking why the Senator had come to a forgotten man's funeral, decides
not to print it: "This is the West, sir. When the legend becomes fact,
print the legend." The initial frame, which began with the train's
arrival in Shinbone, is mirrored by the final frame, as Ranse and Hallie
ride the train back to Washington. Ranse's deception is underscored
in this final scene: the conductor accompanies his efforts to please the
Senator with the words, "Nothing's too good for the man who shot
Liberty Valance." The film closes with the melancholic faces of the
two spouses and a final shot of the train.

The Senator's narrative evokes an age the character of which
has passed away forever, only to be sealed with the death of Tom
Doniphon. A differentiated attitude toward this period dominates the
film. While the young Ransom is inspired by the vision of a better
future, the dominant mood of the old Senator is a mourning of the
past. *The Man Who Shot Liberty Valance* can be contrasted with that of
a work which deals with a similar problem, the *Oresteia*. Aeschylus's
trilogy also treats the transformation of violence to law and order,
from passion to reason, from vengeance to statehood. A process of
rationalization that radically transformed a culture is the subject of both
artworks, but the evaluation is different. Whereas Aeschylus sees only

the positive in the process, Ford's attitude is as ambivalent as that of Vico. The differences in the evaluation result obviously from differences in the two transitions; in the early fifth century BC none of the dangers of hyper-rationalization was visible; the negative side-effects of the Industrial Revolution, on the other hand, have escaped very few of this century's great artists. *The Eumenides* does not simply end with the triumph of the forces of law and rationality over those of vengeance and blood; the drama culminates in the integration of the Eumenides into the political and religious system of Athens. The ancient rationality acknowledges being rooted in the pre-logical; it takes strength from the emotional powers, which are not excluded, but recognized as a necessary moment of every culture. This process of recognition occurred in Greek culture (in a certain sense, it was its essence); therefore, the poet could mirror the reality of his culture and celebrate it in a temporal attitude that was clearly related to the present.

The essence of modernity, on the other hand, is the rash elimination of the pre-rational, the quick triumph of restricted technical and functional rationality over the deeper emotional needs of the human soul. Since the result is not an equilibrate synthesis of passions and reason, past and present are divided by a deep gap, and the poet can no longer identify with the present, but has to recall the past *against* the tendencies of his own time. This leads to the elegiac character of *The Man Who Shot Liberty Valance*: recollection is the main mood of the film. But it is the recollection of a time which, at least for Ransom Stoddard, was deeply characterized by the hope for a better future.[4] Ransom never relates in an unproblematic way toward his present; immediacy in relating to the present can be ascribed only to Tom Doniphon.

The lack of a synthesis in modern culture deprives art of the possibility of identifying with its own time. This means that it divests the artist of one of the most important sources of happiness accessible to humans: the art of modernity is no longer in harmony with its culture. This disharmony, however, gives art a special function, which was alien to a work like the *Oresteia*. It has to hold alive something which, in the real world, has disappeared. It has, therefore, a particular responsibility toward the past. Against public opinion, Ford reminds us who *really* shot Liberty Valance; he gives us both legend and reality. He preserves thereby a heroic virtue: faithfulness, understood here as faithfulness toward the truth and the past. Ford's film has a vindicating function—a function which has become necessary because the age of men has forgotten the heroes without whom it could not have succeeded.

Ford's ambivalence toward the age of heroes is shown by his introduction of two representatives: a good hero and an evil one, Tom Doniphon and Liberty Valance. The moral difference between them is the reason for their conflict; that they are two aspects of the same culture, on the other hand, links their fates together. Tom has an important social function as long as Liberty Valance lives; with Liberty's death he becomes, in a sense, superfluous. The killing of Liberty Valance would have had bad consequences for Tom, even if his action had not meant the loss of Hallie, and the fact that it triggers his personal catastrophe is only an intensification of the intrinsic problem of the good hero: in order to be himself, the hero needs something evil he can negate. The fact that, in the night after the duel, both the corpse of Liberty Valance and the body of Tom Doniphon are thrown on a buckboard expresses in a symbolic way the link between the two.

As toward the heroes, so toward Ranse the attitude of Ford is deeply ambivalent. Surely, there are few doubts about his being a positive figure. In Ranse's classroom we see young and old, male and female, whites and blacks, learning that "all men are created equal" and that, in the United States, power is determined not by the individual's gun but by the voting electorate. Together with the town's other intellectual, Dutton Peabody, Ranse works to bring statehood to the territories; justice, education, and progress to the people; and protection from violence. Beyond his good intentions, the young lawyer risks his life several times and can therefore claim a certain heroic attitude. But the hero is not only willing to fight evil—he is, at least in the majority of cases, also successful. Ranse would never have been able to get rid of Liberty Valance by himself (the fact that after the duel Ranse actually believes he shot Valance evidences an unrealistic and somewhat vain self-perception), and although Ranse's act of risking his life gives him a high moral value, it doesn't yet make him a hero. His weakness is apparent not only in his inability to conquer Liberty Valance, but also, symbolically, in his unmanly wearing of an apron (even to the gunfight) and his waiting on tables.

The young teacher's patronizing attitude toward his class is especially disturbing, as he insists on equality. When Tom's black servant Pompey forgets the words "all men are created equal," Ranse comments that many people forget that line. Ranse is cleverly ironic toward racists, but the text is also ironic toward Ranse, who is patronizing toward Pompey.[5] Implicitly, Ranse shows that in the new culture differences will remain—based, however, on education, not force. The question will no longer be who is quicker at shooting, but who is better at speaking. The intellectual superiority his knowledge of writing and reading give him with regard to most inhabitants of Shinbone (Hallie is not yet literate when he arrives, and Tom reads with obvious difficulties) will become the ground of a new inequality, the overcoming of which had been the promise of the age of men. Ranse corrects the English not only of Pompey, but also of Hallie; and the condescension that characterizes the young lawyer becomes even more pronounced in the old Senator (think of the scene when he gives Pompey money). Only by way of Hallie's poetic gesture of putting the cactus rose on Tom's coffin does the Senator grasp how much has been lost in the passage to the age of men; he recognizes how deeply the world of men, which he helped to bring about, differs from the ideals of his youth and how little right he had to feel superior to the survivors of the earlier age.

"You talk too much, think too much," Tom says to Ranse in the crucial scene when he informs him about the true identity of the person who shot Liberty Valance. Ranse, indeed, lacks the sense for preverbal communication which both Hallie and Tom share. When Tom brings Ranse to his ranch and tells him to take a look, he expects Ranse to grasp his meaning, but, for Ranse, Tom must spell it out in words. Symptomatically, Ranse pays his tribute to Tom by making a long speech to the press, while Hallie puts the cactus rose on the coffin. When Ranse wonders whether he should talk with the journalists, Hallie doesn't speak, she only nods her head. In the last scene in the train, very few words are spoken between the spouses, and the Senator, rather than answering Hallie's question, as to whether he is proud about the transformation of the wilderness into a garden, instead asks her whether she put the cactus rose on the coffin. By asking his question, Ranse implies that Hallie's comment lacks sincerity. She has shown by her deed that the cactus rose means—if not more—at least as much to her as the real roses which in the meantime she must have gotten to know.

The adequate gesture for depicting the passage from the age of heroes to the age of men is not literature, but film, for the passage has also to do with the transition from non-verbal to verbal communication, and only film can mirror both. The filmmaker Ford, not being a novelist, keeps alive the idea, forgotten in the age of men, that some dimensions between human beings transcend words. The feeling that words cannot convey the essential meaning becomes even stronger when the railway conductor speaks with the Senator. His words lack the depth of Hallie's glances; and, even worse, they end with a false statement. Not only is the Senator disturbed by the fact that the merit of another person is ascribed to him (he cannot, for example, light his pipe), he finally grasps that not only his existence, but also the age of men as a whole is based on a lie.[6] The men of this age have forgotten to whom the age owes its existence; the civilizing hero in the modern world is not acknowledged in the way the Eumenides are in the *Oresteia*; and therefore the last image and the first are of the train, that impersonal power of modernization which moves history forward and deprives humankind more and more of the moral and emotional richness of the age of heroes.

Ford's ambivalence toward the characters, his sense of their greatness and limits, is enriched by structures of recognition between the characters, which contain not only tragic but also reconciliatory moments. The film suggests a "unity" of Tom and Ranse. In fact, the title contains the conflict (or opposition) as unified. *The Man Who Shot Liberty Valance* is at once realistic or literal (Tom did, in fact, shoot Liberty Valance) and figurative or representational (to the populace, it was the Senator who shot Liberty Valance).[7] In this non-literal meaning, we see the moment of abstraction or representation which belongs to the spirit. If in the primary content of the film the two characters are opposed, the title unites them, as does a close reading.

Tom and Ranse do not merely compete with one another; each figure indirectly recognizes the value of the other. Tom shoots Liberty Valance, thus giving up the West and making possible the paradigm shift toward the new era of justice. The fact that Tom does not consciously give up the West (he later states: "I wish I hadn't" [saved Ranse]) does not undermine his role in this process; on the contrary, it only reinforces for us the applicability of Vico's thought to the film. As in Vico's theory of divine providence, the end of history transcends the willing of its agents. Tom calls the political meeting to order, arranges that Ranse run it, and seconds the nomination of Ranse for representative ("not only because he knows the law but because he throws a good punch"). Tom recognizes the validity of Ranse as a representative partly because he uses force, a mode privileged and acknowledged by heroes. Further, Tom keeps the meeting democratic (with a display of power). In the period of transition, force and representation are not so easily separated. Knowing that "votes won't stand up against guns," Tom makes sure that votes stand up *with* guns.

Ranse succeeds only as a hero, as the man who shot Liberty Valance; that is, as Tom Doniphon. Yet, Ranse himself shows glimmers of heroism to the extent that he asserts that nobody fights his battles for him, slugs Tom, and, most importantly, is willing to put his life on the line with Liberty Valance. Ranse must accommodate himself to the age of heroes. Tom and Ranse each move into the other's realm—even when they are not fully at home there: as when Tom reads aloud Ranse's sign, or Ranse attempts to learn how to shoot. Each mirrors the tension of the two poles within himself. Ranse succeeds as a politician partly because he is a thinker and a good representative, but he is a representative also because he has the charisma associated with power and the law of nature. This appearance of heroism is necessary for the transition to statehood. The populace admires Ranse because he appears to be a synthesis of the two worlds. Ranse, however, does not kill Liberty Valance; Tom does. Ranse is too ineffective, but this very ineffectiveness is a further presupposition for the development of civilization. If Ranse had killed Liberty, he might not have succeeded as a man of justice, a herald of the new order. Shooting Liberty Valance would have upheld the law of power. Moreover, Ranse would have been incapacitated by pains of conscience, as we see at the territorial convention.

In his confession, Ranse would reveal the truth about himself and Tom; he would erase the tragic structure of his life, the fact that, though he has not built his life on killing a man, he has built it on a lie. In the West, however, "legend" triumphs over "fact," and the film closes with the Senator being heralded not for his government service but for his supposedly having shot Liberty Valance; that is, for the old morality, which lives on in the people and which the Senator has worked to replace. The structure is ironic, for Ranse has been successful in his overarching goal of bringing democracy and good government to his people. But he is recognized not for his democratic service but for the old morality to which he owes his success and which he has knowingly worked to replace. We recognize in Ranse's facial expressions a certain sadness at his having used this lie, but Ranse never expressly regrets his duplicity. This suggests, first, that he may not be fully aware of his Machiavellian actions and, second, that his awareness—expressed only in glances—is a throwback to an earlier age of greatness. Only as a nonverbal person, a hero, does Ranse come to full recognition of the crisis of his identity and the transgression of justice contained in his lie. In allowing Tom's actions to be ascribed to him, the Senator is no longer free to be fully himself. Ranse must not only renounce the truth, he must relinquish his self and his identity in order to become a representative. This is at the core of Ranse's embarrassment at the end; he recognizes that there is something wrong with his identity.

By not lighting his pipe in the final scene, Ranse makes a nonverbal gesture to the earlier period, for light may be taken as the symbol of the new world, the world of spirit, and Ranse acknowledges that light presupposes the darkness associated with the age of heroes. Whereas the earlier age is visible only in darkness, the age of men is consistently filmed during daylight—not only in the frame, but also in the schoolroom and the electioneering scenes. When the Senator and his wife arrive in Shinbone, the journalists tell him to come "out of the sun"; later, in the darkness of the undertaker's shop, he recalls the past. The light of reason has destroyed the passions of the past, bringing the rational bleakness of modernity: there is so much light that one can no longer "see" the true basis of the age.

Politics in this new age is no longer a simple and immediate exertion of physical power. Power, now representational, is mediated by figures who have gained the respect of others. Within this paradigm, appearance and reality do not always coincide. Because of its capacity for deception and the range of its impact, political power can be even worse than the immediate assertion of physical power. The break between seeming and being is already present at the convention in its circus atmosphere; it is the reverse side of progressive spirit. The cattle ranchers appear to be simple-minded with their stage rituals, including their band and their parading a horse on stage, but they are, in fact, very oratorical (especially in their rhetorical anti-rhetoric) and they know precisely how to hurt the opposition (that is, by rendering Ranse vulnerable). We see the dangers of a political theatre that focuses not on any essence but on representation and form alone, and with this hides its blind lust for power.[8] Spirit contains within it the possibility of abuse.

Ranse is weakest at the convention. Not only does he not come clean, he doesn't react with gratefulness toward Tom. Though Ranse may not approve of Tom's cold-blooded murder, he nonetheless takes advantage of it. Ranse uses the lie and his position as hero without fully recognizing the greatness of Tom, who made his success possible. Ranse fails to see that it was he who put Tom in an impossible situation.[9] Although one could argue that Ranse is even more guilty for having morally obliged another person to commit a cold-blooded murder, after Tom's confession Ranse loses his sense of guilt. We see in Ranse a structure typical in politics: the externalization of responsibility (which in this case also means a lack of faithfulness toward the past), a structure analyzed so well by Shakespeare, for example, in *Henry V*. One causes others to act immorally and then reproaches them for having acted so or at least doesn't thank them for it, although one owes one's life or one's power to them. In taking advantage of an act he condemns, Ranse is not only opportunistic, he is hypocritical. And yet not only in Tom's action, but also in this hypocrisy lies a force, namely, the articulated ideal, alien to the age of heroes, that will eventually lead toward the greater realization of justice.

If Ranse's weakest moment is at the convention, his strongest is on the train. The Senator could become Vice-President, but he will return to Shinbone—clearly owing to his love for Hallie. He will finally offer her what Tom had wanted to give her much earlier, when he refused the nomination. The Senator returns to Tom's example, but only after his work is mostly done. In an act of renouncement, Ranse tries to give Hallie back as much as possible of what she relinquished. An important symbol here is the cactus rose, which dissolves on the screen only after we move to the scene in the train. The hat box, which appears to tell us that Hallie is no longer a woman of the wilderness, actually exhibits her bond to the world of heroes, for it is empty, and she uses it to collect the cactus rose. Hallie has kept an emotional link to the world of heroes, which Ranse seems to lack.[10] The cactus rose, which for Hallie is a clear gesture toward the past, triggers in the Senator a process of recognition. It reminds him, first, of Hallie's love for Tom and thus of her great self-renouncement, and second, of how much he owes to Tom.

Each character enacts a sacrifice, but Tom's sacrifice contains moments that clearly exhibit Ford's elevation of Tom over Ranse, and his nostalgia for the world of heroes. Tom is not just a stubborn hero of the past, a man of formal virtues, he is also a self-sacrificing hero. In silently rendering Ranse a hero, Tom makes possible the new age. This sublimity renders him superior to Ranse, who was unable to acknowledge the greatness of Tom's gesture during the convention. It belongs, however, to the idea of heroism that the hero sacrifice himself and receive no credit for it. The film is clear in telling us that Tom could have beaten Liberty Valance in a draw of guns. That he kills him in a cold-blooded way is, in a paradoxical sense, even more admirable, for it robs him of a chance for public heroism and thus exhibits a certain renouncement. It is symbolic that when Tom comes through the door to find Ranse and Hallie embracing, he is visually in dark colors and in the far background. His importance now recedes. Time passes Tom by, and only a handful of people remember his name. The passing of the age of heroes is also symbolized in the marshal's statement that Tom had worn no handgun for years; even he no longer practiced Western law. Tom is a hero only when the community needs him to protect it. With the introduction of legality and the elimination of Liberty (and the forces he symbolizes), the hero becomes superfluous. Tom's killing Liberty consummates the Western in the very specific sense that it renders the hero unnecessary. Another consequence of the death of Liberty—related to our earlier reflections on the ambiguities of the world of spirit—is that evil is no longer easy to recognize. It is sublated in the more shaded world of men, diffused among the crowd of cattlemen and seen to lurk even in the world of light.

Tom, a transitional figure, may very well sense that by killing Liberty Valance he is giving up the West, but what he doesn't know is that his action also means the loss of Hallie. Tom's sacrifice has immediate consequences. In saving Ranse's life, Tom relinquishes the woman he loves. The shooting does not simply perpetuate the competition for Hallie insofar as it means preserving the life of Ranse. The moment is more tragic still. It means his giving Hallie to Ranse. He does Hallie a favor and thereby loses her.

Though a hero, Tom is in no way brutal, and he would have made Hallie at least partially happy. He is tender toward her, and he is—as we have seen—self-sacrificing. But, for several reasons, Tom doesn't fully express his love for Hallie. First, it's not Western-like; the strong hero does not easily exhibit sensitive emotions. This is symbolically conveyed in Tom's not being at home in the kitchen: Tom burns his finger on the coffee, and Hallie takes the bottle out of his hands. More importantly, Tom doesn't see Hallie when she looks after him from the kitchen door. Not a man of words, Tom does not speak his love, and not a reflexive person, he doesn't turn around to see if his love is encountered, reciprocated. Whereas other persons would be motivated to look back—conscious of their position in the love relationship, Tom simply loves her. Tom's lack of concern, which is a weakness, also contains a moment of greatness: he is indifferent to the games of love and love's moments of self-glorification and sentimentality.

Hallie did not want Ranse to leave Shinbone, and her sin of omission, not encouraging his departure strongly enough, contributes to his endangerment. She thus expresses her love all the more after the duel, for Ranse has become vulnerable partly because of her actions. Heroes, on the other hand, are never weak, and thus never in a position where love is so easily expressed. Unjustly, the hero who saves the other is the loser, and ironically, being the loser, he deserves (or needs) the love much more than the other. Throughout, Tom is hard on Hallie and stoic within himself. He does not *show* his need for Hallie. Hallie is attracted to Ranse precisely because he seems so vulnerable (first, when he arrives; second, after the altercation in the restaurant; and, finally, after the gunfight); only in the end does she grasp that, in truth, Tom was far more vulnerable. Tom, part of a disappearing age, needed her much more than Ranse, who would have had a successful life also without her: Tom without Hallie can only stay with Pompey.[11] The feminine aspect of Ranse is here significant. While heroes are worshipped and longed for, we can relate to men. Thus, although Ranse, unlike Tom, can exist without Hallie, it is Ranse who can benefit from Hallie's pointing out his weaknesses and who, unlike Tom, can adapt.

Second, it belongs to the idea of the hero that he sacrifice all love relations; this is the ideal of the knight, who is thus free to do heroic things. The knight, however, does not forgo all intersubjective relations. Pompey has a prominent role throughout as the caring servant and loyal friend. The relationship between Tom and his black servant is stable, if not fully symmetrical. One is reminded of Tom's ordering Pompey out of the schoolroom. Tom's relationship toward Hallie is clearly asymmetric; he treats her as if she were his property. Hallie's mother, unlike her father, favors Ranse over Tom; the woman has an interest in symmetry. Ranse treats Hallie as an equal, helping out in the kitchen, for example. After Tom has lost Hallie, Pompey gains in importance—he repeats Hallie's gesture of taking the bottle away from Tom; he even saves his life. Pompey becomes the person who cares for Tom, as Hallie might have. The relationship becomes more symmetrical. When we see him beside the coffin, he seems almost a widow, and Hallie—not the Senator—recognizes this.

Third, the hero and quester Tom must seek the perfect ideal before he is ready to ask Hallie to marry him, and so he works on the house he will never finish. Significantly, Pompey stops working on the addition because he is in school with Ranse. Pompey is loyal to Tom, but his people's destiny is with the idealism Ranse represents, even if this affiliation means disrupting a stable relationship for something less secure and momentarily patronizing. Pompey, not unlike Hallie, sees his future not with the hero whom he continues to admire, but with the man who will bring him equality.

Tom's self-sacrifice causes him great pain. He eventually burns the house, even endangering his horses, knowing that his earlier actions have eliminated any chance for bliss with Hallie. The fire represents both the passage of time and the all-consuming light of spirit. Self-destruction and a return to the pure power of nature, symbolized in the horses he orders freed, are Tom's reactions against the inexorable passage toward rationality.[12] In a certain sense, the railroad, which opens the outer frame, represents civilization and the age of men; the stagecoach, which opens the inner frame, represents the frontier, the transition period; and the horse is, of course, nature. Whereas Ranse takes the stagecoach and later sits on a buckboard, Tom rides a horse. Tom's contact with nature is immediate; Ranse's relationship is mediated. The futility of Tom's affirmation of the horse (as nature) is unveiled to the viewer when, at the statehood convention, the horse becomes a mere prop. Nature gives way to (a corrupt) spirit.

Another way to recognize the superiority of the heroic age is to contrast Peabody and the modern newspaperman. Peabody risks his life in pursuing and printing the truth; the modern reporters neither risk their lives nor print the truth. A dominant aspect of the modern newspaperman is their intruding on others. Peabody is a heroic and sympathetic character. He is also very cultivated: his literary allusions range from Homer to Shakespeare. Particularly fitting is his description of Liberty Valance's thugs as "myrmidons," which implies that the setting is still that of the age of heroes. The myrmidons are the obsequious soldiers of Achilles, and Achilles is *the* hero—also, for Vico, both in the positive and negative sense. Also of interest are Peabody's various comic exchanges with Tom, the Marshall, and Hallie. The modern newspapermen are not as substantial or human. On the contrary, they are banal and indiscreet. Especially tactless is their address to the Senator, when they show no respect for the deeper emotional needs of human beings. Like much of modernity, the journalists rely too much on speech. While Ranse is at home with them in their office, Hallie and the Marshall say very little, but in those few words there is a wealth of meaning. Similarly, while Ranse tells the reporters his tale, Hallie, Pompey, and the Marshall sit in silence.

The newspapermen associate the West with legend, but the lawless past was in truth very real, also in its often fatal consequences. Peabody tells the truth and does not speak of legends, for he is still part of the West. The legend exists only for the modern consciousness, which looks back on the West. The older West, the earlier stage, is in fact less legendary, more realistic than the deceptive modern spirit. For the archaic mind, there is no difference between reality and legend. The legend exists not in the West itself, but in the modern world, which looks back on the West, speaks of it, reflects on it—and then denies it.

The universal opposition between the law of nature and the law of spirit is beautifully intertwined with the private love story. Hallie briefly wavers between Tom and Ranse, but eventually chooses Ranse and, with this, the future. She longs for equality and intellect, but also for security and home. It is obvious that love has, in part, to do with identity search and the decision as to which type of life one wants to lead; by marrying a certain person, one cannot live the same life as by marrying another. Marriage always signifies a certain renouncement. In choosing, Hallie limits her possibilities. Already in the schoolroom we see a more subdued, less vocal Hallie; as J.A. Place notes, "she is dressed in darker shades than previously, her hair up under a hat instead of free in pigtails."[13] These details are symbolic of Hallie's movement—like that of the West—in the direction of civilization. Hallie's choice is not without a moment of tragedy. She clearly loves Tom: she would like to be with the hero, and she would like to stay in Shinbone. Yet, Hallie also loves Ranse, who has brought her the world of spirit, the world of reading and writing. To go with Ranse, as she does, Hallie must renounce Tom, and she must leave Shinbone for Washington. A tragic moment of self-sacrifice surfaces here as well, for Hallie still loves Tom: she puts the cactus rose on his coffin and longs to be back in the village. Indeed, she may love Tom in ways she never could have loved Ranse. Spirit demands sacrifices. Like Tom and Ranse, Hallie, too, is a transition figure; in fact, she bridges the two eras in a way that neither Tom nor Ranse can. She is at home both in the old Shinbone—where Ranse cannot feel at home, and in the new era—where Tom could never have been at home. Nonetheless, Hallie cannot have both simultaneously; she, too, must choose.

Liberty Valance is a film about transition—the movement of history from heroes to men. The characters move history forward, yet the most interesting aspect of this development is the transition itself. Tragic is that the characters seek a better future, but when they reach it, they recognize that not what they achieved, but the process toward this future, was the greatest aspect, not the change from the primitiveness of the age of heroes to the superficiality of the age of men, but the richness of the time when both worlds were present, as they are present in the artwork itself, which is a synthesis, an ideal, and in this sense does not mirror contemporary society but breaks from it. The film seeks a synthesis of both modes, but it is a tragic synthesis: on the narrative level, it is too late for Ranse to undo his lie; on the thematic level, the film returns to the past knowing that history has already transcended it. The film tells us that force has given way to representation, the stagecoach has been surpassed by the railroad, the wilderness has become a garden, and yet, in this advance, an era of greatness, the age of heroes, has passed away.

Notes

1. This article originally appeared in *Clio* 23(2) (1993): 131–47, and is reprinted with permission of the authors.
2. *The New Science of Giambattista Vico*, trans. Thomas Goddard Bergen and Max Harold Fisch (Ithaca: Cornell University Press, 1984), section 951. Cited by section, hereafter, in parentheses in text.

3. See the comparisons between *Liberty Valance* and Ford's earlier Westerns which are developed by Joseph McBride and Michael Wilmington in *John Ford* (London: Secker & Warburg, 1974): 178–81.

4. Significant in this context is "the Ann Rutledge theme," first used in *Young Mr. Lincoln* (1939) whenever Lincoln reflected on the death of his young love. David F. Coursen notes the contrast with *Liberty Valance*: "In *Lincoln*, the theme evokes a consistent set of feelings, first for Ann and later for her memory and her dreams for Abe, which remain vital and will come to fruition when the mature Lincoln assumes his mythic role as the embodiment of America's highest ideals. In *Valance*, however, the theme is associated exclusively with feelings that are remote and idealized, whether for Tom's memory after his death, or for Ranse's hopes for the future, which are only imperfectly realized. The music is invariably linked to an ideal, promised or remembered, its melancholy sound and its context alike suggesting that ideals are, by their very nature, unattainable" ("John Ford's Wilderness: *The Man Who Shot Liberty Valance*," in *Sight and Sound* 47 (1978): 240).

5. William S. Pechter also has commented that "Stoddard's relation to Pompey smacks unmistakably of paternalism" (*Twenty-Four Times a Second: Films and Filmmakers* (New York: Harper & Row, 1971): 234.)

6. Ranse's being shamed into not lighting his pipe ironically echoes an earlier scene in the classroom when Ranse shames one of the adults into not smoking. Here, Ranse is on the receiving end of a far more subtle lesson.

7. The third person to whom the titular verb refers is John Ford: in shooting the film, he unites the virtues of each.

8. The critique of mere oratory is one of Ford's dominant themes, beginning already with *Judge Priest* (1934).

9. We see in Ranse a certain carelessness toward others. Consider, for example, his decision to set up his law practice inside the office of the *Shinbone Star* just after it is made clear that doing so might antagonize Valance, and thus endanger Peabody and the security of his office.

10. This is also evident in Ranse's easy departure with the journalist, which contrasts with Hallie's depth of emotion during her ride to Tom's home, and in the funeral parlor, where Hallie rushes to greet Pompey and does so with great emotion, while Ranse stands aside in the bright light.

11. Pompey's name alludes to the Roman statesman Pompey, who was defeated by Caesar and represented the last attempt to defend the old Roman aristocracy (in an age of heroes); Pompey is, in this sense, the symbol of an era doomed to disappear. Pompey plays a major role in the dissolution of Tom's relationship with Hallie also insofar as it is he who—at Hallie's behest—helps Tom save Ranse and eventually tosses him the gun. On the symbolism of the names "Liberty" and "Ranse," see Tag Gallagher, who notes that Tom's name doesn't mean anything: "in contrast to whatever one may read into Stoddard's name, Tom Doniphon is just plain Tom Doniphon" (*John Ford: The Man and His*

Films (Berkeley: University of California Press, 1986): 407). Tom is the only person who is not a mere representative; he is the heroic man.

12. This progression might be said to have three stages: first, Tom gets Liberty Valance to leave the restaurant in response to an attack on his personal property (Liberty has led Ranse to drop *Tom's* steak); second, Tom shoots Liberty Valance not for himself, but for another—namely, Hallie; third, Ranse works for an abstract, less passionate and personal, but more comprehensive concept of justice.

13. J.A. Place, *The Western Films of John Ford* (Secaucus, NJ: Citadel Press, 1974): 220.

8

Anatomy of a Shipwreck: Warner Bros., the White House, and the Celluloid Sinking of *PT 109*

Nicholas J. Cull

At around 2 a.m., August 2, 1943, the powerful Japanese destroyer *Amagiri*, ploughing through the sea off the coast of the Solomon Islands, struck and sank a flimsy American patrol boat, PT 109. For the surviving members of the PT crew, it marked the beginning of a week-long struggle as they clung to the wreckage, sought refuge on a succession of desert islands, and waited while their commanding officer swam to get help. It was only one of many stories of endurance to emerge from that ocean that year. What made it newsworthy was the identity of their heroic commanding officer: Lt. (j.g.) John F. Kennedy, the second son of millionaire businessman, sometime Hollywood mogul and Ambassador to the U.K., Joseph P. Kennedy. Ambassador Kennedy pulled strings to maximize coverage for the incident, getting *Reader's Digest* to abridge and reprint "Survival," John Hersey's dramatic account of the episode for the *New Yorker*.[1] The PT 109 story became an essential element of JFK's postwar political campaigns all the way to the White House. With this level of emphasis on the story, it was only to be expected that the wartime accounts would be supplemented by new versions to reflect the destiny of Lt. Kennedy. So it proved.

As of 1961, there had already been a television adaptation of the PT 109 story as an episode of the ABC series *Navy Log*.[2] Two books, a model kit, a comic book, a TV documentary and a motion picture—Warner Bros.'s *PT 109*—followed.[3] While some Kennedy-themed popular culture proved wildly successful, the film flopped. Yet, the reasons for that failure and the attitudes revealed during the making of the film are instructive, more especially given the intervention of the White House in the process, the full story of which is reconstructed here for the first time.

According to its credits, *PT 109* was an adaptation of a non-fiction book: *PT 109: John Kennedy in World War Two* (1961) written by the head of the *New York Herald Tribune*'s Washington bureau, Robert J. Donovan. Telling the story in 1966, White House press secretary Pierre Salinger recounted how Kennedy had been so impressed by Donovan's completed book that he asked his father to do the author a good turn and see if his old friend Jack Warner might buy the film rights. Unfortunately, neither the chronology of the book's publication nor the studio documents support this version of events; rather, the movie seems to have two points of origin brought together by Ambassador Kennedy's phone call.[4]

Robert Donovan's book began in the days following the inauguration, when an editor at McGraw-Hill books in New York named Edward Kuhn Jr.—whose credits included the memoirs of both presidents Hoover and Truman—knowing that Donovan had an entree at the present White House, proposed that the journalist write a full account of Kennedy's war.[5] Donovan raised the idea at a meeting with JFK on February 10 and found the President initially resistant—calling it "flogging a dead horse." The journalist proceeded regardless.[6] The Warner Bros. film emerged quite independently.

The originator of the Warner Bros. film was a veteran producer named Bryan W. Foy: by 1961, Foy had over two hundred films to his name.[7] He had begun his career in vaudeville as one of the "Seven Little Foys" singing family and progressed from early silent work as a director/producer at Universal to Warner Bros. In the 1930s and 1940s, he had presided over the studio's famous B-picture unit, earning the soubriquet "keeper of the Bs."[8] Foy had produced the critically acclaimed *Guadalcanal Diary* (1943) but his real forte was the exploitation picture: the low budget, fast-made film which turned news stories into profits for the studio. *I Was a Communist for the FBI* (1951) was a Bryan Foy production, as were the studio's first sound and 3D films. Kennedy's war record seemed like obvious territory for similar treatment, though Foy raised eyebrows later in the process by referring to the film as an "exploitation" picture.[9]

Foy's initial inspiration was a newspaper article on Kennedy's life written in the summer of 1960 by Vincent X. Flaherty of the *Los Angeles Examiner*, and syndicated by the Hearst Headline Service. Flaherty, a legendary sports writer and flamboyant man-about-town, is now best remembered for his role in lobbying for the relocation of the Brooklyn Dodgers to L.A. in 1958. He had previously written the screenplay for Warner Bros.'s sports biopic *Jim Thorpe, All American* (1951). His Hearst piece had been made possible by his friendly relations with the Kennedy family, and Foy apparently hoped to harness these contacts for the film. Foy sounded out Flaherty on a possible film at the time of the article and officially recruited him in early March 1961.[10] Flaherty immediately fired off requests for help to Joseph P. Kennedy and White House Press Secretary Pierre Salinger, and set to work seeking out survivors of the incident as he would team members for a baseball story.[11]

Foy's project needed a champion at Warner Bros. and, in this case, his champion was none other than the studio president himself, Jack L. Warner. Exactly why Jack Warner seized on Foy's suggestion for the movie is unclear. He had publicly backed Nixon in the election, taking full-page advertisements in the *New York Times* and elsewhere, and perhaps was now seeking to court the winning camp. Warner's approach to the movie veered towards a prestige product—shot in Panavision wide-screen and Technicolor—rather than a quick and dirty exploitation picture. He recognized a project to bring glory to the studio, and perhaps upstage Twentieth Century-Fox's elaborate D-Day epic *The Longest Day*, announced with fanfare by rival mogul Daryl F. Zanuck in December 1960. The first news of the Warner project was a note in *Variety* on March 6 to the effect that the studio had registered the title *PT Boat 109* with the MPAAA.[12] Then, on March 9, 1961, Jack Warner personally declared his intent to "produce an epic dramatization wartime action involving Lt. John F. Kennedy, now president of the United States . . . To be filmed on a sweeping scale commensurate with the importance of Kennedy's legendary wartime adventures." Warner confessed that he had not decided if he would cast a star in the role of Kennedy or conduct a "nation-wide search" for a newcomer, but he predicted "the player who is awarded the part certainly will win one of the greatest motion picture roles of all time."[13] Warner remained unusually central to the making of the film, which studio publicity always billed as "produced under the personal supervision of Jack L. Warner." *PT 109* was Jack Warner's vanity project.

The production process had barely begun when the first crisis hit in the form of a blunt phone call from Robert Donovan's agent at MCA introducing his authorized book project and asserting that Donovan had a monopoly on cooperation with the White House. As a studio lawyer put it: "We will not be permitted to portray Kennedy or refer to him in the motion picture, unless we acquire the rights to Donovan's book."[14] Joseph P. Kennedy personally called Warner to negotiate a deal. Warner agreed that Donovan's history would be the source for the screenplay. He took an option on the unwritten book and prepared to wait for Donovan to finish it.[15] The prospect of a delay to production did not please Joseph Kennedy, who had an obsessive interest in the minutia of his son's public image. Perhaps hopeful of the electoral advantages that might accrue from the film, then projected to be released in time for the 1962 election season, he called Warner a second time to request that Flaherty be kept on the project.[16] Foy duly commissioned Flaherty to write the first draft of the screenplay and back-fill with Donovan's material when it became available.

In mid-April 1961, Donovan delivered a sketch of his approach to the PT 109 story. His treatment, as his McGraw-Hill editor explained, diverged from his proposed book. Whereas the book would focus on the sinking, rescue and Kennedy's role in a subsequent evacuation of marines from the island of Choiseul, the film treatment focused on "lighter moments as the crew remembers them," and anecdotal render- ings of the early bombings, and "minor skirmishes."[17] This remained the blueprint of the picture, to the chagrin of some involved. In July 1961, Warner formally purchased the rights to Donovan's book for $145,000, with the understanding that that price would bring with it the endorsement of President Kennedy, waivers from all survivors of the incident, and special permission of four of the PT 109 families to represent specific real crewmen in some detail in the film. At the President's request, some money would go to the PT 109 families.[18] Despite Joe Kennedy's role as a go-between, to move to a full contract without all permissions in hand was an act of faith on Warner Bros.'s part, or, as one studio lawyer put it, "a calculated business risk."[19]

As Joseph Kennedy had requested, Flaherty pressed ahead with his own treatment of the PT 109 story. Working with Foy's assistant, a veteran of the Fox B-movie factory named Howard Sheehan, he threw himself into interviews with the crew. By April 22 they had 125 pages of interviews and by May 13, 62 pages of a treatment.[20] The odd writing arrangement worried Flaherty, but he pressed on, asking the elder Kennedy to broker some sort of information sharing agree- ment with Donovan and pull strings to open doors with the navy. Flaherty warned Joseph Kennedy about creative differences within the production team (transparent code for Foy). Flaherty mentioned that he had had to struggle to ensure that the term "Jap" would not be used and that the Japanese would be sensitively depicted. He also recounted his dismay at a suggestion that he include a blatantly racist remark about native girls "getting lighter and lighter" the longer one served in the Pacific. "I could see the NAACP applauding that immediately," he noted ironically. His bottom line was to warn Joe Kennedy to "take complete control of the completed script, so as to delete anything off color . . . Keep a firm hand on the script, even more so than on the book. The movie will be exposed to millions of people while the book won't." It was an ill omen. Joseph Kennedy forwarded the note to Salinger at the White House. Salinger would be on his guard.[21]

Working with crew testimony, basic naval information, and their ingenuity, Flaherty and Sheehan had produced a 242-page estimating script by August 19.[22] While the script took shape, Warner and Foy turned their attention to hiring a director. The first choice was John Ford, who had filmed the war in the Pacific for real as a documentary filmmaker, and in fiction as the director of the PT boat drama *They Were Expendable* (1945). In a memo of June 23, Foy strategized that Ford might be more amenable to directing the film if he knew about the planned guest stars: Bob Hope had expressed an interest in recreating one of his USO shows for the film and Warner wanted James Cagney to appear in the role of Admiral Halsey. Foy learnt that, while Ford was likely to be free from the fall of 1961 for a couple of months, a serious offer from the studio would need to be in the vicinity of $250,000—ideally including a percentage. Either Ford's price or his existing commitments obliged Foy to look elsewhere. Cagney and Hope also passed on the project.[23] A synopsis of the film dated June 15, 1961 survives among the papers of George Stevens, suggesting that he might have been offered the helm.[24] By August, the preferred (but unconfirmed) candidate was the veteran director Raoul Walsh.[25]

Although willing to proceed without Donovan's book, the studio needed the final go-ahead from the White House and the sign-off of the survivors. Weeks passed with no news. Jack Warner's legal team became increasingly nervous. Then, on September 14, Donovan's editor, Kuhn, contacted the studio to say that the permissions were in hand and the book was in its final phase.[26] While the galleys arrived as promised, the permissions did not and, to make matters worse, the studio realized for the first time that the book would be titled *PT 109* rather than their own announced title of *PT Boat 109*. Warner Bros. switched its title to conform.[27]

Donovan's book appeared in mid-November 1961 to positive reviews.[28] Sales were brisk and multiple translations followed. Many Americans read the book in serial form in the *Saturday Evening Post* over five weeks from November 18. While the magazine mentioned the planned movie, progress at the studio remained slow. The all-important final signatures from the PT 109 families arrived only in December, suggesting that the White House might have been quietly applying the brakes.[29]

The White House used (or engineered) the delay to establish ground rules for its input into the movie. In October, *Newsweek* revealed, "JFK sought and got veto rights on the actor who will be picked to portray him."[30] In November, Warner did his best to court Kennedy by hosting three PT 109 survivors at a gala dinner at the L.A. Palladium held to benefit Pat Brown's run for Governor of California.[31] President Kennedy spoke at the dinner and Warner persuaded him to pose for a photograph with his crewmates. He did not discuss the film project, so Warner followed up in early December in a letter to Joseph Kennedy explaining: "We are getting along very well with the script. It is in the home stretch and in the next couple of weeks we will start seeking the proper person to portray the President when he was in the Navy." Warner reassured Kennedy: "Before anything is done, we will go through the proper channels so that the President will have the final approval of everything we will be doing, not only the person who will portray him, but the story itself." By return, Ambassador Kennedy promised to pass on Warner's assurances to his son:

> I should think that if you want to get any action fast, and you can't reach me by telephone, you call Pierre Salinger, and he'll get any information to the President at once. I'll arrange this with the President when he arrives here Tuesday.

Just a few days after writing this letter, Joseph Kennedy suffered a major stroke. He played no further part in the making of *PT 109*.[32]

As Ambassador Kennedy had promised, White House Secretary Pierre Salinger managed the White House input into the making of the film. He, in turn, recruited Alvin Cluster, President Kennedy's former commanding officer in the PT boats, to act as go-between with the studio. By 1962, Cluster was an aircraft components executive in Southern California. He had been disappointed not to join the administration as Assistant Secretary of the Navy and was eager to be of use. He had already helped with the Flaherty/Sheehan script, and joined the studio as a fully-fledged technical adviser on $250 a week from December 11. He would shuttle back and forth on night flights between Los Angeles and the White House.[33]

Salinger also asked the newly appointed Director of the United States Information Agency for Motion Pictures, George Stevens Jr., to join him in an *ad hoc* committee on the film. Arriving in Washington in February 1962 with a brief to manage the US government's use of documentary film to influence international audiences, Stevens's presence reflected a hope that this feature film might also play a significant role in projecting the image of JFK to a global audience.[34] As Stevens recalled in later years, Kennedy himself asked him to help with the film. He approached Stevens at a party at Sargent Shriver's house saying "I have something I want to talk with you about." Stevens was stunned, recalling: "I didn't know he knew who I was."[35]

The interest of the White House in shaping the film was only one of the challenges facing Warner at the beginning of 1962, but it added urgency to the other problems. Warner had yet to announce his star or his director, and sensed that the screenplay was still not all it should be. In mid-December, the studio laid off Flaherty. In Flaherty's place Foy hurriedly engaged Richard Breen, a veteran of the naval war in the Pacific, to rewrite the script. A former president of the Screen Writer's Guild, Breen had won an Oscar for *Titanic* (1953). The studio hoped Breen could pull the script into shape in two weeks.[36] He ended up working for more than three months and earning the principal writing credit for the film.[37] Foy also moved forward on the question of a director, persuading Raoul Walsh to take the helm. On December 27 Walsh and veteran Warner art director Leo "Kay" Kuter left L.A. for the Florida Keys to scout for suitable locations.[38] The question of the star remained to be answered.

Initially, Warner milked the question of his star, plainly hoping for a male equivalent of the search for Scarlett O'Hara. The studio and White House alike had been deluged with letters from people expressing opinions as to who might play the role.[39] One came from Supreme Court Justice William Douglas. In a note which reached the studio in March 1962, the great defender of the first amendment suggested that his son be tested for role of Kennedy. "His resemblance to Kennedy at least from the mouth upward should put him in a good position for the role if he turns out well on the screening." The studio arranged a test and cast Bill Douglas Jr. in the role of one of the 109's crewmen.[40] Despite the clamor of volunteers, Warner and Foy began their search for their star among the ranks of America's successful young TV actors. The first batch of actors tested for the role of Kennedy included the star of ABC's Western series *Bronco* (1958–62), Ty Hardin, and teen heart-throb, Ed Byrnes, who played "Kookie" the parking attendant-turned-detective on *77 Sunset Strip* (1958–64).[41] Byrnes believed that he lost the role because President Kennedy did not want to portrayed by someone known to the American public as "Kookie." Hardin at least won the role of JFK's second-in-command. Meanwhile, the President had developed his own casting ideas. The Kennedys had recently seen *Splendor in the Grass* (1961), and JFK was persuaded by Jackie that he should be portrayed on screen by that movie's striking young star, Warren Beatty. Despite Bryan Foy's immediate misgivings that Beatty was "mixed-up," Warner Bros. rushed a copy of the Donovan book and the first 75 pages of the revised script to Beatty and scheduled him for a screen test.[42] Pierre Salinger and Robert Donovan both met Beatty in Los Angeles to feel him out for the part. Beatty not only declined the role, he told Salinger exactly what he thought of the script. Jackie Kennedy hoped that a visit to Washington might change his mind. Beatty was unpersuadable and ignored her invitations.[43]

The next candidate for the young Kennedy was Peter Fonda, who was flown in from New York for a week of tests.[44] The studio was plainly enthusiastic about the idea of the acting torch being passed to a new generation of Fondas and arranged full publicity to the test, including journalists on the set and photographs of Fonda in costume duplicating archive pictures of Kennedy. Foy seemed as unhappy with Fonda as he had been with Beatty and, for his part, Fonda was appalled to be subjected to long sessions with a dialogue coach to train him to speak with a Boston accent. He hated being required to perform the part in the manner of a "night club comedian" and burnt his bridges by asking for "under protest, actor," to be chalked onto the clapperboard for the test. His candidacy ended with Warner roaring at the screen, "That silly son of a bitch—he'll never work in this town."[45] The search went on, and the test reels traveled east for review at the White House.[46]

As if the frustration of the search for a star were not enough, the White House unexpectedly questioned the choice of director. At USIA, George Stevens Jr. was deeply unimpressed by Raoul Walsh's most recent film: a Korean War drama called *Marines Let's Go!* Stevens feared that the veteran director was so far past his prime that he would do a similarly poor job with *PT 109*. He arranged a screening of *Marines Let's Go!* at the White House and was relieved when the President himself halted the film show with a sailor-ly exclamation, "Tell Jack Warner to go fuck himself." But this was easier said than done. An uncomfortable lunch with Foy, Warner, Salinger, and Stevens in Washington followed. Foy was incensed when Stevens passed on Kennedy's preferences for a director—Fred Zinnemann or John Huston—telling him that he did not need to be told how to make an "exploitation" picture by Stevens. With paperwork citing only "circumstances beyond the control of each of us," the studio dutifully paid off Walsh with $100,000. Warner Bros. tried to hire Zinnemann, but found that, despite an explanation that "certain pressures" had been brought to bear in Washington, the director was too involved in his present project to move.[47]

Kennedy's interest in Zinnemann or Huston demonstrated a desire to keep the film to the highest standards. The studio plainly needed to try to find a prestigious director. Warner hired Lewis Milestone, whose reputation with military subjects included the landmark *All Quiet on the Western Front* (1930). He informed Salinger of the appointment by telegram on March 19, and also expressed frustration that so much time had been lost. "This delay endangers our entire production," he complained, "and makes it more difficult to attract other competent people to this production."[48] The delay notwithstanding, Warner was able to recruit other first-class talents to the team including the multi-Oscar winning cinematographer, Robert Surtees and (for the time being) composer, Max Steiner.[49]

Milestone recommenced screen testing potential stars. His candidates for the role of Kennedy included Jeffrey Hunter, who had just finished playing the role of Jesus Christ in *King of Kings* (1961) and Cliff Robertson. Despite a succession of critically acclaimed TV roles (which had become movie parts for other actors), Robertson was not an obvious choice for Kennedy. He was in his late thirties and bore little physical resemblance to the wiry Kennedy of 1943. Undeterred, Cluster dutifully carried the reels of his test back to the White House. Kennedy took an immediate shine to Robertson, in part because he did not look as young as Kennedy had been in the war. As Cluster told Robertson, "The President approved you not only because you're a fine actor but because you're young looking, and yet mature enough so that the world won't get the idea that he's being played by a parking lot attendant or something." Kennedy suggested that Robertson might lighten his hair and part it on the left as he did, and that Milestone's assistant, Lew Gallo, who had pitched the lines in the test reel, also be given a part, which he was. To the relief of Milestone and Robertson, Kennedy also made it clear that he preferred not to be played with a Boston accent. The battle of the dialogue coach had been won.[50] On April 9, 1962 Jack Warner announced that Cliff Robertson had been cast.[51]

Two further issues of concern to the White House loomed large at that point: the script and the studio's relationship with the US navy. Hollywood had long counted on the armed services for help in staging military spectacle for the screen. In exchange for review of the script and free prints of the final product, the Pentagon loaned hardware, stock film, advisers and even servicemen as extras.[52] *PT 109* certainly needed this kind of help, but all concerned sensed the potential for a political trap.[53] In January, Pierre Salinger was extremely careful in the wording of his note to Secretary of the Navy, Fred Korth, requesting Pentagon cooperation with the film. He pointedly asked that the navy "should not extend a single bit more cooperation to this movie than it would to any movie in which it determined that the interests of the Navy as a fighting Service were involved." He quoted the document to the press whenever he spoke of the film to head off complaints of taxpayer resources going to create an elaborate Kennedy campaign poster.[54]

The navy assigned its own technical adviser—Captain Jack E. Gibson—to watch over the production and write weekly reports to the Chief of Information (CINFOS) at the Office of the Chief of Naval Operations. Gibson had commanded MTB squadron 10, to which Kennedy was assigned after the loss of PT 109. His first duty on the film was to transmit the studio's request for assistance—including the loan of a destroyer, and the quartering and feeding of 160 men from June 4 to August 30 at US naval station Key West, including "fifteen members of the navy or Marine Corps of Japanese extraction to act as Japanese soldiers and sailors in several scenes."[55]

One vital item which the navy could not provide was a PT boat. The studio was startled to learn that the boats were no longer in service and none had been officially preserved. Undeterred, the art director Kuter purchased three old air force rescue boats at auction and set about converting them into something resembling PTs.[56] The finished boats were an impressive sight cutting through the sea off Florida in tight formation; so impressive that locals assumed a repeat of the Bay of Pigs invasion might be imminent.[57]

The navy's technical adviser was just one of the parties working to pull the script into shape. In the first instance, the studio looked to its own research department where the head, Carl Milliken Jr., was himself a veteran of the same Rendova naval station from which PT 109 operated. Writing in January, Milliken confessed himself "in awe" of Breen's screenplay, and especially the way that it captured "the slightly hysterical humor which was part of that wartime experience." His biggest concern was of Kennedy's own use of language. During the war, Kennedy had been known by the nickname of "Shafty." Cluster went so far as to say that, if he were not referred to by this name at that time, his comrades would not know who was meant. The origins of the nickname were variously explained. Some said that Kennedy was thin as a propeller shaft. Others that it sprang from his characteristic use of the phrase "we were shafted," made memorable by his elongated "a" vowel. Breen had accordingly had Kennedy lament "we were shafted" at several points in the script as a running gag. Milliken was concerned, writing, "I want to respectfully suggest that we violate accuracy in this instance. *Because of the office John F. Kennedy now holds!* [his emphasis] And because of the offensive vulgar derivation of this slang term." He helpfully included a definition from Wentworth and Flexner's *Dictionary of American Slang* (1960) as: "An act or instance of being taken advantage of . . . Figuratively, the image is the taboo one of the final insult, having someone insert something, as a barbed shaft, up one's rectum." "Shafty" disappeared shortly thereafter. Milliken also thought that it might be better if Kennedy's crew where not shown fishing for dolphins with hand grenades, as killing dolphins is considered bad luck by sailors.[58] The reminder did not prevent at least one cast member from catching and eating dolphin for sport during the location shooting. Appropriate luck followed.[59]

Meanwhile, Richard Breen's script went forward to the White House. Jack Warner heard that Kennedy read it on February 20, 1962 while John Glenn orbited the earth.[60] The White House approved the script subject to a number of changes, including dropping all references to Kennedy's elder brother, Joe Jr., for the comic elements of the scene in which Kennedy accidentally crashed his PT boat into a dock to be toned down, and for the deletion of a scene in which Kennedy orders his crew to shoot up the (unoccupied) outhouses on the Japanese-held island of Gatu. The copy of the script which survives in the Kennedy library includes terse annotations in Kennedy's hand: "Ramming dock—shooting up privy: NO," and marginal marks wherever the issue of Ambassador Kennedy's ability to influence his son's career was mentioned. Breen received more nuanced guidance. Breen noted of the outhouse incident: "They acknowledge that this happened and in much this fashion. However, they feel it is not prudent to include it in a film account. They urge that it be replaced by the Marine rescue described in the last part of Donovan's book. The time discrepancy does not distress them." The incident had actually taken place after the sinking, when Kennedy captained PT 59. More generally, Breen reported: "Their general views can be best summarized in this way; any legitimate action which can be added will be appreciated; humor and light-heartedness are to be sought if not 'pratfall' in nature."[61] In late March, Bryan Foy received a letter endorsing his new version from Undersecretary of the Navy and PT veteran Paul B. Fay, who predicted "a very exciting movie." Fay—a close confidante of the President—may have been delegated to review the script on Kennedy's behalf. Certainly, Fay copied his reply to the studio to the President. The approval of Washington strengthened Bryan Foy's confidence in the script, and the specific wishes of the White House for an emphasis on humor underscored his own instincts. Unfortunately, Foy's director felt differently.[62]

Lewis Milestone was never comfortable with the script for *PT 109.*[63] On March 23 he attempted to quit the project, but was persuaded to remain by a generous new contract which offered $150,000 for the film, including contingency payments if the studio either cancelled the film or asked someone else to finish it.[64] Milestone had enjoyed Robert Donovan's book but felt that the screenplay had little in common with it. He read Breen's revisions of the script with alarm.[65] Breen was expanding the humor, while Milestone believed that the film should be a "universal story of combat . . . A story of the way men grow larger and stronger inside when caught up in the awesome, impersonal machinery of war." In a bid to bring the film closer to Donovan, Milestone and his assistant Lew Gallo extracted about 100 typewritten pages of material from the Donovan book and presented them to Foy for integration into the script. Breen devoted only four days to the task of blending these ideas into the script and with negligible results. Appalled, on April 30 the director wrote a stiffly worded memo to Foy enumerating the screenplay's failings:

1) Character development: still non-existent.
2) Inter-relationships: still non-existent.
3) Historically correct dramatic facts have been substituted by mediocre fiction.
4) In the entire time that the eleven men are ship-wrecked we do not have a single sustained dramatic scene.
5) The drama of war, the fear of the enemy and general suspense are constantly destroyed by weak attempts at humor.

He begged Foy to hire a new writer "while there is still time."[66] Nothing changed and so, two weeks later, Milestone decided Foy would need to hire a new director. On May 15, he walked out of the studios and summarily resigned from the picture. Jack Warner persuaded Milestone back for a conference at 9 p.m. that evening and, as Milestone recalled, "gave the necessary orders to alter the screenplay in keeping with the views I held." Mollified, Milestone resumed work, but not before the press reported the fracas.[67]

Although the screenplay was still in flux, Jack Warner insisted on the agreed production schedule and on completing location work during the coming summer. None of the surviving studio or White House documents explain exactly why. Milestone was told it was due to a previous studio contractual obligation.[68] The Kennedy administration raised no objection to keeping to the schedule, and may have been the reason for it. It is possible that the White House wanted the film to be ready for 1963 and the run-up to the re-election campaign, but more likely that Salinger feared a negative press if the navy extended its aid to the film beyond the agreed dates.[69] For whatever reason, in the early summer Milestone, the cast, and crew moved to Florida to begin shooting the film with what the director still considered a flawed script.

The location was an eight-acre isle near Key West called Munson Island, upon which the resourceful art director Kuter had recreated replicas of Talagi and Rendova, the two South Pacific outposts necessary for the story. President Kennedy reportedly viewed and approved scale models of these, and of the reconstructed boats. The location was no beach picnic. The studio used fifteen gallons of insecticide a day to keep the mosquitoes at bay. The rats and bats remained.[70] Problems were never far below the surface. There were panics over locating props and continued problems with the coast guard, who worried that the PT boats might be Cuban intruders. There were casting problems. The film required three Pacific Islanders, and efforts to bring the actual rescuers of Kennedy to the US to re-enact their wartime roles failed.[71] Other survivors of the saga proved easier to manage. A number of 109-ers visited the location with their wives. Barney Ross played a cameo role as a gruff Chief Petty Officer accidentally doused with a bucket of oil by JFK. Leon Drawdy and Gerald Zinser had walk-on parts, and John Maguire served as consultant during the island survival scenes.[72] The Australian coast-watcher Reg Evans, who coordinated the rescue, sent a revised page of dialogue and earned $500 for his trouble.[73] But there were limits to the studio's quest to involve real people. Following a legal panic in July, the studio cut all non-essential identifications, even deleting a casual mention of Bing Crosby in the dialogue.[74] Such concerns paled against the ongoing issue of the script. Milestone hoped that being three thousand miles from Burbank might allow him a little licence and began discreetly cutting some of the more clunky humor. He had not reckoned with Jack Warner's obsession to stick to his "orders" from Washington.[75]

On June 23, Foy and White House liaison Cluster met with the ultimate authority on the PT 109 project, President Kennedy himself. The meeting was short—lasting just from 11:00 a.m. to 11:18 a.m.—but seems to have motivated Warner to tighten his hold on production. Warner was apparently disappointed by first sight of the rushes, alarmed by reports that journalists had been visiting the location in search of a story, and worried by the suggestion that the director had been drinking. He promptly unleashed a barrage of phone calls and letters in the direction of Florida. On June 23, he called Foy and Cluster in Washington, and on June 26 he wrote a formal note to Milestone warning that, because of Kennedy's status as president, "every action of the cast and crew during the making of *PT 109* will be constantly scrutinized" and, hence, "we cannot permit the actions of the usual Hollywood company, good or bad as they may be on location." Warner ordered Milestone, Foy and Cluster immediately to assemble a meeting of all cast and crew and lay down a new set of rules insisting on the "'highest standard" of conduct on set and off. "Avoid liquor and unnecessary visitors," he cautioned, continuing: "Above all, I do not want any stories given to reporters that can or will reflect upon the people playing in the picture, the director or anyone else . . . I have never written a letter like this before," he concluded, "I am writing it because we are dealing with the President of the United States and I want no stone unturned to see that propriety and dignity are upheld."[76] The micro-management had begun.

Barely a week later, on July 6, Warner pushed back against Milestone's wish to change the script: "Please do not cut out lines that have a chance for humor and for good characterization . . . Inasmuch as we are willing to put up the money please shoot it and if it does not work after we put the picture together we can correct it with a thing known as the scissors!" He noted that yet another writer named Bill Driskill (who had helped Milestone on *Mutiny on the Bounty*, 1962) was on his way to help. Warner concluded by instructing Milestone on the best camera angles when shooting scenes of crew dialogue, which was something of a slight to the veteran director's professionalism.[77] More of the same followed. On July 11 Warner forwarded "two sets of changes I talked to you about on the phone Tuesday." Noting, in probable cryptic allusion to the White House: "We must comply with these for reasons I do not want to go into in this letter."[78]

Milestone initially agreed to retain the humor in the script, writing on July 14, "If this is what you want, you shall have it."[79] But, when Warner objected to other changes, Milestone's irritation boiled over. In an angry letter the following day, he explained certain cuts as actually being at the request of Captain Gibson, the navy adviser, whose standing instructions for the production included the removal of all derogatory language towards the Japanese. To this end, Milestone had cut short an air raid scene during which a regular Japanese patrol plane was referred to as "Louis-the-Louse." Milestone also explained that Warner was not seeing the close-ups he expected in the rushes because one simply could not do TV-type close-ups of noses and eyes when working in Panavision. He concluded, "Never before have I worked under conditions where the company shows so little trust in what I am doing."[80] In despair at Warner's attitude, Milestone defied Warner's order and vented his frustration in an interview with Karl Fleming of *Newsweek*.

The *Newsweek* story blew the lid off the problems on *PT 109*. The magazine quoted Milestone saying: "A lot of the script is cornball jokes" and Foy's raging back, "It's a damn good script and its not going to be changed. I'm a Democrat who found something he could use. I'm always looking for an exploitable idea. This is a wonderful script and it's going to be a good movie. Milestone is all wrong." Caught in the middle, Cliff Robertson told the paper: "I don't think this will be a great picture, but I think it can be a good one."[81] Warner did not wait for the piece to appear to act. Milestone had embarrassed the studio in front of the nation and the President. Warner hired a substitute and fired the director on July 21.[82] The studio cover story blamed Milestone's slow progress and an argument over the budget of $4,000,000 and rising, but Milestone issued a press release that underlined his worry over the script.[83] The cast and crew were sympathetic to his position and signed a touching hand-made farewell card, but had no alternative but to soldier on.[84]

Warner made no attempt to find a prestigious successor for Milestone; rather, he hired a younger director known mainly for television work named Leslie H. Martinson. Martinson had been drafted from M–G–M and served in the army in the Pacific in World War II. His recent films for Warner Bros. included *FBI Code 98* (1963), a low-budget film which required close cooperation with the FBI and won the appreciation of J. Edgar Hoover and, as a consequence, of Warner as well. Martinson had been investigated by the bureau as part of the preparation for that film and was, hence, considered "cleared" for a project requiring utmost discretion. He could be expected to follow instructions more exactly than a high-maintenance star director. He relocated to Florida on a few hours' notice.[85] Jack Warner gave the unit publicist, Ted Ashton, strict orders to turn away all journalists: "This is one picture on which I don't want any more publicity." No one doubted the challenge facing Martinson. He responded admirably. On his first day, he rallied the troops with an impressive speech and set right to work filling in Milestone's gaps with retakes and added scenes.[86] By the end of the month, Martinson was ready to shoot new scenes and only the local Miami press seemed interested in running negative stories on the film.[87]

Milestone's mantle of chief worrier over the script passed to the film's star, Cliff Robertson, who felt keenly the responsibility of all involved in the film to project the best possible message to America and the world. He had sought to alert the White House to Milestone's firing through a back-channel telegram to Kennedy's brother-in-law, Peter Lawford: "It is as an actor citizen and not least of all a Democrat that I implore you to help in any way you might deem judicious to all."[88] On August 12, he set out his concerns in a four-page letter to Foy. Robertson knew better than to ask for a new script, but he made an excellent case for three new scenes and the revision of two more. He began by pointing out that the film had a central problem—a complete lack of suspense. The whole world knew who Kennedy was and what he became. The engine of the film had, rather, to be Kennedy's development as a character. "This is not just a story of battle sequences and incidental anecdotes or jokes," Robertson noted,

> It is the Story of Kennedy the Man. *It is the story of his relationship to other men.* The audience knows who he is—we must show who he was. The audience knows *what* he did—we must show *how* and *why* he did it. The audience knows he commanded men—we must let them *know* those men. The audience knows he *grew* as a man—we must show the beginnings of that growth.

To this end, Robertson called for a reworking of the opening scene in which Kennedy speaks of having pulled strings to get into action, to stress his inner need to prove himself to his family and his peers. He suggested a scene in which the crew's initial attitude to Kennedy could be established, so that the film could show a growth of their respect and his authority. He suggested developing the scene in which Kennedy successfully rallies a man with a premonition of death by showing others fail. He suggested showing the "fight in Kennedy" with a clash between him and the defeatist character, Ross. Finally, he wanted a new "summation scene," which could display his own realization that he had proved himself and "he was on the move and the move was forward."[89] It was a brilliant analysis which, if applied, could have established a structure akin to that of John Hersey's first telling of the story, rendering it a rite of passage. Foy saw no reason to follow the suggestions. Robertson was left, as he later put it, "like a painter who is given three pots of paint and told to come up with twelve colors."[90]

Martinson managed the location work with aplomb. The navy adviser noted that the complex action scenes were "hair-raising" to watch being staged, but went without a hitch.[91] Martinson's impact on the movie included a toning down of Kennedy's actual heroism to make the incident more believable. His Kennedy only personally rescued two crew members in the immediate aftermath of the sinking, rather than four. He also sped up the response time of the US navy to the loss and generally re-engineered the script.[92] Breen returned to make his own adjustments.[93] Foy showed his own limits by muddling up the versions of the screenplay and giving the wrong pages to the director to film. Back in Burbank, Warner's assistant, Steve Trilling, wrote in despair on September 5, "For a first-class shooting company and a multi-million dollar production it certainly has been handled in a slip-shod, sloppy manner. I intend sparing no words with Foy . . . half the confusion is his fault—Milestone was bad but Foy is worse."[94] There is no record of exactly what was said to Foy, but he immediately became ultra budget conscious. Capt. Gibson, now reporting the new CINFOS, Rear Admiral John McCain, registered disquiet on learning that Foy had suddenly announced that there could be no further use of the PT boats. The following week, he announced that he was ending all use of the first camera unit on location early.[95] There was no longer talk of a Max Steiner score for the film. It was too late to prevent the budget running over $5 million. This was around half of Fox's expenditure on *The Longest Day* (1962), a third of Columbia's budget for *Lawrence of Arabia* (1962), and one-quarter of M–G–M's outlay on *Mutiny on the Bounty* (1962). There were clear limits on Warner's willingness to indulge his pet project.

The picture relocated to Burbank for studio work. Jack Warner reiterated orders to bar all journalists from the set and forbade all cast interviews.[96] Admiral McCain and PT 109 survivor Patrick McMahon were invited to view the last leg of shooting, which provided something for the press office to release.[97] By the end of October, the filming was complete.[98] Captain Gibson for one breathed a sigh of relief, noting later: "It was easier fighting World War II than making this picture."[99] Foy made a half-hearted attempt to build a case for negligence against Milestone to prevent payment of the $50,000 still due under his generous contract. He found the cast and crew unwilling to testify.[100] In the event, the final economy on the film was at Foy's expense. On December 4, the studio informed Foy that he would be on a "vacation without pay" from January 1 until the end of his contract period, and would be expected to do any publicity around the release of *PT 109* for expenses only.[101] Bryan Foy never produced another film.

As completed, *PT 109* followed the original formula outlined by Donovan in the spring of 1961, bringing character comedy and anecdote to the fore. While most of the characters were real, two were invented: Commander Ritchie (James Gregory), a tough boat maintenance officer with a grudge against the young PT-ers who actually engaged the enemy; and Yeoman Rodgers (Lew Gallo), a purveyor of rumor who lived in hope that he could persuade Kennedy to use his influence to transfer them both away from the war zone. Lt. Kennedy's struggle to restore PT 109 and win round Ritchie provided the trajectory for the pre-sinking portions of the film. The final third of the movie concerned the sinking and survival story. While the film had its moments, including well-staged action sequences and impressive shots by Surtees, it seemed that much of the effort had gone into things that would mean little to the audience. The technical advisers knew enough to appreciate a realistic recreation of the Rendova base, but the audience did not. The audience wanted a story. As Robertson and Milestone before him had feared, that story failed to show any development of Kennedy's character during the film. He arrived in the story fully-formed, with iron resolve and an instinctive understanding of his men visible in the half-smile that met every adversity. As Robertson predicted, the dramatic tension was minimal and the whole thing unwound with the inevitability of clockwork.

Judging by the two batches of thank-you letters in the White House files, the White House organized two advanced screenings of the film. The first took place in February, including such expert eyes in the audience as the Federal Maritime Commissioner, a retired Admiral named John Harlee. The screening seems to have generated some tweaks to the final film.[102] The second screening took place in May and included Donovan and his family.[103] Kennedy's own family was sufficiently impressed with the finished product to take a hand in the release festivities that June. The west coast premiere on June 26 was a gala event at the Beverly Hilton in support of the Kennedy family's children's charity. Jack Warner was in his element, meeting Kennedy's mother and sisters. That event (together with the world premiere in Boston the previous week) raised over $108,000.[104] Warner was reluctant to acknowledge any creative hand but his own in the making of the film. He was the only non-actor mentioned in the theatrical trailer, and he excluded Leslie Martinson from the premiere in Boston on pain of suspension.[105] The studio reported encouraging early box office business, which Salinger passed on to the President.[106] Jack Warner's reward was a thank-you lunch at the White House with Kennedy, during which the President called the picture a "fine job."[107] While others also reported Kennedy's enjoyment of the film, the President was not above quipping in the other direction to please an interlocutor. Warren Beatty recalled that, meeting Kennedy shortly after the film's release, the President remarked, "You were right."[108]

Warner felt sure that the world would adore the film. He would be bitterly disappointed. Domestic opinion divided on its merits, with reactions for and against perhaps colored by politics. *Variety* judged *PT 109* "see worthy" and predicted good business among the "Little League crowd and male action buffs."[109] In the *New York Times*, Bosley Crowther dismissed the film, pouring particular scorn on the characterization of the young Kennedy as "pious and pompous."[110] Warner still had high hopes for the international reception and travelled to England to premiere the movie personally in the presence of Lord Mountbatten and various other notables.[111] British opinion proved unrestrained it its dismissal. One review headline ran: "Tarzan Kennedy beats the Japs and surrenders to clichés." British critics all agreed that Kennedy came across as insufferably priggish. The left-wing *Daily Herald* found the "great dollops of sentimental dialogue ... frankly laughable." The US press reproduced these reviews with suitable horror.[112]

The American public largely stayed away, despite creative marketing. The flop baffled Warner. He wrote in his memoirs, "I don't understand why it missed."[113] Warner continued to court the Kennedy White House with messages of support for particular speeches. Warner hoped that Kennedy might speak at a gala dinner honoring the studio boss in October 1963, but the President declined.[114] When Kennedy died a month later, the film was still only three-quarters of the way around the circuit. Jack Warner withdrew it immediately.[115] Three months later, with due decorum observed, Warner felt able to re-release the film—oddly choosing Dallas as the first major city for screening. Kennedy's death gave the film a small boost internationally. The *New York Times* reported traffic jams to see the film in Lusaka, Rhodesia on a drive-in double bill with the made-for-television documentary *The Making of the President*.[116] In the end, international exhibition raised $2,100,000 which, when combined with the $3,316,000 grossed domestically, still could not match the $6,494,000 which the film had cost. Jack Warner's pet project had lost his studio $1 million.[117]

Poor box office did not prevent legal difficulties. In the summer of 1964, one Sarah Albert—the mother of Seaman Raymond Albert, a member of the PT 109 crew who had died later in the war—sued both McGraw-Hill and Warner Bros. for over $1 million in damages stemming from the unauthorized representation of her dead son. The case of *Albert v. Warner Bros. et al.* was settled out of court in the spring of 1967 when the studio paid Mrs Albert $4,500 ($2,000 of which passed to her lawyers), which gave her parity with payments to the survivors featured in the film. The studio watched the case with anxiety, given the danger for similar litigation arising from relatives of the real people due to be depicted in their high-profile project *Bonnie and Clyde*, due for release that summer.[118]

PT 109 took a heavy toll on its older participants. Milestone, like Foy, never made another film. Warner attempted nothing on that scale again. Martinson had proved himself and built a solid career in TV. He is now best remembered as the director of the camp classic *Batman* (1966). The only real winner was Cliff Robertson, who found that merely being cast in the role of the President provided the career break that had eluded him for so long. A new contract led to a string of parts worthy of his talents, culminating in the title role in *Charly* (1968) for which he won his Academy Award.[119]

What can be learnt from the celluloid sinking of *PT 109*? The film is a milestone in the evolution of the depiction of the American president; a half-way house between the reverence of the back-view-only portrayal of FDR in Warner Bros.'s *Mission to Moscow* (1943) and the no-holds-barred onslaught of Oliver Stone's *W* (2008). By 1962, times had changed enough to allow the representation of a sitting president, but not enough to allow the film to be done properly with a full characterization, or to allow either the studio or the White House to relax during the production process. Few commentators objected to the taboo-busting.[120]

Warner Bros. had handled any number of high-profile films before, and successfully rescued weak scripts and brokered peace between awkward directors and producers. The studio system had no shortage of checks and balances to prevent the kind of meltdown which occurred on the *PT 109* set. What was unique about *PT 109*, and beyond the capacity of the studio system to cope with, was intervention of the Kennedy camp and attempts by Foy and others to conform to their understanding of the White House wishes. The archives reveal clearly that, despite Salinger's claims at the time, the White House had an influence on more than just casting. Foy's fixation with comic content was affirmed and sustained by Kennedy's staff, and must have met with the general approval of President Kennedy himself. What were they thinking? Why steer the film in this direction? The best explanation is that the White House, in pushing the story forward, was seeking not only to present Kennedy as a hero, but also—by insisting on the inclusion of humor and character interaction—as a regular person able to share a joke with his crew. The movie was expected to both valorize and humanize Kennedy at the same time. This would be a difficult act for anyone to pull off, and it proved beyond the capacity of the team of studio veterans assembled by Jack Warner for the task. To borrow a metaphor from the incident which started the whole thing, they were at sea in a flimsy craft and were broken in two by the impact of a powerful oncoming vessel; ironically, in the case of the movie that vessel was the Kennedy White House.

Notes

1. For a study of John Hersey's "Survival," see John Hellmann, *The Kennedy Obsession: The American Myth of JFK* (New York: Columbia University Press, 1997): 37–61.
2. The TV version of *PT 109* was the sixth episode of the third and final season of *Navy Log* (1955–58). It first aired on ABC on October 23, 1957, produced by Sam Gallu with John Baer in the role of JFK.
3. Jack Gould, "Jack Paar Returns," *New York Times* (September 22, 1961): 51.
4. Salinger's version is in his memoir, *With Kennedy* (Garden City, NY: [Doubleday, 1966]): 102–3. It is the foundation for Bob Thomas, *Clown Prince of Hollywood: The Antic Life and Times of Jack L. Warner* (New York: McGraw-Hill, 1990): 237–8. The account of the film in Warner's memoir—Jack L. Warner, *My First Hundred Years in Hollywood* (New York: Random House, 1965: 325–7)—errs wildly.
5. Walter H. Waggoner, "Edward Kuhn Jr., Editor, Dies at 55," *New York Times* (December 22, 1979): 28.
6. Robert J. Donovan, *Boxing the Kangaroo: A Reporter's Memoir* (University of Missouri Press, 2000): 95–7. Kennedy's appointments diary (John F. Kennedy Library) records meetings with Donovan on February 10, 1961 11:30 a.m. to 12:06 p.m., May 27, 1961 from 2:00 p.m. to 2:20 p.m. and July 6, 1961 from 1:25 p.m. onwards.
7. This claim is made by the film's original writer Vincent X. Flaherty in letters to Pierre Salinger. See Flaherty to Salinger, March 27, 1961, box 722, PP 13–11, JFKL WHCSF.
8. "Bryan Foy, Vaudevillian and Producer, 80, Dies," *New York Times* (April 22, 1977): 51.
9. Thomas (338) notes that Foy's show-business family had links to Joe Kennedy from his time running the vaudeville circuit.
10. Studio press release, March 21, 1961, box 658, file *PT 109*, Warner Bros. Archive (hereafter WBA); Michael D'Antonio, *Forever Blue: The True Story of Walter O'Malley, Baseball's Most Controversial Owner, and the Dodgers of Brooklyn and Los Angeles* (Riverhead, 2009). Joseph P. Kennedy's private papers confirm his contact with Flaherty through the journalist's thank-you note for tickets to JFK's inauguration, Flaherty to JPK January 26, 1961, box 219, file F, 1945–1963, Joseph P. Kennedy papers, JFKL.
11. Studio press release, March 20, 1961, April 17, 1961, box 658, file *PT 109*, WBA. Flaherty to Warner, March 20, 1961, box 722, PP 13–11 (General), WHCSF.

12. "Biopic JFK as war hero," *Variety* (March 6, 1961).
13. Studio press release, March 9, 1961, box 658, file *PT 109*, WBA.
14. Walter MacEwen to Warner, March 15, 1961, box 2179, file *PT 109* (story 1 of 2), WBA. Robert Donovan misdates the alarm over the rival projects to May 1961, some time after the Warner press office reported a deal (105).
15. Salinger to Ted Strauss (April 17, 1961, WHCSF name file: Warner Bros., JFKL) describes the deal: "I understand that Warner Bros. has dropped all plans to film the original PT 109 project until Donovan's book is available. The President did not want to have his war exploits filmed unless they were based on authentic information."
16. Joseph Kennedy to Salinger, May 1, 1961, WHCSF box 722, PP 13–11, JFKL; Flaherty to Joseph Kennedy, May 7, 1961, *ibid*.
17. Outline by Donovan, April 15, 1961, box 2180, file *PT 109* outline, WBA.
18. Contractual correspondence filed box 2179, file *PT 109* (story 1 of 2). Kennedy's personal concern that the families benefit is stated in Sue Mortensen (WH press office) to Nell Hickey (*American Weekly*), July 16, 1962, WHCSF box 722, PP 13–11, JFKL.
19. MacEwen to Orr, July 13, 1961, box 2179, file *PT 109* story (1 of 2), WBA.
20. The chronology is recorded in O'Steen to MacEwen, September 11, 1962, a statement for a Writer's Guild adjudication, box 2179, file *PT 109* (story 1 of 2), WBA.
21. Joseph Kennedy to Salinger, May 1, 1961; Flaherty to Joseph Kennedy, May 7, 1961, WHCSF box 722, PP13–11, JFKL.
22. O'Steen to MacEwen, *passim*.
23. Foy to Orr, June 23, 1961; Orr to Foy, June 26, 1961, box 27, file *PT 109*, Jack L. Warner collection, housed in the USC Cinema Collection (hereafter JLWC).
24. Walter Hartman, Synopsis of *PT 109* by Robert J. Donovan, June 5, 1961, *Execution of Private Sovik* synopsis # 3241, George Stevens Papers, Academy of Motion Picture Arts and Sciences (hereafter AMPAS).
25. Walsh is first mentioned in MacEwen to Orr, August 21, 1961, box 2179, file *PT 109* (story 1 of 2), WBA, in the context of the studio's anxiety waiting for the endorsement of JFK.
26. Kuhn (McGraw-Hill) to Mayer (Warner Bros., New York), September 14, 1961, box 2179, file *PT 109* story (1 of 2), WBA. Kuhn's account is not confirmed by the White House appointment diary.
27. MacEwen to Mayer, September 19, 1961, box 2179, file *PT 109* story (1 of 2), WBA.
28. John Toland, "A Profile in Courage; A Background of War . . .", *New York Times* (November 19, 1961): BR3.
29. Vivienne Nearing (WB, New York) to Obringer, December 19, 1961, box 2179, file *PT 109* story (1 of 2), WBA.
30. "Behind the News, Newport RI," *Newsweek* (October 9, 1961): 17.
31. Studio press release, November 17, 1961, box 658, file *PT 109*, WBA.

32. Warner to Kennedy, December 8, 1961; Kennedy to Warner December 14, 1961, box 238, file W: 1960–63, Joseph P. Kennedy Papers, JFKL.

33. Cluster to Howard, July 3, 1961, box 2179, file *PT 109* story (2 of 2), includes a note that during the war the men conversed mainly about "booze, women, rumors and their mail" and that they all expected Kennedy to become a writer. On Cluster's bid for a post in the Kennedy administration, see President to Cluster, February 20, 1961, name file: Cluster, WHCF.

34. Interview: George Stevens Jr., April 10 and 14, 1998. See Bill Davidson, "President Kennedy Casts a Movie," *Saturday Evening Post* (September 8, 1962).

35. Stevens to author, March 23, 2010.

36. MacEwen to Obringer, December 15, 1961, box 2179, file *PT 109* story (1 of 2), WBA.

37. Mary Dorfman (WGA) to MacEwen, October 24, 1962, folder 2179, file *PT 109* story (1 of 2), WBA, delivered final arbitration of the writing credits: Screenplay by Richard L. Breen; adaptation by Howard Sheehan and Vincent X. Flaherty; from the book by Robert J. Donovan. Uncredited writers included William L. Driskill and Vincent Fotre. Connie Martinson recalls that she and her husband also wrote additional material.

38. Trilling to Foy, December 27, 1961, box 27, *PT 109* file 2, JLWC. Kuter's relevant credits included art direction on *Destination Tokyo* and *Operation Pacific*.

39. Casting, March 13, 1961, box 630, file *PT 109*; for similar letters to the White House, see WHCF name file: Warner Bros.

40. Bill Douglas to Max Gordon, forwarded to Trilling, March 21, 1962, box 27, *PT 109* file 1, JLWC.

41. Press Release, December 14, 1961, box 630, file *PT 109*, WBA.

42. Trilling to Beatty, January 4, 1961 [sic], box 27, *PT 109* file 2, JLWC.

43. For a full account, see Suzanne Finstad, *Warren Beatty: A Private Man* (New York: Harmony Books, 2005): 281–2; John Parker, *Warren Beatty: The Last Great Lover of Hollywood* (New York: Carroll & Graf, 1994): 89; Ellis Amburn, *The Sexiest Man Alive: A Biography of Warren Beatty* (Harper-Entertainment, 2002): 46–7. Donovan recalls JFK telling him Beatty was Jackie's choice (Donovan, *Boxing the Kangaroo*: 105–6).

44. Trilling to Peter Knecht, January 19, 1962, box 27, *PT 109* file 1, JLWC, making arrangements for testing Peter Fonda not later than January 26, 1962. See also Bowers to accounts payable, February 6, 1962, file 2, JLWC.

45. Peter Fonda, *Don't Tell Dad: A Memoir* (New York: Hyperion, 1998): 160–2. For sample press coverage, see UPI "Fonda's Son 'Best Bet' to Play Role of Kennedy," *Las Vegas Sun* (January 26, 1961): 22; *Hollywood Reporter* (February 23, 1962); Stevens to Salinger, February 26, 1962, box 722, PP 13–11 (general), WHCSF.

46. Warner to Salinger (telegram), March 2, 1962, name file Warner, Jack, JFKL, WHSCF.

47. Interview: Stevens; Trilling to Warner, March 9, 1962 and on the pay-off to Walsh: Steve Trilling to Hal Holman, July 13, 1962, box 27, *PT 109*

file 1, JLWC. For the contract with Walsh, see legal file, 1 of 6, Studio to Walsh—May 1, 1962 and Obringer to Warner, May 23, 1962, box 2849A, WBA.

48. Warner to Salinger, March 22, 1962, box 810, PR12 motion pictures (exec.), JFKL WHCSF; press release, March 28, 1962, box 630, file *PT 109*, WBA.

49. Steiner is listed on the "Final Credits," August 9, 1962, box 27, file *PT 109* file 1, filed at JLWC. The completed film was credited to David Buttolph, Howard Jackson, and William Lava.

50. Bill Davidson, "President Kennedy Casts a Movie," *Saturday Evening Post* (September 8, 1962); Don Alpert, "Cliff Robertson on *PT 109*—US image," *Los Angeles Times* (December 30, 1962): A6.

51. Press release, April 10, 1962, box 630, file *PT 109*, WBA, includes "It is understood that Robertson's casting has the warm approval of the White House," deleted in pencil. For coverage, see "Kennedy role is filled," *New York Times* (April 10, 1962): 44.

52. Donald D. Baruch chief production branch, audio-visual division, to George Fishman, February 9, 1962, box 27, *PT 109* file 1, JLWC, notes permission from White House has been received.

53. This concern is obvious as early as April 1961 with the studio's first inquiries about Pentagon holdings of footage of PTs in action; George Fishman (Warner Bros., DC office) to Bill Hendricks, April 6, 1961, box 27, *PT 109* file 2, JLWC.

54. Salinger to Korth, January 6, 1962, box 810, PR 12—Motion Pictures (exec.), JFKL WHCSF; Bill Davidson, "President Kennedy Casts a Movie," *Saturday Evening Post* (September 8, 1962).

55. Gibson to Chief of Information (Navy), Ref (a) CNO 052304Z, April 4, 1962, folder 217, *PT-109*, Leo Kuter Collection, AMPAS; Bill L. Hendricks to Foy, April 3, 1962, *ibid.*

56. For full details and original plans, see folder 217, *PT-109*, Leo Kuter Collection, AMPAS.

57. Murray Schumach, "Warners Dispels Invasion Rumors, Key West Activities Linked to Kennedy War Film," *New York Times*, April 5, 1962.

58. Carl Milliken, Jr. to Foy, January 26, 1962, box 27, *PT 109* file 1, JLCW. For input into the script from the Marine Corps, see *ibid.*, Baruch (Department of Defense) to Hendricks (Warner Bros.), April 13, 1962; for final script see "Final" screenplay, December 22, 1961, folder 2180 *PT 109*, WBA.

59. Lew (Gallo) to Milestone, July 31, 1962, *PT 109* production, folder 78, Lewis Milestone Papers (hereafter LMP), AMPAS.

60. Warner: 326.

61. Richard Breen to Trilling, March 1, 1962, box 27, *PT 109* file 1, JLWC. At this time, the studio reassigned writer Howard Sheehan. MacEwen to Knecht, February 15, 1962, notes Sheehan was to complete the script by February 23, 1962. In the screenplay of December 22 (box 2180, WBA), the mentions of Joseph Kennedy Jr. included a scene inserted

on February 1, 1962 in which JFK receives a letter from Joe stating that when he returns from war he is going to run for office; the Gatu Island scene is #109 (56), January 26, 1962; White House copy box 1144, PP 13–11 (exec.), JFKL, WHCSF.

62. Fay to Foy, March 27, 1962, box 810, PR 12 motion pictures (exec.), JFKL, WHCSF.

63. Milestone statement, July 23, 1962, *PT 109* publicity, folder 79, LMP.

64. Edward Lasker to Steve Trilling, March 23, 1962, *PT 109* legal, folder 77, LMP, Lasker to Hastings (inter-office memo), March 26, 1962 and contract dated March 28, 1962, LMP.

65. Autobiography research (Lew Gallo), folder 326, LMP. Breen, as Milestone's assistant Lew Gallo put it, "Seemed to be getting closer to Sergeant Bilko (a manic TV comedy of the era set in the army) and further from President Kennedy."

66. Milestone to Foy, April 30, 1962, *PT 109* production, folder 78, LMP.

67. Autobiography research (Lew Gallo), folder 326, LMP; Milestone statement, July 23, 1962, *PT 109* publicity, folder 79, LMP, AMPAS; *Hollywood Reporter* (May 16, 1962). The hiatus prompted an agent for John Farrow to write to the White House recommending him as a substitute. John Bennett to Salinger, May 22, 1962, box 722, PP 13–11 (general), JFKL, WHCSF.

68. Milestone Statement, July 23, 1962, *PT 109* publicity, folder 79, LMP.

69. George Stevens Jr. was not consulted about the schedule (Stevens to author, March 23, 2010). The White House and USIA had already incurred criticism for their creation of documentary film about Jackie Kennedy's trips to India and Pakistan. See Nicholas J. Cull, "Projecting Jackie: Kennedy administration film propaganda overseas in Leo Seltzer's *Invitation to India, Invitation to Pakistan* and *Jacqueline Kennedy's Asian Journey* (1962)," in Bertrand Taithe and Tim Thornton (eds.), *Propaganda: Political Rhetoric and Identity, 1300–2000* (Stroud, Gloucestershire: Sutton 1999): 307–26.

70. "On location with *PT 109*," *Newsweek* (July 23, 1962): 72; "*PT 109*: The Man JFK Picked to Play His Wartime Role," *Look Magazine* (June 18, 1963): 50.

71. Trilling to Milestone, July 12, 1962, folder 78, *PT 109* production, LMP; Bowers to Harry Mayer (NY office) June 26, 1962, box 27, *PT 109* file 1, JLWC.

72. Studio publicity, September 10, 1962, box 2179, file *PT 109* story (1 of 2), WBA; Maguire wrote to Kennedy expressing concern over distortions and "over dramatization," see Maguire to President Kennedy, September 28, 1962, box 722, PP 13–11 (general), JFKL, WHCSF.

73. Reg Evans to Donovan, August 1, 1962, box 2179, file *PT 109* story (1 of 2), WBA.

74. Obringer to Foy, July 10, 1962, box 27, file *PT 109* file 1, JLWC.

75. *PT 109* script, folder 76, LMP, contains pages of the script of June 15, 1962 with excisions by Milestone.

76. Warner to Milestone, June 26, 1962, President's appointment diary, JFKL; *PT 109* production, folder 78, LMP; Connie Martinson to author, February 26, 2010, noted allegations that Milestone was drinking, and reported learning later after the fact that Bryan Foy had bugged cast and crew phones during the location work.

77. Warner to Milestone, July 6, 1962, *PT 109* production, folder 78, LMP. Driskill worked on the film for the next month, primarily revising the marine evacuation scenes. For materials, see *PT 109* revisions July 11, 1962 to August 16, 1962, box 2180, WBA.

78. Warner to Milestone, July 11, 1962, folder 78, LMP, also filed box 27, *PT 109*, file 1, at JLWC.

79. Milestone to Warner, July 14, 1962, folder 78, LMP.

80. Milestone to Warner, July 15, 1962, folder 78, LMP.

81. "On Location with *PT-109*," *Newsweek* (July 23, 1962): 72.

82. First mention of the new director, Warner to Ashton, July 20, 1962, box 27, *PT 109* file 1, JLWC.

83. William Tucker, "Director Fired: Feud Rocks *PT 109*," *Miami News* (July 22, 1962): 1; "Martinson Replaces Lewis Milestone as *PT 109* Director," *Hollywood Reporter* (July 23, 1962): 1; "Milestone Charges Poor *PT 109* Script," *New York Times* (July 24, 1962): 17; *Hollywood Reporter* (July 24, 1962): 1. Milestone's rebuttal of July 23, folder 79, LMP. Ten news outlets received it and he called six movie journalists to explain.

84. Folder 78, *PT 109* production, LMP; card includes 85 cast and crew signatures and 45 from navy personnel.

85. Connie Martinson to author, February 26, 2010.

86. Ashton to Latham, July 24, 26 and 31, 1962, box 695, file *PT 109*, WBA.

87. Ashton to Latham, July 31, 1962, box 695, file *PT 109*, WBA.

88. Lawford to Salinger, n.d., filed August 11, 1962, box 722, PP13–11 (general), JFKL WHCSF.

89. Robertson to Foy, box 27, *PT 109*, file 1, JLWC.

90. Lawrence Suid, *Sailing on the Silver Screen: Hollywood and the US Navy* (Annapolis, MD: Naval Institute Press, 1996): 155.

91. Gibson to RADM John McCain (CHINFOS), August 8 and 16, 1962 and file 2, Gibson to McCain, September 11, 1962, box 27, *PT 109*, file 1, JLWC.

92. Connie Martinson to author, February 26, 2010.

93. Revisions, August 19, 1962 to September 5, 1962, box 2180, file *PT 109*, WBA.

94. Trilling to Charles Greenlaw, September 5, 1962, box 27, *PT 109*, file 1, JLWC.

95. Gibson to McCain, September 11 and 15, 1962, box 27, *PT 109*, file 2, JLWC.

96. Max Bercutt to Martinson, September 14, 1962, file 695, file *PT 109*, WBA.

97. Press releases, September 25 and 26, 1962, file 630, file *PT 109*, WBA.

98. Gibson to McCain, final report, October 22, 1962, box 27, *PT 109* file 2, JLWC.

99. "*PT 109*: The Man JFK Picked to Play His Wartime Role," *Look Magazine* (June 18, 1963): 50.

100. Note from Lewis D. Gallo, November 15, 1962, folder 78, *PT 109* production, LMP; Warner Bros. to Milestone, January 6, 1965, folder 77, *PT 109* production, LMP.

101. Trilling to Foy, December 4, 1962, box 27, file 1, *PT 109*, JLWC.

102. Harlee to Salinger, February 4, 1962 and annotated transcript of stateroom scene (received February 4, 1962), box 277, PP 13–11 (general).

103. Donovan to President, May 22, 1963, POF personal secretary's files, *PT 109* correspondence, JFKL.

104. Jack Warner, personal scrapbook, box 27, *PT 109*, JLWC.

105. Trailer, Warner Bros Classics video edition of *PT 109* (rel. 1997); Connie Martinson to author, February 26, 2010. Martinson and his wife paid for their own tickets for the Los Angeles gala premiere.

106. Salinger to President, July 8, 1963, name file: Warner Bros., JFKL, WHCSF.

107. Warner (1962): 327. This lunch is not recorded in the White House diary.

108. Parker: 90; Amburn: 47, *The Sexiest Man Alive*: 47.

109. *Variety* review of *PT 109* (March 14, 1963).

110. Bosley Crowther, "*PT 109*," *New York Times* (June 27, 1963).

111. The premiere was the cover story of Britain's *Kine Weekly*, July 25, 1963, featuring a cover portrait of Warner in front of crossed UK and US flags.

112. "Movie critics bomb *PT 109* in London," *Los Angeles Times* (July 27, 1963): B7.

113. Warner: 327.

114. Name file, Warner, Jack, various, JFKL WHCSF.

115. "JFK's Naval Heroics Film Withdrawn," *Weekly Variety* (December 4, 1963).

116. "Warner to Reissue Film about Kennedy," *New York Times*, February 19, 1964; "*PT 109* draws Rhodesians," *New York Times*, September 5, 1964.

117. Warner Bros.'s comparison of negative cost and gross income, release number 266, *PT 109*, William Schaefer Collection, USC.

118. "Mother sues *PT 109* (books and film) for affront to late son," *Variety*, August 19, 1964. The legal papers are located WBA Legal Papers, file 12543A, *Sarah Albert v. Warner Bros. Pictures, Inc. et al.* (*PT 109*), pleadings and correspondence, especially Knecht to Levinson, December 7, 1966 (with note about *Bonnie and Clyde*) and Smith Warder to Kenneth Kulzick, May 8, 1967 with details of proposed settlement.

119. Hedda Hopper, "Robertson Breaks Career Impasse: Kennedy Role Brings Actor New Contract at Columbia," *Los Angeles Times* (May 1, 1962): C10.

120. See Morrie Ryskind, "Kennedy Movie: Question of Taste," *Los Angeles Times* (February 27, 1963): A5, who evokes the cult of personality around Stalin.

9

The Long Road of Women's Memory: Fred Zinnemann's *Julia*

J.E. Smyth

In a corner of one of his pages of film notes on *Julia*, Fred Zinnemann wrote, "I am in a totally false position," and then circled it for emphasis. Part of a tapestry of sketches for camera set-ups, script jottings, commentary, and phone numbers written in several varieties of his handwriting, it is initially very difficult to see the small note. There are hundreds of pages of the director's production notes in his archive. But as with all of Zinnemann's films, every detail counts. When Zinnemann signed to direct *Julia*, he had already made two other films about the history of the European resistance to fascism (*The Seventh Cross*, 1944; *Behold a Pale Horse*, 1964), and six others about the Second World War and its aftermath (*The Search*, 1948; *The Men*, 1950; *Teresa*, 1951; *From Here to Eternity*, 1953; *The Nun's Story*, 1959; *The Day of the Jackal*, 1973). *Julia*'s 1930s Resistance context was perfect Zinnemann material, and was destined to become one of Hollywood's most complex and powerful historical films about women. He had one problem, however: Lillian Hellman. Although adapting Hellman's "memoirs" posed significant difficulties for the film as a traditional Hollywood biopic, Zinnemann's discomfort, articulated in his production notes, enabled him to explore the very real struggle for historical legitimacy plaguing women's history in film. Though less studied than masculine biopics, Westerns, and period gangster films, Hollywood's historical films about women explore issues in adaptation, narration, editing, and agency as complex as their male counterparts. Yet, despite its strong connections with these studio-era films, ironically *Julia*'s deepest links are with the great "revisionist" men's biopic, *Citizen Kane* (1941). But while *Citizen Kane* addressed the entrenched tradition of "Great Man" biopics and a historiography founded upon objectivity, careful chronology, and public heroism, Fred Zinnemann's adaptation of *Julia* represented a complete and timely redefinition of the content and form of women's history on screen.

Pentimento

Despite starring two of world cinema's most prominent and politically engaged actresses—Vanessa Redgrave and Jane Fonda—*Julia's* biggest star was arguably its subject, left-wing playwright and screenwriter, Lillian Hellman. Cold War revisionism had transformed the formerly blacklisted screenwriter's public reputation and, by the 1970s, Hellman had made a new career as a memoirist. Her perspectives on women's liberation in the 1920s, golden-age Hollywood, liberalism, and the anti-communist witch-hunts were constructed as critical correctives of the traditional historiography, and did not go unchallenged by her contemporaries and colleagues.[1] But it was her story of childhood friend "Julia" which raised the most public controversy.

In *Pentimento* (1973), Hellman remembers her childhood best friend as a heroic maverick. Born to wealth and privilege, Julia spurns her family, attends Oxford and later medical school in Vienna, and becomes a committed socialist and anti-fascist leader. Though the two women's lives diverge, they keep in touch largely through letters. But while on a trip to Europe in the mid-1930s, Julia asks Hellman to bring some money across the German border for her anti-Nazi organization. Hellman, though terrified, agrees, and the friends meet once more before Julia's murder at the hands of the Gestapo some months later in Frankfurt. Hellman's memory of Julia comprised only one of several stories in *Pentimento*, but critics would focus on it almost to the exclusion of the other stories. Some even argued that she invented the courageous, anti-Nazi heroine and her connection with Hellman.[2] At present, all evidence strongly suggests that Hellman did invent the friendship, but she patterned "Julia" after the lives of several real women. Dr. Muriel Gardiner, the only known American to work in the Austrian underground during the 1930s, was the primary historical basis for Hellman's heroine, although one-legged American master spy Virginia Hall was doubtless another source. Alliance chief and divorced mother of two Marie Madeleine Fourcade had Julia's fabled Hollywood looks and durability; she also made train journeys through occupied territory wearing a hat stuffed with Resistance money.[3] Hellman would "adapt" all of their stories to suit her own ends.

Questions about Hellman's veracity, Julia's identity, women's history, and memory would become more complex with the release of Fred Zinnemann's film in late 1977. The director knew there were expectations for any historical or biographical film and that, for a number of reasons, *Julia* could not be a heroic biopic along the lines of his acclaimed *A Man For All Seasons* (1966) or even his other major biographical film, *The Nun's Story* (1959). Zinnemann wrote that on one level, he was anxious to avoid making *Julia* seem "slick or manicured or polished" because it was based on one woman's shifting memories of another woman.[4] But he was well aware of the problems with Hellman's veracity. In a 1996 interview for *Cineaste*, the director commented, "*Julia* . . . was not true. Lillian Hellman . . . would portray herself in situations which were not true . . . [S]he was a phony character, I'm sorry to say. My relations with her were very guarded and ended in pure hatred."[5] Undoubtedly, with Zinnemann's name attached to Hellman's, the story acquired a public patina of historical truth. The worldwide success of *A Man For All Seasons* had made Zinnemann the twentieth-century Hollywood equivalent of its hero, Sir Thomas More. Quite simply, if you worked for an organization that could market your integrity without damaging it, then you had to be Fred Zinnemann.

It is perhaps too easy to become absorbed by questions of fiction, history, and film, and whether Hellman lied about Julia. But Zinnemann was understandably worried about what would happen if the filmmaker most associated with truth and objective vision in Hollywood productions were adapting a historical film based on a false premise and constructed by a former Hollywood screenwriter. Even more importantly, so many of Hollywood's historical films about women had been undermined by a false romanticism and soft focus on historical truths. These films are often tied to a legacy of historical fiction which has both enabled women to appear as active, even transgressive protagonists (*Cimarron*, 1931; *Gone with the Wind*, 1939; *Duel in the Sun*, 1946), while paradoxically trapping the films as inaccurate Hollywood kitsch, masscult romanticism, and "women's" history. It was equally crucial for a film about the Resistance to avoid this type of criticism. Historical relativism and creative license had damaging historiographic consequences for a movement which defined itself in opposition to fascism, the mass falsification and destruction of documents, racial propaganda, and Holocaust denial.[6] Films are repeatedly criticized for their failure to adhere to the standards of textual accuracy, but what happens when the text itself is corrupt? In *Julia's* case it is particularly important to recognize the consequences of Hellman's construction of history because her memoir, and especially the film, memorialize a great woman, a Resistance leader, and do so through the legitimization of oral history—a mode crucial for much of women's historiography and certainly to that of the Resistance.[7]

Upon its release and before the controversy over Julia's identity attracted widespread press attention, *Julia* represented a unique view of America in the 1930s, a historic friendship between two women, and a self-conscious cinematic effort to rescue a truly heroic woman from historical obscurity. Despite a recent surge of women's films in Hollywood's advertized "Year of the Woman" (*Annie Hall, An Unmarried Woman, Three Women*, all 1977), the film was a major gamble for Twentieth Century-Fox. As Jane Fonda (Lillian) commented during production, "'The old female roles have been done away with, but the financiers of movies—those men who run the multi-national corporations—can't figure out which new female stereotypes are bankable.'"[8] Although historical women were an important part of Hollywood filmmaking from the silent era onwards, neither of *Julia's* two main female characters was a traditional biographical film subject. Julia and Lillian are both articulate, educated, politically empowered, confident women, without any conventional romantic dependencies.

Historical Fictions and the Voice of Women's History

However, *Julia* entwines many of the themes from studio-era Hollywood's historical women's pictures and, in fact, self-consciously links itself to the classical period in which Hellman and Zinnemann worked. Many critics, regardless of whether they endorsed the film, viewed *Julia* as a throwback to studio-era filmmaking. Some highlighted the film's ties to the 1940s women's genre; others noted the obvious connection with studio-era filmmakers Hellman and Zinnemann; and others identified the lavish sets and period polish with old Hollywood glamor.[9]

For Jane Fonda, *Julia* represented a return to the studio which made her father, Henry Fonda, a star. During the latter half of the 1930s, he became one of Hollywood's most popular and critically respected stars, largely through performing in American historical productions under studio head Darryl F. Zanuck (*The Farmer Takes a Wife*, 1935; *Way Down East*, 1935; *Jesse James*, 1939; *The Story of Alexander Graham Bell*, 1939; *Drums Along the Mohawk*, 1939; *Young Mr. Lincoln*, 1939). While her father had made traditional American heroes such as Abraham Lincoln human and reassuringly flawed, in making *Julia*, Jane Fonda was both historicizing her father's era and creating a new generation of twentieth-century American screen heroines. But *Julia's* protagonists and film style differed fundamentally from traditional Hollywood historical epics which, even by the early 1970s, still lionized individualism and courageous public lives in a chronological and progressively-styled format (*Patton*, 1970; *Dillinger*, 1973; *Serpico*, 1973).

Julia's opening image of a grainy black-and-white Twentieth Century-Fox logo made a direct link between its narrative and studio-era Hollywood. But the logo is not accompanied by the famous trumpet fanfare; instead, a single drum beats as the credits begin. Jane Fonda's voiceover as Lillian begins the film with Hellman's original introduction to *Pentimento*: "Old paint on canvas, as it ages, sometimes becomes transparent. When that happens it is possible, in some pictures, to see the original lines: a tree will show through a woman's dress, a child makes way for a dog, a boat is no longer in an open sea. That is called pentimento, because the painter 'repented,' changed his mind."[10] Besides affirming its faithful adaptation of Hellman's memoirs and introducing the narrative's underlying conflict between the accuracy of history and the creative work of the writer, *Julia*'s opening foreword recalls the tradition in studio-era history films of introducing the narrative with either a text foreword or a voiceover. While forewords often established a conventional historical period, they were also capable of highlighting a historical controversy or question (*Young Mr. Lincoln*, 1939; *Citizen Kane*, 1941) or underscoring the film's project to rescue an event or person from obscurity or infamy (*The Prisoner of Shark Island*, 1936; *Blossoms in the Dust*, 1941; *Spartacus*, 1960; *Bonnie and Clyde*, 1967; *The Day of the Jackal*, 1973).[11]

Fred Zinnemann had made several films featuring female protagonists, three of them with extensive subjective narration and use of voiceovers—and based in the period immediately before, during, and after the Second World War. In *The Search* (1948), Mrs. Stevens (Aline MacMahon), the UNRRA director of postwar "unaccompanied" children's services, tells much of the story of a lost child survivor of Auschwitz (Ivan Jandl). In 1953, Zinnemann's *From Here to Eternity* gave army wife Karen Holmes and prostitute Lorene the time to tell their own unique stories in a narrative about the pre-Pearl Harbor armed forces, and verbalized the gender and class inequities rife within American society. A few years later, *The Nun's Story* narrated the experiences of Belgian nun Gabriel van der Mal (Audrey Hepburn) as she failed to reconcile her own need to defend her country from the Nazis with the Catholic Church's tolerance of Hitler. Very often, Zinnemann's work recuperates the historical importance of a woman through the power of the voice, creating an authentic "oral history" for relatively unknown women.

Julia's foreword is not an impersonal third-person narration by an unnamed journalist or historian, as in *Citizen Kane*; it is personal and, most importantly, it is a woman's voice. It introduces not only the film's central questions about authorship and memory, but of history and women's role in writing it. Most importantly, Hellman's voiceover doesn't merely introduce the film like a perfunctory historical gloss; it is sustained throughout the narrative. Classical Hollywood cinema has long been criticized for its inability to invest female characters with visual agency and power. Over the past forty years, psychoanalytic and feminist film studies have explored the range of Hollywood's male gaze and its punishment, both through narrative and visual means, of the transgressive woman.[12] Yet, in foregrounding the work of directors Alfred Hitchcock and Douglas Sirk, scholars have often ignored the preponderance of women's historical films in the studio era, and the degree to which these female protagonists articulated a memorable and often critical voice. In mainstream historiography, the link between women's history and oral history is clear.[13]

A fair share of research has already uncovered the importance of women's historical fiction to prestigious Hollywood productions, and David O. Selznick's adaptation of Margaret Mitchell's *Gone with the Wind* (1939) remains one of the most powerful historical explorations of female subjectivity in American cinema. *Gone with the Wind* and other prominent women's historical films of the studio era underscore the paradox of women's cinematic history: while the female protagonists dominate the narratives, motivate camera movement, and change major currents in history, very often they are based on works of fiction (*Cimarron*, 1931; *Ramona*, 1936; *Jezebel*, 1938; *Duel in the Sun*, 1946; *Maverick Queen*, 1956; *Soldier Blue*, 1971). Adaptations of historical novels (including *Gone with the Wind*) often focused on "fictional" characters who, nonetheless, represented key but comparatively voiceless groups and minorities sidelined by traditional historiography (*A Tree Grows in Brooklyn*, 1945; *Saratoga Trunk*, 1945; *Duel in the Sun*, 1946; *Pinky*, 1949; *Giant*, 1956).[14] Historical fiction's formal deviations from the chronologies and public achievements upholding traditional biography and history enabled Hollywood filmmakers to reshape the social content and critique of historical filmmaking.

But, all too often, Hollywood films with "historical" female protagonists such as Norma Desmond (*Sunset Boulevard*, 1950), Calamity Jane (*Calamity Jane*, 1953), Annie Oakley (*Annie Get Your Gun*, 1950), Ruth Etting (*Love Me or Leave Me*, 1955); and Jeanne Eagels (*Jeanne Eagels*, 1957), were either narrated and controlled by male characters or structured within a traditional omniscient use of intertitles. Films about Hollywood women are particularly revealing of the boundaries of female subjectivity and narrative power. In these films in which

Hollywood historicized itself, women often appear as paranoid or abused actresses (Desmond, Etting, Eagels) or as powerless secretaries. There are no film histories about women such as writers Frances Marion, Anita Loos, or Lillian Hellman, filmmakers who authored their own and other people's stories. Even films such as *A Tree Grows in Brooklyn* and *Giant*, adapted from historical literature which featured the female protagonist as narrator, tended to remove or edit women's voices.[15] But a handful of major Hollywood films—among them Dalton Trumbo and Sam Wood's *Kitty Foyle* (1940), *So Proudly We Hail* (1943), George Stevens's *I Remember Mama* (1948), Darryl Zanuck's productions, *Cheaper by the Dozen* (1949), *Belles on Their Toes* (1950), *A Letter to Three Wives* (1949), and *All About Eve* (1950), and the adaptation of Harper Lee's *To Kill a Mockingbird* (1962)—employ the woman's voice as a structuring historical device throughout the film. Zinnemann's construction of Lillian Hellman's voiceover in *Julia* would connect the divisions between women's fiction, history, and memory while paradoxically fracturing both traditional historical film structures and critical expectations for the historical film.

Julia and Charlie

Though it is easy enough to trace *Julia*'s lineage back through Zinnemann's work and the voices of women in other adapted historical fictions, *Julia*'s closest antecedent is the biopic *Citizen Kane*.[16] Both films share unconventional narrative structures which probe the limits of historical knowledge and create complex interplays of sound and memory. Both productions were affected by public controversies over the protagonists' identities. Fred Zinnemann shared many of Orson Welles and Herman Mankiewicz's problems with negotiating the historical details of *Citizen Kane*—but with one key difference. William Randolph Hearst and his associates were unhappy with the amount of historical and biographical material in the "fictional" tale of Charles Foster Kane,[17] while records reveal Hellman wanted more historical detail attached to her fictional memoir. Hellman looked at early versions of Alvin Sargent and Zinnemann's scripts and knew that it was not going to be the type of biopic popular during her tenure as a screenwriter for Samuel Goldwyn. As she complained to Zinnemann: "There are times when I had trouble understanding what period it was and why. But O.K. if it seems clear to other people who have not read the story. *But this is not a work of fiction and certain laws have to be followed for that reason.*"[18] Already Hellman sensed that Zinnemann was not following traditional rules.

Both films make use of non-chronological narration to deconstruct ideas about historical continuity and certainty. *Citizen Kane*'s multiple character flashbacks complement *Julia*'s female narrator. Thompson's search for "Rosebud" resembles Lillian's search for traces of Julia's life in an increasingly fascist political climate in Europe and America. While *Citizen Kane*'s historical space returns briefly to the mythic West as a site of historical certainty before Kane's gradual moral disintegration, Hellman has her own mythic spaces with Julia—childhood sleepovers in Julia's Fifth Avenue mansion, camping trips in the mountains, Oxford. But while *Citizen Kane* reworked and critiqued a tradition of men's biopics known from the silent era and especially popular in the 1930s,[19] *Julia* was built upon a much more ambiguous historical presence of women in Hollywood. Newspaper documents avidly depict the life and death of media mogul and "shaper" of public history Charles Foster Kane, but Julia avoids documentation. Zinnemann never even inserts shots of her letters to Lillian. And though both Julia and Charles Foster Kane belong to the establishment, Julia revolts against everything that Kane stands for in the 1930s.

As Hellman's older voice articulates the changing nature of memory and intention, Zinnemann shoots her in long shot in a dory, her back to the camera. Only Hellman's outline shows in the shadowy shot. She may be the author of this unusual dual biography but, from the outset, the filmmakers project her own self-reflective distance from her narrative.[20] Voice and image are separated (i.e. we do not see Hellman speaking the foreword or even see her face). Sound cues drift across images; the cry of a gull is echoed by the menacing scream of a train engine at night. Again, Hellman's voice returns, "I am old now, and I want to remember what was there for me once, and what is there for me now." We see her eyes, but not her lips (Illustration 9.1). This disjunction between word and image, history and myth, oral history and visual history, is something that *Citizen Kane* explores in a more elaborate juxtaposition between the journalistic bombast of the *News on the March* narrator and the relative silence of Kane. But while Kane's biopic relies on the contrast between reportage of his public life and private memories, *Julia* explores the memory of a life in the absence of traditional textual documentation. Indeed, one might argue that this is Zinnemann's very point: Lillian is the hollow celebrity, the well-known woman, the writer, and the embodiment of historical distortion; Julia, the other side of the "great woman," is not known to contemporary history, or only imperfectly. She keeps no written historical records. She is one of the "army of shadows," as Alliance chief Marie Madeleine Fourcade once put it, "that army . . . who

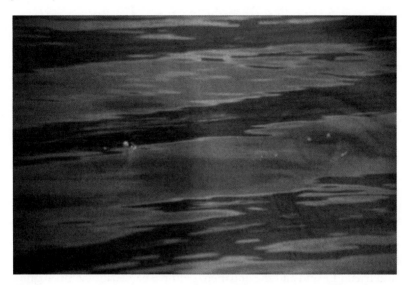

Illustration 9.1 Separation of word and image: Lillian Hellman (Jane Fonda) in *Julia*
© Twentieth Century-Fox

shifted and succeeded one another and changed places like images in
a film, fading and being replaced by others to ensure continuity."[21]
    Alvin Sargent and Zinnemann's script makes extensive use of
Hellman's non-chronological, fragmentary sequences in *Pentimento.*
However, while Hellman's narrative contains one large flashback narrat-
ing the outline of Julia's life in chronological order (roughly 1905–36),
from the outset, Sargent and Zinnemann splintered Hellman's memories and the chronology, creating a complex interplay between Hellman's
life in the 1930s and her memories of Julia.[22] This choice replicates
Herman Mankiewicz and Orson Welles's decision to insert multiple
and contradictory flashbacks of Kane throughout the contemporary
hunt for "Rosebud."[23] Hellman's creative life in 1934, when she was in
the midst of constructing *The Children's Hour*, triggers memories of her
childhood and young adulthood with Julia in New York. Zinnemann
pushed Hellman's attitudes toward the past still further, accentuating the
narrative's refusal to follow a traditional, chronological format in which
image and sound work in sync to support and authenticate the truth
of the recorded events. The form of traditional masculine biography
and biopics would not work for the content of women's history, so
Zinnemann simply shattered it.
    Like *Citizen Kane's* exploration of heroism and relativism, *Julia's*
non-chronological format becomes a kind of historical choice, and the

film foregrounds the editing of memories—central to the historical process, women's history, and narrative filmmaking—more than any other major feature film of its period. Often, Zinnemann drags sound cues from the past into Hellman's workaday life in 1934. As Bernard Dick comments, this recalls Welles's sequence in which Thatcher's cold Christmas greeting to young Charlie Kane ("Merry Christmas, Charles") bridges the next sequence in which Thatcher dictates a letter to his college-age charge ("And a Happy New Year").[24] However, while *Citizen Kane*'s sound bridge serves little historiographic purpose beyond affirming Charlie's cold upbringing, Zinnemann's sound bridges articulate the ways in which history and memory are in constant dialog with the present. Hellman's voiceover in old age comments on sequences from the 1930s, yet historical clarity is rarely given to these earlier sequences.

While Gregg Toland's famous long shots, deep-focus photography, and use of shadow often represent Kane's isolation from wife Susan and friend Leland and the anti-hero's elusive personality, Zinnemann's camera is often deliberately placed too close to his protagonists. This distances Hellman and Hammett (Jason Robards) in their shot-reverse shots while establishing a need for closeness to Julia—a closeness which paradoxically separates Hellman and Julia in the frame. Zinnemann heightens Hellman's resentment of Hammett's literary reputation and dictatorial attitudes by rarely shooting them in a two-shot. Instead, he follows a distinct shot-reverse shot format, both long and close-up, which accentuates their personal separateness. Even when Hammett finally approves the second draft, calling it "the best thing that's been written in a long time," Zinnemann refuses to unite them in a single shot. Wooden spars and piling separate them (Illustration 9.2).

This sequence is in stark contrast to the fireside chats she had with Julia at the latter's Park Avenue mansion. In two sequences, one when they are teenagers and the other several years later, a fire warms their room as they create a chain story. Zinnemann shoots them both in close two-shots. Even when Lillian (Susan Jones) cannot understand a French quotation of Julia's (Lisa Pelikan), Zinnemann keeps them together (Illustration 9.3). There is love, companionship, and a shared creative power between these two young women. The older Lillian comments on these sequences: "I think I have always known about my memory . . . But I trust absolutely what I remember about Julia" and, later, "I cannot say now that I had ever used the words gentle or strong or delicate, but I did think that night that it was the most beautiful face I had ever seen." While editor Walter Murch believed the film replicated Zinnemann's attitude toward Julia and Hellman's material

Illustration 9.2 Divided in the frame: Lillian with Hammett (Jason Robards) in *Julia* (1977)
© Twentieth Century-Fox

Illustration 9.3 Together in the frame: young Lillian (Susan Jones) with young Julia (Lisa Pelikan) in *Julia* © Twentieth Century-Fox

("The narration here challenges the audience to find Vanessa [Julia] to be perfect, which I think may be an impossible goal"), Zinnemann was quick to correct him.[25] The director's visualization of Julia via Lillian's narration is ironic. That face is seen through a nostalgic haze. Cinematographer Douglas Slocombe used special filters on his lenses when shooting the two young girls and later Fonda and Redgrave precisely because he wanted to emphasize Hellman's nostalgia—even historical fantasy. While Lillian's scenes with Hammett have a cold clarity, the shots of Lillian and Julia together are misty, glowing, and even blurred.

Zinnemann's close shots of Julia reveal his and Hellman's need to establish her historical presence. And as much as *The Children's Hour* and her years with Hammett are matters of recorded literary history, for Hellman, it is Julia's memory which allegedly gives Hellman the confidence to remember the past with personal accuracy and commitment. Hellman's memories of Julia at Oxford accentuate the latter's connection to the past, but it is a past which Zinnemann deliberately over-frames. The director chose to shoot Redgrave framed in a succession of Oxford doorways, and as she approaches, her perfect beauty and grace and power seem to rival the architecture. She walks closer and closer to the waiting camera, which remains stationary even when Redgrave's luminous eyes threaten to swallow up the screen (Illustration 9.4).[26] In this sequence, Zinnemann argued that the camera was replicating Hellman's perspective and "It is Lillian who remembers Julia as being perfect."[27] But as she pauses in the final doorway, Zinnemann's slow dissolve makes her "framed" image look like a superimposed photograph in the Oxford landscape, giving the sequence a constructed look, like a photograph superimposed on another photograph. When Julia later attacks fascism for the first time in the February 1934 riots, Zinnemann replicates the shot of the over-framed colonnade, replacing the process of prewar nostalgia with that of anti-fascist heroism. Was this another of Zinnemann's knowing constructions of Resistance history?

Through many of these memories, Zinnemann struggles, like Lillian, to keep the two women together in one frame. The camera moves only to keep the pair in a two-shot aboard the boat that will take Julia to Britain and Oxford. Later, as Lillian tells of her gradual understanding about Julia's warnings about fascism, the camera pulls into a crane shot, following the two as they cross the quad to Julia's rooms. Yet, paradoxically, we cannot hear what Julia says and what Lillian says she now understands. There isn't even an illusion of historical unity between evidence and interpretation. Hellman's "historical" voice has

Illustration 9.4   An overdetermined and overframed image of beauty: Vanessa Redgrave as Julia in *Julia* © Twentieth Century-Fox

obliterated Julia's original voice.

Zinnemann also highlights the problem of historical translation as one of the film's key themes. Lillian cannot comprehend Julia's dislike of Cairo and her wealthy family's refusal to help the poor, and later Julia's enthusiasm for Vienna's Floridsdorf district in the 1920s. Hellman also reveals that she cannot understand the threat of Hitler, despite Julia's early warnings. When she visits Julia in a Vienna hospital, Julia tries to communicate silently with her hands that Lillian must go and seek someone; Lillian replies despondently, "I don't know what you mean." Zinnemann follows this scene with a silent shot of the two sailing in upstate New York. Again, we cannot hear their words. When Hellman returns to consciousness, Julia has disappeared. A note related in voiceover makes nothing clearer to Lillian. As Hellman wrote in *Pentimento*, Julia's note included the phrase, "Something else is needed," something she realized only later related to their school days when they were translating Latin and missed a word.[28] Hellman's efforts to piece together her memories with Julia and bring order and sense to them are the struggles of a playwright and memoirist translating experience into history. For history itself is an imperfect effort at making the past live again, an effort which involves tricky editing and attempts at authenticity. Nothing is perfect in this narrative—or polished. It, like Hellman's *Children's Hour*, is mostly a work in progress. The film's refusal to go in chronological order, to separate time and space into distinct sequences, to invest the narrator with omniscience, are all choices which break down traditional boundaries between history, fiction, and memoir. Arguably, Welles and Mankiewicz did this for Charles Foster Kane/William Randolph Hearst in 1941. Yet, the stakes are arguably higher for revisionist women's history on screen—narratives of methodological resistance to traditional (masculine) biopics. Zinnemann went still further, casting his film loose from the corrupted text of Hellman's "biographical" Resistance tale, blurring his focus, muting dialog, separating sound and image. Late in the film the Gestapo's attack on Julia and her death are juxtaposed with Lillian's bored response to a Moscow performance of *Hamlet*. As the assassin drives the knife through Julia's body, applause erupts, waking a sleepy Hellman. For Zinnemann, Hellman's Julia, her heroic life and death, and "History" itself are staged events like *Hamlet* or *The Children's Hour*.

A Casualty of Relativism?

While audiences and many small-time reviewers loved *Julia*, major film critics Vincent Canby, Andrew Sarris, Pauline Kael, and Molly Haskell disliked it.[29] Popular auteurism, championed by Sarris since the late 1960s, had always snubbed Zinnemann's work. But Sarris also loathed Hellman and what he perceived to be the recent Hollywood project to heroize her; Haskell and Kael resented Hellman and the film's canonization of Julia. Though the revelations about Hellman's historical inventions were in the future, Canby complained that the film was "an illusive narrative fragment in desperate need of further amplification," and poked fun at the "conventional" soft-focus flashbacks of Julia, little realizing that, according to Zinnemann, the camera was replicating Hellman's perspective and "It is Lillian who remembers Julia as being perfect."[30] Even more than Canby and Sarris, Haskell and Kael resented Hellman's simplistic and often fragmented memories. Haskell wrote, "Who can believe in the idealized portrait of a Madonna of the Left that Hellman paints?" Kael, a long-time defendant of *Citizen Kane*'s screenwriter, Herman Mankiewicz, and the film's status as a Hollywood biopic, almost perversely ignored *Julia*'s script innovations and meditations on women's history and memory. Haskell—whose much-quoted *From Reverence to Rape* (1977) lambasted Hollywood's alleged stereotyped portrayal of women (in the days before feminist film criticism transformed the study of Hollywood cinema)—also resisted the film's obvious appeal as a prestige film about two American women and the way important women have been lost to the historical record. For some, *Julia* would be an abstruse fragment; a frustrating enigma which fell short of being the standard impressive historical epics *A Man For All Seasons* and *Lawrence of Arabia* (1962), and lacked the complexity and critical accolades of *Citizen Kane*. For others, its portrait of female heroism was too impressive to be credible. To a certain extent, this was true: Hellman, who had made a career of not naming names, was eventually discredited by her former public virtue in refusing to identify Julia. But had Hellman written truthfully about American heroines Muriel Gardiner and Virginia Hall or about Marie Madeleine Fourcade, would Twentieth Century-Fox have filmed the property as a major historical film? Would Gardiner, Hall, and Fourcade's lives have been "appropriate" and "believable" historical subjects for Haskell and Kael? Would the lives of truly heroic women always be too unbelievable for film critics?

In the early 1970s, several prominent feminist historians had written that traditional explorations of women's history which heroized the individual did so because they resembled men in their public achievements.[31] They argued, to paraphrase Julia, that something else was needed. The exploration of formerly unknown women needed a new content and a new form of historiography. Some, like historian Sherna Berger Gluck, argued that memory and oral history were the answer. As Gluck summarized: "Women's oral history, then, is a feminist encounter, even if the interviewee is not herself a feminist. It is the creation of a new type of material on women; it is the validation of women's experiences; it is the communication among women of different generations; it is the discovery of our own roots and the development of a continuity which has been denied us in traditional historical accounts."[32] In *The Long Road of Women's Memory* (1916), Jane Addams looks at the pasts of poor immigrant women and focuses on the impact a spurious tale has on prompting the revelation of women's stories which otherwise would have been lost to posterity. Regardless of accuracy, Addams believed, memory and oral testimony were key in both "interpreting and appeasing life for the individual, and . . . its activity as a selective agency for social reorganization."[33] Is *Julia* another such paradox—an invented historical text which soothed Hollywood with a sense of political self-righteousness and histori-cal worth while giving audiences a new content, form, and social meaning for women's historical cinema? Or in the end, will it, like Charlie Kane's Rosebud, be cast into the fire as another casualty of relativism?

Notes

1. Lillian Hellman, *Three: An Unfinished Woman, Pentimento, Scoundrel Time* (Boston: Little & Brown, 1979); Diana Trilling, *We Must March My Darlings: A Critical Decade* (New York: Harcourt Brace Jovanovich, 1977); Martha Gellhorn, "On Apocryphism," *Paris Review* 23(79) (spring, 1981): 280–301.

2. Carl Rollyson, *Lillian Hellman: Her Legend and Her Legacy* (New York: St. Martin's Press, 1988): 503–28. See also Justus Reid Weiner, "Lillian Hellman: The Fiction of Autobiography," *Gender Issues* 21(1) (2003): 78–83.

3. Muriel Gardiner, *Code-Name "Mary"* (New Haven: Yale University Press, 1980); Michael Davie, "The Life and Lies of Lillian Hellman," *The Observer* (October 26, 1986): 64; Margaret Rossiter, *Women in the Resistance* (New York: Praeger, 1986): 189–98; Marie Madeleine Fourcade, *L'Arche de Noé* (Paris: Fayard, 1968). See also transcribed interview with Professor Maria Jahoda collated by Tom Pevsner, May 19, 1976: 1–3, with notations by Fred Zinnemann, *Julia*, Research (Vienna), box 40, folder 525, Fred Zinnemann Papers, Academy of Motion Picture Arts and Sciences Library (hereafter AMPAS).

4. Fred Zinnemann to Douglas Slocombe, undated editing notes, box 40, folder 547, Zinnemann Papers, AMPAS.

5. Zinnemann with Brian Neve, "A Past Master of His Craft: An Interview with Fred Zinnemann," *Cineaste* 23(1) (1997): 15–19, 19.

6. Hayden White, "Historical Emplotment and the Problem of Truth," in Saul Friedlander (ed.), *Probing the Limits of Representations: Nazism and the "Final Solution"* (Cambridge: Harvard University Press, 1992): 37–53; Peter Novick, *That Noble Dream: The "Objectivity Question" and the American Historical Profession* (Cambridge: Cambridge University Press, 1988): 625–8.

7. H.R. Kedward, *In Search of the Maquis* (Oxford: Clarendon, 1993) and Margaret Collins Weitz, *Sisters in Resistance* (New York: Wiley, 1995).

8. Judith Weinraub, "Two Feisty Feminists Filming Hellman's *Pentimento*," *New York Times* (October 31, 1976) section 2: 17.

9. See Joe Baltake, "A Tale of Two Women," *New York Daily News* (October 12, 1977), AMPAS clipping file; Tom Dowling, "The Trouble with *Julia* is Lillian," *Washington Star* (October 12, 1977), section C, C5.

10. Sargent's original first draft script and all subsequent scripts begin with Hellman's voiceover. See box 34, folder 438, Zinnemann Papers, AMPAS.

11. For more discussion of the historical foreword, see Smyth, *Reconstructing American Historical Cinema from Cimarron to Citizen Kane* (Lexington: University Press of Kentucky, 2006): 1–3, 7, 36–9.

12. Laura Mulvey, "Visual Pleasure and Narrative Cinema," *Screen* 16(3) (1975): 6–18; Mulvey, "Afterthoughts on 'Visual Pleasure and Narrative Cinema,' Inspired by *Duel in the Sun*," *Framework* 15/16/17 (summer,

1981): 12–15; Molly Haskell, *From Reverence to Rape: The Treatment of Women in the Movies* (New York: Penguin, 1974); Mary Ann Doane, *The Desire to Desire* (Bloomington: Indiana University Press, 1987); Tania Modleski, *Women Who Knew Too Much: Hitchcock and Feminist Theory* (London: Routledge, 1988).

13. Weitz: 15. See also Paul Thompson, *Oral History: The Voice of the Past* (Oxford: Oxford University Press, 1978): 87–8.

14. For more on American historical fiction and the representation of racial minorities and women, see Smyth, *Edna Ferber's Hollywood* (Austin: University of Texas Press, 2009) and Camilla Fojas and Mary Beltran (eds.), *Mixed Race Hollywood* (New York: New York University Press, 2007).

15. For *A Tree Grows in Brooklyn*, see Tess Slesinger and Frank Davis, scripts October 7, 1943 through December 21, 1944, Twentieth Century-Fox scripts, FX-PRS-802 and FX-PRS-733, UCLA Arts Special Collections. For a discussion of the adaptation of *Giant*, Smyth (2009): 191–227.

16. *Julia* also resonates strongly with another key Welles film in its projection of a naïve American visiting a mysterious friend in the wilds of Vienna—*The Third Man* (1949), although this parallel arguably operates at a narrative level without impacting the film's construction and attitude toward history.

17. For more on the Hearst controversy and *Citizen Kane*, see Pauline Kael, *Raising Kane and Other Essays* (London: Marion Boyers, 1996): 159–266; Ronald Gottessman (ed.), *Perspectives on Citizen Kane* (New York: G.K. Hall, 1996); and Smyth: 317–35.

18. Hellman to Fred Zinnemann, undated, 4pp., *Julia*, box 38, folder 491, Zinnemann Papers, AMPAS.

19. Smyth (2006), especially ch. 11. See also Kael (1996); Morris Dickstein, "The Last Film of the 1930s: Nothing Fails Like Success," in *Perspectives on Citizen Kane*, Ronald Gottesman (ed.) (New York: G.K. Hall, 1996): 82–93; and Dennis Bingham, *Whose Lives Are They Anyway? The Biopic as Contemporary Film Genre* (New Brunswick, NJ: Rutgers University Press, 2010).

20. Bernard Dick, *Hellman in Hollywood* (East Brunswick, NJ: Associated University Presses, 1982): 140–5. For another view, see Stephen Prince, "'Do You Understand?': History and Memory in *Julia*," in Arthur Nolletti Jr. (ed.), *The Films of Fred Zinnemann: Critical Perspectives* (Albany: State University of New York Press, 1999): 187–97.

21. Fourcade: 8.

22. See first, revised, and final drafts of scripts, box 34, folder 437 through box 35, folder 445, Zinnemann Papers, AMPAS.

23. For more on the development of *Citizen Kane*'s scripts, see Robert L. Carringer, *The Making of Citizen Kane* (Berkeley: University of California Press, 1985).

24. Dick: 147.

25 Walter Murch, editing notes annotated by Zinnemann, undated 12pp, box 38, folder 487, Zinnemann Papers, AMPAS.

26. Sargent felt that this shot was "too obviously a gimmick" and wrote to Zinnemann asking it to be cut. Zinnemann ignored him (AMPAS); Alvin Sargent to Zinnemann, May 12, 1977, box 40, folder 528, Zinnemann Papers, AMPAS.

27. Zinnemann, handwritten notes to accompany editing notes, p. 3, box 38, folder 487, Zinnemann Papers, AMPAS.

28. Hellman: 427–8.

29. For previews, see box 39, folder 506, 507, Zinnemann Papers, AMPAS. See Vincent Canby, "Julia," New York Times (October 3, 1977); Andrew Sarris, "Good Intentions Are Not Enough," Village Voice (October 10, 1977); Molly Haskell, "Julia," New York Magazine (October 19, 1977); Pauline Kael, "Julia," The New Yorker (October 1977).

30. Zinnemann, handwritten notes to accompany editing notes, p. 3, box 38, folder 487, Zinnemann Papers, AMPAS.

31. Ann D. Gordon, Mari Jo Buhle, and Nancy E. Schrom, "Women in American Society: An Historical Contribution," Radical America 5(4) (July–August 1971): 3–66.

32. Sherna Berger Gluck, "What's So Special About Women? Women's Oral History," Frontiers: A Journal of Women's Studies 2(2) (summer, 1977): 3–17, 5. See also From Parlor to Prison: Five American Suffragettes Talk About Their Lives (New York: Vintage, 1976). John A. Neuenschwander's Oral History as a Teaching Approach was also published that year.

33. Jane Addams, The Long Road of Women's Memory (Urbana: University of Illinois Press, 2002): 5.

10

Inventing Historical Truth on the Silver Screen[1]

Robert Rosenstone

The problem is that we historians have it backwards. Or sideways. At the very least, seriously out of alignment. What I am talking about is the relationship between the historical film and written history. Particularly the dramatic historical film. And because we can't get it straight, nobody else can either. For the notions of what constitutes history held by the culture—and here I include film critics, reviewers for newspapers and magazines, politicians, pundits, TV talking heads, students of cinema studies, high school teachers, students, and the general public (at least as sampled in letters to the editor columns)— are entirely consonant with, and no doubt derive from, the assumptions underlying the college and university courses that we teach. And what we have been teaching is not so much wrong as, simply, a particular view of the past that insists on a certain kind of historical truth and tends to exclude others. We may pay lip service to the oral tradition, to good historical museums or especially noteworthy exhibits, even to the occasional film, usually a documentary. But we have little doubt that historical truth resides in a certain kind of empirically-based discourse, one that developed over the last two centuries, was drummed into us in graduate school, and is constantly reinforced by the norms of the profession.

What I mean by backwards, sideways, or out of alignment is this: for twenty-five years now, or ever since historians have begun to think and write about historical film, we have essentially been trying to make the dramatic feature fit into the conventions of traditional history, to force what we see into a mold created by and for written discourse. Such an approach ensures that history on film will come off as a largely debased and trivial way of representing the past. Those of us who have studied the topic (along with my own work, one

might include such historians as Pierre Sorlin, Natalie Davis, and
Robert Brent Toplin) and wished to make claims for the historical
film have too often found ourselves on the defensive, explaining away
the mistakes and inventions of filmmakers to skeptical colleagues,
journalists, and students. Here, I want to end that defensive posture by
suggesting a different way of looking at historical films. One based on
the notion that the historical film is already a way of doing history, *if
by the phrase "doing history" we mean seriously attempting to make meaning
of the past.* The visual form of historical thinking cannot be judged by
the criteria we apply to what is produced on the page, for it exists in
a separate realm—one which relates to, comments upon, and often
challenges the world of written history.

We must, in short, stop expecting films to do what (we imagine)
books do. Stop expecting them to get the facts right, or to present
several sides of an issue, or to give a fair hearing to all the evidence on a
topic, or to all the characters or groups represented in a historical situation,
or to provide a broad and detailed historical context for events. Stop,
also, expecting them to mirror a vanished reality that will show us the
past as it really was. Dramatic films are not, and will never be, "accurate"
in the same way as books (claim to be), no matter how many academic
consultants work on a project, and no matter how seriously their advice
is taken. Like written histories, films are not mirrors but constructions,
works whose rules of engagement with the traces of the past are
necessarily different from those of written history. How could they be
the same (and who would want them to be), since it is precisely the task
of film to add movement, color, sound, and drama to the past?

(Let me confess, as an aside, to being tired of hearing and dubious
about the kind of assertions that have been repeated in many essays, or
on panels at conferences and academic meetings over the last decade;
namely, that we will be able to take the historical film seriously when
more academics are advising filmmakers on projects, or when historians
pick up the camera and begin making their own films. Such may or
may not be a good idea, but one thing adding historians to production
teams will not do is to remove the problematics from the dramatic
historical film. Hosts of historians will not prevent such works from
essentially being works of fiction in which inventions of characters,
situations, and dialog will always play a major role.)

We have been conditioned to see History as something as solid and
weighty as the thick tomes of those national and world history textbooks
in which it too often gets buried. But it isn't. History is, rather, a genre
of writing, one with certain conventions and practices which have often
changed over the last two plus millennia (even if they have held fairly

steady for the last century or so) and will do so again. Historical film is
also a genre with conventions, but one which has had but a century in
which to develop. Both genres have as their goal the attempt to make
the past meaningful for us in the present. For the historian who works
in words, this means selecting certain traces of the past as important,
"constituting" those traces as "facts," and then making them part of a
larger historical picture and argument. For the filmmaker who must
create a past that fits within the demands, practices, and traditions of
both the visual media and the dramatic form, this means having to go
beyond "constituting" facts to inventing some of them.

This process of invention is not, as some might suggest, the weakness of the historical film but, in fact, a major part of its strength.
Drama, as Hitchcock famously said, is life with the boring parts left
out. This is certainly true of the historical feature. Without its many
inventions—the condensations which collapse several characters into
one, the displacements which move an event from one time frame
to another, the alterations which let one character express sentiments
that may have belonged to a different historical figure or to no one at
all, the invented dialogue that allows us to understand characters and
situations—the historical would be more sprawling and formless and
far less able to make us interested in the past. Even when based on
historical people, characters are essentially an invention—for, except in
the case of contemporaries, whose voices and body language we may
to some extent know, it is the actor who creates and gives meaning to a
historical figure through invented movements, gestures, and intonations.
Finally, the created intensity of dramatic situations, which compress
events or even ideas which happened over time into a narrow compass,
is yet another form of invention, one that allows the screen to bring us
history in the present tense, involve us through the unique, embodied
quality of the film experience in the proximate realities of events and
situations, and serve to move us emotionally and intellectually.

To say fiction, and particularly invention, are crucial to history on
the screen may seem counterintuitive (and is sure to anger some),
but it only expands upon a suggestion made by theorist Frank
Ankersmit—that the truths of historical discourse are not located
primarily in the individual details of a work, but in the arguments
and metaphors that allow us to think about and understand that past.[2]
Along with its powerful experiential quality, the feeling that while
viewing the screen we are virtually living in the past, the contribution
of the historical film lies precisely at the level of argument and metaphor, particularly as these engage the larger discourse of history. By
which I mean how the films relate to, comment upon, and critique

the already existing body of data, arguments, and debates about the topic at hand.

To keep this from sounding hopelessly abstract, let me use the film *Glory* (1989) as an example of what I mean. Based on the story of the 54th Massachusetts Regiment, one of the first black units in the American Civil War, the film invents characters, situations, events, and even the letters (ostensibly written by the unit's commander, Robert Gould Shaw) which are delivered as voiceovers and help to provide both a psychological and moral dimension to what we see on the screen. The four main African American troopers do not originate from regimental histories but, rather, represent four distinct types—the wise elder, the country boy, the intellectual, and the angry black nationalist—whose presence works to generalize the experience beyond the 54th to all African American units in the war (and, by extension, to later periods of history). Cabot Forbes, the second-in-command of the unit, is also an invented character, one who plays the role of Shaw's alter ego and adds to our understanding of the complexity of black–white relations within the Union. This is best shown during a scene at a social gathering in Boston, when Shaw, offered command of this regiment by the governor of Massachusetts, walks away to mull the issue; while he remains silent, all his doubts about becoming the first commander of black troops are voiced aloud by Forbes. This entire sequence is another invention, since the offer actually came by letter to Shaw, camped with his unit in Maryland, but what is lost here in factuality (he was reluctant to accept the command) is clearly gained in dramatic truth. Similarly, an invented incident—in which a quartermaster who disdains black fighting abilities, first refuses to provide boots for the 54th, then is forced to do so by Shaw—serves to dramatize the well-documented racism of many in the Union Army, and simultaneously show how the martinet, Shaw, slowly gained acceptance by his men.

Such invented incidents and characters help to make *Glory* a powerful work of history. They are also inextricably tied up with the argument of the film and its metaphoric thrust—that undergoing the brotherhood of arms and the risks of death on the battlefield helped African Americans to recognize themselves and, to some extent, be recognized by part of the white community as full-fledged men, partners, and citizens of the United States. The moral clearly urged is that if African Americans have not yet achieved that actual equality (as we know they have not), it is certainly due them not only as fellow human beings, but also for the sacrifice they have made for the country. This theme is underscored in the final image of the film as black and white soldiers are shoveled together into a mass grave, and the two chief antagonists—Shaw and the black nationalist—roll in death into each other's arms. A debatable metaphor insofar as it suggests complete black–white reconciliation, but one that, like the larger argument, draws and comments upon the ongoing discourse of both the Civil War and race relations in America.

It is this discourse which helps us both to distinguish a "historical" from a "costume drama," and to judge the usefulness of the inventions in a film. A "historical," I would argue, engages the discourse insofar as it poses and attempts to answer the kinds of questions that surround a given topic (at the time the question was "Will the Negro fight?", while now it can be seen as "What was the effect of black military partici- pation in the Civil War on both African Americans and Whites?"), though its answers are not contained within and must be read out of the dramatic form. The discourse also helps us to judge the values of the inventions which, to promote historical truths, must be apposite; that is, within the possibilities and probabilities of the given period. An inven- tion that showed the 54th winning the battle of Fort Wagner, rather than being decimated (nearly fifty percent casualties), would violate what we already know from the discourse (which includes data, as well as arguments), though the invention that shows the unit advancing on the fort from the north, rather than from the south, is harmless to the larger meaning of the work—perhaps setting the cameras there allowed the director to better render visually the difficulty and bravery of the 54th's assault. There is, of course, no formula for rendering such judgments, which must be—as in all historical judgments—decided on a case-by-case basis. The discourse also governs the inventions of a kind of film which is less common, one which, rather than depicting documented historical figures, places fictional characters into actual past events or situations (e.g. the films of Theo Angelopoulos or the Taviani brothers that I mention below).

That the dramatic film has for some time been "doing history," that certain films have been (sort of) recognized as contributions to the historical understanding, and that certain filmmakers can been seen as some species of historian—surely such ideas have been recognized in print by a few scholars, and in the classroom by the actions of hundreds (thousands?) of historians, not only in the United States but also around the world, who now teach history in film classes on topics that range from the ancient world to slavery to the Middle Ages to Oliver Stone's America. Such courses, which often use film as a way of luring students into historical topics, hedge these works about with written texts, but no work of history (film or book) should be allowed to stand on its own as the complete word on the subject. Every historical argument is always situated within that larger discourse, from which it draws much of its meaning.

The importance of the dramatic film becomes clearer if one looks away from Hollywood and toward Europe and the Third World. With lower budgets, often government support, and a stronger sense of the burdens that history places on the present generation, filmmakers in other parts of the world have a more continuous and better record of dealing with historical issues on the screen. In the United States, our only recent, persistent practitioner of history on film has been Oliver Stone. Here, I won't repeat the details of my own essay in the anthology *Oliver Stone's USA*, where I argue that he is, in fact, a historian— that is, a man who has wrestled on the screen with the meaning of the Vietnam War for the United States (above all in *Born on the Fourth of July* (1989), which uses the coming apart of the protagonist's family as a metaphor for the coming apart of America in the late 1960s), as well as with the life (or the death) of two presidents who bookend the war.[3] Doing so, he not only brings alive the issues of the past but, in *JFK* (1991), also raises the issue of to what extent the past is knowable and representable. (This work also stands as a perfect example of what seems to me another possible task of the historical film: to be provocative. To create a past on the screen so outrageous or controversial that it forces a society to openly debate important historical issues.)

Had I the space available, it would be possible to explicate other films as I have done briefly with *Glory*, to show how their inventions and/or arguments flow out of and engage the discourse of history. Elsewhere, I have undertaken this task for Sergei Eisenstein's *October* (1927) and Alex Cox's *Walker* (1987).[4] (Okay, I have a taste for the offbeat.) The former, usually seen as no more than propaganda, situates its dramatized arguments about such topics as the roles of the people, the Bolshevik Party, Lenin, and the famed July Days well within the boundaries of half a dozen classic interpretations of the Bolshevik Revolution, from John Reed's *Ten Days That Shook the World* to the recent, acclaimed work by Orlando Figes, *A People's Tragedy*. The latter film, seen as a kind of quirky, black comedy, full of ahistorical anachronisms, turns out to engage the 150-year tradition of writing about William Walker in newspapers, magazines, journals, and biographies, starting with his own work, *The War in Nicaragua*, and ending with the most recent, multicultural interpretation of the man's exploits written in the 1970s.

Because so few historians have looked seriously at film, we do not have the studies that could take this approach into other areas of the world. But such investigation should and could easily be done. Clearly, such directors as Andrzej Wajda, Ousmane Sembene, Margarethe von Trotta, Theo Angelopoulos, and Vittorio and Paolo Taviani (to name but a few) have been obsessed by historical questions. Claims for some of these as historians have already been staked out in excellent studies by film scholars. The films of Angelopoulos, as Andrew Horton describes them, are at once meditations on the past and explorations of what has been repressed by official narratives. Clearly "fictions," they are, at the same time, powerful narratives that trace the history of Greece from the turn of the twentieth century through the civil war of the late 1940s, and taken together, constitute an "attempt to see clearly through the dark window of Greek history . . . with all of its internal conflicts, external pressures and ancient baggage from past empires and eras so that we experience . . . how individuals and their destinies are absolutely woven into and from the fabric of their culture and their times."[5] The Tavianis, Marcia Landy argues, are similarly broad in their historical aims. In films which cover episodes from the early nineteenth century all the way to the mid-twentieth, the brothers deal with the kinds of questions posed by historians—questions of subalternity, regionalism, and class struggle. And they do so in works that neither sentimentalize nor monumentalize the past, but engage in a "treatment of history (that) is predominantly interrogative, analytical, and ironic."[6]

If dramatic films can successfully meditate upon, interrogate, and analyze the past, or explore that which has been repressed by official histories, as I believe they can, then surely they are playing at least a part of the role we assign to traditional History. More than fifteen years ago, Marc Ferro, the father of the field of history and film, edged towards this issue. In a chapter title of his book, *Cinema and History*, he poses the question: "Does a Filmic Writing of History Exist?" His first answer to the question is no, on the grounds that historical features offer "no more than a filmic transcription of a vision of history which has been conceived by others"—that is, such films do no more than "reproduce" the dominant historical discourse or the opposition (usually Marxist) discourse without adding anything.[7] But having some second thoughts, Ferro goes on to explain that some "opposition" filmmakers do produce worthwhile works of history, while other directors who manage to maintain an "independent or innovative" view of society are able to provide an interpretation of history "which is no longer merely a reconstruction or reconstitution, but really an original contribution to our understanding of past phenomena and their relation to the present." Among those he lauds are

Andrei Tarkovsky, Hans Jürgen Syberberg, Luchino Visconti, Ousmane Sembene, and the directors of "most Polish historical films."

Picking up on one of Ferro's most important suggestions, that film provides a kind of "counter narrative" to contemporary society, and using it in a different way, I want to suggest that historical film at its best provides a kind of counter-discourse on the past. One which includes not only the independent thinkers among directors, or those whose work reflects oppositional views, but some traditional filmmakers as well. For it is necessary to get beyond Ferro's implicit notion that somehow the medium is neutral, that a topic can be translated from the page to the screen without undergoing significant alterations. To change from the oral or the written to the screen, to add images, sound, color, movement, and drama is to alter the way we read, see, perceive, and think about the past. All these elements are part of this practice of history on film for which we do not yet have a decent label. Nor do we have a good sense of its coordinates, how and where it sits in time, space, and in relation to our other discourses.

Ultimately, this form of telling the past is at once a challenge, a provocation, and a paradox because its ostensibly literal rendition of the world can never be taken literally. The historical film creates rich images, sequences, and visual metaphors to help us to see and think about what has been. It does not provide literal truths (as if our written history can provide literal truths) but symbolic or metaphoric truths, which work, to a large degree, as a commentary on and a challenge to traditional historical narratives. In a sense, film returns us to a kind of ground zero with regard to history—a realization that we can never really know the past, but can only continually play with, reconfigure, and try to make meaning out of its traces.

Notes

1. This article was originally printed in *Cineaste* (2004) and is reprinted by permission of the copyright holders.
2. F.R. Ankersmit, "Historiography and Postmodernism," *History and Tropology* (Berkeley: University of California Press, 1994): 162–81.
3. Robert A. Rosenstone, "Oliver Stone as Historian," in Robert Brent Toplin (ed.), *Oliver Stone's USA: Film, History, and Controversy* (Lawrence: University Press of Kansas, 2000): 26–39.
4. Robert A. Rosenstone, "*Walker*: The Dramatic Film as Historical Truth," *Film Historia* 2(1) (1992): 3–12; reprinted in Rosenstone, *Visions of the Past: The Challenge of Film to Our Idea of History* (Cambridge: Harvard University Press, 1995): 132–51; Rosenstone, "*October* as History," *Rethinking History* 5 (summer 2001): 255–74.

5. Andrew Horton, *The Films of Theo Angelopoulos: A Cinema of Contemplation* (Princeton: Princeton University Press, 1997): 55–7.
6. Marcia Landy, *Italian Film* (Cambridge: Cambridge University Press, 2000): 165.
7. Marc Ferro, trans. Naomi Greene, *Cinema and History* (Detroit: Wayne States University Press, 1988): 161–3.

11

"This Is Not America: This Is Los Angeles": Crime, Space, and History in the City of Angels

Ian Scott

Movies about Los Angeles have been characterized by their bleak, noirish urban landscape, circumvented by larger-than-life loner detectives, glamorous femme fatales, and sociopathic underworld crime bosses. The characteristic distinctions of the people inhabiting Los Angeles have been metaphors for the extremities of the city itself; at once sexy, famous, and full of possibilities, but offset by bleak back streets, tired and tatty neighborhoods, and desperate low-lives running from someone or something. But these characteristics also highlight something else about the kind of films set in Los Angeles: they frequently attempt, through character, place, and time, to convey a sense of the city's fractured pasts, heightened by its image of an urban frontier town and site of detective fictions and film noirs. As David Fine points out, "Crime fiction is one place that foregrounds history," yet Los Angeles and the West's mythology is often predicated on an escape from another past and the construction of a new identity.[1] In *Chinatown* (1974), *Mulholland Falls* (1996), *L.A. Confidential* (1997), and more recently *Changeling* (2008), the most obvious of cinematic signifiers return the city to its glamorous and dangerous heyday; but, in a whole series of other noirs from *Double Indemnity* (1944) to *The Blue Gardenia* (1946) and on to more modern interpretations such as *To Live and Die in L.A.* (1985) and *Collateral* (2004), these films also register the historical evolution, spatial tensions, and cultural antitheses that are at work in the city, a jumble of concerns rarely articulated in movies about other parts of America. This chapter examines the ways narrative, character, and setting work to condition, usurp, and mythologize the history, politics, and development of Los Angeles, and why the films might be the best and most reliable of chroniclers for a city determined by, and built out of, its movie-set origins.

One of the most striking moments in *Changeling*, Clint Eastwood's historical melodrama set in Los Angeles in 1928, is not the grim facts of the story of a telephonist (played by Angelina Jolie) who finds her child missing when she returns home one day, only to be reunited some weeks later with a stranger paraded as a miracle discovery by the city authorities. Nor is it the extraordinary denouement of the movie where a host of "lost" children who have been kidnapped and killed by the psychotic and itinerant Gordon Northcott (Jason Butler Harner) are having their stories relayed back to the negligent police force by one who escaped and then returns seven years later, revelatory and shocking as both these moments are. No: arguably the most affecting moment in the film is the sight of Jolie's character, Christine Collins, stepping onto and riding one of the Pacific Electric Railway's "Red" trolley cars that weaved their way around the city's environs during the first half of the twentieth century.

The impressive nature of these scenes is made all the more pertinent by the knowledge that the production team actually acquired some of the old trolley cars, restored and then used them as living, breathing artifacts in the picture, rather than wholly recreate the imagery through CGI technology. Their significance, however, over and above the implanting of a historical urgency and authenticity onto a film that is typically acute by Eastwood's standards in its attention to period detail, is that the very presence of the cars confers upon the film, its story, and setting, many of the mythic overtones that have defined the history of Los Angeles on screen. The cars almost seem invented for the image of a city in another time and place; they resonate with San Francisco's trolley cars and a city that possessed a history and culture without having to invent it. The trolley cars remain a vibrant signal throughout *Changeling* that this is a Los Angeles not just lost to history, but almost one that never seemed to exist at all; or, if it did exist, only in the pages of the history chronicled in other sources and at subsequent times. As this chapter argues, therefore, a series of films demonstrate where the real and reimagined Los Angeles intersect and provide the context for the mythic saturation of legend and rumor that stretched across the twentieth-century growth of the city. The result has not only been the cinematic reclamation of a metropolis lost in the city annals, but also the articulation of a story of its people, institutions, and history that reveals schisms, controversies, and excesses at every turn; a city of imagination and degradation buried in the idealized and cinematic City of Angels.

The story of the "Big Red" and "BigYellow" cars (the former actually serving the region, the latter the city) that suffuse Eastwood's film is part and parcel of that lost edenic entity that was the prewar—really the pre-automobile—history of an L.A. already mired in political scandal and social violence. "This myth of a lost urban Eden, like the biblical myth," explains the state historian Kevin Starr, "had a villain: General Motors, which was alleged to have conspired and bribed the Big Red and BigYellow Cars out of existence."[2]

As Starr asserts, the truth was somewhat more prosaic. The trolley cars simply couldn't compete with the automobile, on a financial as well as accessibility footing, even by the 1930s. In 1924–25, the Pacific Electric's service peaked in terms of its popularity with 110 million passengers; but it was running the same routes at this time that it had a decade before.[3] No further development had taken place, and claims were already beginning to be made for roads and highways to supersede the trolley cars and join together burgeoning new communities in the greater Los Angeles area.[4] At the same time, over 300,000 automobiles had already been registered in California and, almost overnight, L.A.'s intersections became some of the busiest thorough-fares in America. The trolley cars, traveling along the same streets, were caught in the same congestion and quickly began to lose an edge on their transportation rival.[5] But Starr's conclusion to the myth that superseded this more perfunctory geographic and ethnographical explanation of the changing urban environment is also interesting from a further twofold perspective. First, he compares the trolley car experience and the GM invasion as a villainous story every bit as rich and inviting as the idea of water as culprit in Hollywood's classic take on this myth: Roman Polanski's 1974 period drama *Chinatown*. Second, Star argues that both the *Chinatown* and the trolley car myth assumed the same thing: that somewhere in the early twentieth-century period, the entry of these two villains resulted in the loss of a "finer Los Angeles."[6]

What that "finer L.A." might have looked like has never been easy to define. An integrated transport network and, by implication, a more integrated city might have been the result. The creation of "garden suburbs" that would have had distinct communities and offered alternative ways of living beyond some affirmation of the genericity of the place could have been a possibility.[7] Water as environmental gateway to a freely self-sustaining city, rather than as a battleground for competing forces of power and authority, might also have been a legacy. Certainly, the downtown section of L.A., which hit its height ironically enough in WorldWar II, ought to have been saved as a place of glory, commerce, and a figurative if not literal hub of the city. At the time, the downtown area's 50,000 commuters per day enjoyed the architecture of the office buildings, the picturesque movie palaces, and religious centers in the shape of St. Vibiana's Cathedral, dedicated back in 1876.[8] All that could have been a part of Los Angeles in the second half of the twentieth and now twenty-first centuries, but somehow evaporated like the water itself lying on desert floors with nowhere to go, until, the assertion goes, William Mulholland and the patrons of the city moved in at the turn of the last century.

For Hollywood, and for film scholars and critics as well as social and cultural historians examining the impact and implications of films about Los Angeles's past, Roman Polanski's *Chinatown* remains the dominant cinematic chronicler of these changes, battles, mythic constructions, and lost opportunities. Comparing San Francisco's own water project, for example, the Hetch Hetchy Dam, Starr concludes that it "lacked the murky ambiguity of the Los Angeles venture, the sinister suggestions of conspiracy filmed so persuasively in *Chinatown*."[9] In *Chinatown*, a detective's routine investigation of adultery uncovers city-wide conspiracies involving water rights, real estate, police corruption, murder, and incest. Robert Towne's script never overplays these entwined melodramatic odysseys in its progression towards a confused, half-crazed, and convincing conclusion. Indeed, the whole film's ironic attitude toward the city and the construction of its history is summed up by two of the final lines in the script. When Jake Gittes (Jack Nicholson) pleads with Evelyn Mulwray (Faye Dunaway) to tell her story to the authorities as she tries to escape the city with her illegitimate daughter/sister, she retorts that her father, abuser, and architect of the city's water scam, Noah Cross (John Huston), "owns the police." The final line of the movie sees Gittes dragged away from the stationary car after Evelyn's "accidental" shooting by his associate Walsh (Joe Mantell) who famously reasons, "Forget it Jake; it's Chinatown."

Steve Neale has argued that this last line is a signal of *Chinatown*'s deployment of unconventional genre approaches to the detective thriller that defined it as a key example of "the New Hollywood" cinema.[10] Corruption is endemic as well as systemic, suggests Evelyn's comment. Walsh's remark suggests that L.A. is hybridized, unknowing, and unknown.[11] But though he is told to "forget," Gittes has traveled the Southern California landscape dominated by Noah Cross; corruption is not enclosed within the "other" community of Chinatown. The two lines have become something of a signification for the film's contribution to Hollywood's changing dynamics during the 1970s, as well as its political and social stance towards the city's history and its pioneering elite. The lines act as cinematic shorthand for films that have followed in *Chinatown*'s wake, as well as a statement of intent that has produced reams of debate and denunciation beyond the circles of film scholarship and review.

As Catherine Mulholland points out in a biography of her grandfather, head of the Los Angeles Department of Water and Power, William Mulholland, "the fictional and melodramatic movie, *Chinatown*, has come to be regarded by the uninformed as a kind of documentary on the history of Los Angeles, while others who hold the city in disdain see the film as a clever parable on the greed and ambition of an upstart town."[12] Mulholland might be accused of familial loyalty and a frustration with the reproduction of rumor and legend that has slowly built William Mulholland into the beast of Los Angelean excess. Steven Erie and Harold Brackman in their work do their best, however, to offer a slightly different take on this debate. Returning to the scene of the proverbial cinematic crime in what they call a "shadow conspiracy of L.A. water imperialism, *Chinatown* is paraded as a more even-handed allegory for the city's complex emergence.[13] While acknowledging that the film inevitably acts as the enduring cultural staging post for perceptions about water, power, corruption, and Hollywood, Erie and Brackman nevertheless question whether the film is, or ever has been, the "appropriate metaphor" for water development. In fact, as they observe, the picture's *roman à clef* didactics insinuate a larger metaphor at work, "a prostitution of the public good for private greed and ambition," as they describe it.[14] No matter that the approximate characters, both real and imagined, are transported some twenty years into the 1930s; that the diminutive Hollis Mulwray (Darrell Zwerling) of the film is not a fit for the larger-than-life physical and philosophical dominance of his historical counterpart Mulholland; or that old-style Westerner Noah Cross (John Huston) is, in fact, a venal incarnation of several figures—including *Los Angeles Times* proprietor Harrison Grey Otis and quite possibly Mulholland himself, to whom legendary director Huston has more than a passing resemblance. The film, for Erie and Brackman, is not about accurate historical reflection so much as it is approximate cultural reaction. It deals in larger brush-strokes of historical development and construction, even if the true nature of the water story—if indeed it can ever be located—is compromised along the way.

The overwhelming success and attention afforded *Chinatown* since its eleven Oscar nominations in 1975 and a $30 million rental receipt total (much of it garnered on video and DVD where its reputation has not only survived but been enhanced in the last thirty-five years) has made Polanski's film a dominant player in perceptions about L.A.'s past. But subsequent pictures have not only taken up the mantle of legend and fable, visual and narrative reconstructions; they have built upon and enhanced the claims of *Chinatown* as a city dialectically trying to reconcile its past with the future, especially in the crucial decades of the 1920s, 1930s, and 1940s.

Hence, the lasting significance of a film like *Changeling* concerns a contemporary narrative structure much in the mould of *Chinatown* that plays upon, conforms to, but also usurps many of the mistaken assumptions about Los Angeles that resonated when Polanski's film was made and earlier, when the formative history of the city was being written. These assumptions and misnomers can be traced back through Hollywood's own conflicted relationship with the city that has never quite come to terms with its proximity to and dependence on the film industry. Whether it be the film noirs *Double Indemnity* (1944), *Mildred Pierce* (1945), and *The Blue Gardenia* (1946), or the modern interpretations *To Live and Die in L.A.* (1985), *Heat* (1995), and *Collateral* (2004), the notion of L.A. as some unknowable place, of a geographic and cultural frontier "outside of history" that promises much but which disappoints and destroys in equal measure, has been a barely disguised but recurrent textual theme.

It is appropriate, then, that screenwriter Michael Straczynski, well-known for penning multiple television episodes of successful series such as *Murder She Wrote* (1984–96) and *Babylon 5* (1994–98), translated the obscure but true tale of single mother Christine Collins in *Changeling* from contemporaneous court reports and newspaper cuttings. Missing her last trolley bus one night after work, which is the catalyst for the events to follow, Collins arrives home late only to find her young nine-year-old son Walter is missing and nowhere to be seen, despite Christine's subsequent search of the neighborhood. Appealing to the police department to unravel the cause of the mysterious disappearance in the days that follow, Collins watches the LAPD's investigators dither, only for the force's publicity machine to go into full-scale action once the answer is seemingly and conveniently presented to them five months later. A child emerges off a train, having been recognized at an out-of-town diner apparently hanging around with a vagrant, and police chief James Davis (Colm Feore) then escorts the members of the press to the emotional reunion at the station between what turns out to be the imposter Walter and Christine.

In this early exchange between mother and police force, Straczynski and Eastwood cleverly create a curious coda in the duality of performance and investigation by the LAPD that documents the kind of media-savvy environment the city had already become under the spell of Hollywood at this time. In a reflective gesture to institutions integrating and mirroring each other, the presence of the media and the film colony compare here to a similar link established in Curtis Hanson's period drama *L.A. Confidential*, where Detective Jack Vincennes (Kevin Spacey) is presented as a glamorous impersonation of a policeman; unpopular with colleagues and never quite up to the demands and rigor of the job, he spends most of his time distracted by his role as an advisor on a fledgling TV cop show.

Pressured by the mayor's office in *Changeling* to obtain some closure in the case, LAPD Chief Davis takes all the credit when Walter seemingly turns up unharmed, and urges the media, which he corals every time a newsworthy subject like this surfaces, to celebrate a "good news story" in an otherwise increasingly restless and criminal-infected metropolis. But Collins notes immediately that the boy is not her son. When Davis, ably assisted by his Captain, J.J. Jones (Jeffrey Donovan), attempts to insinuate that Christine must be wrong, that Walter has changed in the time away, she quickly begins to realize that the LAPD neither care nor are infused by revelations that somehow a mistake— or, worse, collusion—might have taken place for the sake of positive headlines. Collins thus embarks on a harrowing journey—what critic Philip French calls "the stuff of Kafkaesque nightmares"—that leads to incarceration in a mental hospital, as a result of Captain Jones invoking a penal code whereby somebody can be detained for persistently harassing the police.[15] The series of episodes leading to this point are expertly dissected by Eastwood's cinematographic concentration on story and character that only serves to highlight a city driven by appearance, spooked by foul play, and diseased by crookedness and deception at every turn. Christine's cause is helped by a radio priest, somewhat in the guise of a Francis Townsend or Father Charles Coughlin figure (the former would, indeed, be campaigning across the state of California by the early 1930s), the Rev. Gustav Briegleb (John Malkovich), who broadcasts to the city each week from his pulpit.[16] Briegleb sets the tone for the movie's interpretation of L.A. in these years. Praying for Christine at his Sunday service and castigating the police department for its shoddy attempts to solve the case, he states: "Every day the needs of this city's citizens are put second to greed and gain, every day this city sinks deeper into a cesspool of fear, intimidation, and corruption. Once the City of Angels, our protectors have now become our brutalizers."

Briegleb's reference to Davis's so-called "gun squad" is, again, a tantalizing recall to the city's mythic past. James Davis became

Chief of Police in 1926, with the city already engulfed in turmoil from racketeering and semi-organized crime. His real-life attempts to clean up L.A.'s illegal activities stretched as far as a purge of his own force with an internal affairs division not unlike that insinuated by the film. But Davis's intentions are perceived as less than honorable in a somewhat counter-intuitive move, given the film's reading of his own intransigence on the matter and tacit endorsement of the force's malfeasance. Davis's presence in *Changeling*, as with Nick Nolte's Detective Max Hoover in Lee Tamahori's *Mulholland Falls* and the so-called "Hat Squad" there, as well as Perry Lopez's Lieutenant Escobar in *Chinatown*, offers up a force that is riddled with corruption, unable to shape the moral compass of the city and, ultimately, losing a philosophical battle against its own excesses. It is a vision that has its natural apotheosis in the postwar take on the city in a number of films, notably the adaptation of James Ellroy's *L.A. Confidential*, but it is no less apparent, if somewhat more contrived, in Tamahori's own nod to Hollywood noir. Here, corruption is pervasive even among the good guys, like Max in *Mulholland Falls* and Russell Crowe's somewhat unhinged Bud White in *L.A. Confidential*, both of whom are officers with vestiges of morality but who are only just on the right side of the angels.

So, it is in *Changeling* that the forces of law and order, the state's institutions, its news-hungry media, and its early spatial appearance defined by public transportation and articulated through the contrasting imagery of the city's neighborhoods and downtown area, set against the desert scrubland where Northcott hides out with the abducted young boys, where the film construct an ideological agenda that subdivides the city's competing forces. In the shape of the trolley car service that Christine relies upon for her daily commute and which takes her conveniently past Walter's school—shown as a marker of the city's public service to its patrons—the picture creates a fault line that contrasts for the viewer the historical moment where L.A.'s initial development and evolution is about to come face-to-face with its restless future.

The repetitive visual articulation of fault lines, borders, and frontiers in Hollywood movies about Los Angeles sets up a modern clash between Western savagery and civilization, between civic invention and the personal search for truth. David Fine points to John Fowles and his 1977 story *Daniel Martin* as a clear example of myth and reality working in tandem, not least when the central protagonist living in L.A. as a screenwriter meets a newly arrived British actress at LAX with a sage piece of advice, "You have to decide one thing here—which is real, you or Los Angeles."[17] In *Chinatown, Mulholland Falls*, and *Changeling* those schisms and tensions are hard at work in tales that similarly project the city's fallen Western past set against agents who either actively seek to escape its environs or are desperately hoping to cling to lost values and peaceable futures. Very often, these are gendered conflicts. Thus, the torment of Christine Collins in *Changeling* is mirrored by the desperate and incestuous upbringing of Evelyn Mulwray (Faye Dunaway) in Polanski's film, and the covert but seedy existence of Alison Pond (Jennifer Connolly) in *Mulholland Falls*. Evelyn lives the life of a respectable city patron, married to the Department of Water and Power's architect and engineer, Hollis Mulwray, but riddled by secrets and deceptions that conceal the incestuous relationship she was once forced into by her father, Cross. As he relates to Gittes at the close of the film, Cross does not blame himself for this heinous state of affairs. In another line that could encapsulate much of the picture's ideological venom, he casually states: "You see, Mr. Gittes, most people don't have to face the fact that given the right time and circumstance, they are capable of virtually anything."

In *Mulholland Falls*, Alison Pond is a good-time girl caught up in secrets related to military nuclear testing in the desert outside Los Angeles as she carries on an affair with John Malkovich's nuclear scientist Colonel Timms. Alison Pond's discovery of government and business plots ultimately costs her her life. Alison and Christine in *Changeling* are victimized women invested in the promise of the California Dream and the prospects of a better future embodied by Los Angeles. But "the future" is what men like Noah Cross control. They are ultimately tormented by a collective set of vested interests that have different agendas and alternative visions of the future for the city and its residents.

As David Fine points out, the "tough-guy detective" often identified with Los Angeles noirs is "a reminder that history is inescapable," and yet, like so many Westerners intent on remaking their own past, he is hardly a bastion of historical incorruptibility.[18] If one issue unites the films and their projection of an L.A. evolving swiftly in the interwar years and then coming to terms with its creation and mid-century realization in the late 1940s and early 1950s, then crime is surely it. Statistics of the time show that L.A.'s crime problem was serious enough to replicate the kind of figures that were being racked up in cities like Detroit, Cleveland, and Chicago. But they were not so serious as to amount to the kind of gangland warfare that parts of those cities, at least, were experiencing. They were the crimes of a city not quite urbanized enough for the onset of such depressive metropolitan tendencies as those back east. One journalist summed up the dilemma on a trip there in the late 1920s when he rhetorically contemplated what was worse for Los Angeleans, "the number of crimes or the ruralness of their character?"[19]

As Starr asserts, the LAPD of the 1920s already had an institutional profile every bit as relevant and colorful as the University of Southern California, the Los Angeles Philharmonic Orchestra, and the rather more notorious Department of Water and Power; for many years the fiefdom of William Mulholland. What it didn't and couldn't have was an organization and structure to match. Precincts sprouted up, fields were turned into roads, shops, houses, and whole communities, and police officers never patrolled on foot through areas that had only recently come into existence. Rather quickly, they made their way around in patrol cars, anonymous and, for some, shadowy entities that nominally protected neighbourhoods as they appeared, but who quickly garnered a reputation for aloofness and corruption. It was a reason why, from 1921 until Davis's appointment in 1926, the mayor's office could not keep hold of a Chief of Police long enough to assess the job properly.[20]

In *Mulholland Falls*, the so-called "Hat Squad"—led by hard-bitten, but borderline-corrupt cop Max Hoover (Nick Nolte)—sees its investigation into a series of connected murders in the immediate aftermath of World War II usurped by official institutions. The "Hat Squad" is unlicensed and virtually unregulated, even from within the confines of L.A. law enforcement itself. But when the FBI, military personnel, and the Atomic Energy Commission become accessories after the fact in a cover-up that goes beyond the city's remit covertly to clean up crime and violence, L.A. is paraded as an outsider city, an edge town on the limits of federal control that has spent its developing years up until the war looking after its own, and worrying little about the infringement of official government forces and regulation. Max Hoover, like Gittes in *Chinatown*, is a victim of his own hubris, a man whose destiny was once under his control only for more powerful forces, and of the exposure of his affair with the murdered call-girl, Alison, to come back to haunt his past and threaten his future.

Director Lee Tamahori separates Los Angeles from its technological future by having the collection of officers make recurring visits out into the desert, principally to call upon a failing Colonel Timms, who is dying of cancer as a result of working on the government's top secret nuclear program for a number of years. In a climatic confrontation aboard a transport plane where Timms's minders, led by Colonel Fitzgerald (Treat Williams), are exposed as the real conspirators, Max

Hoover loses his partner Elleroy Coolidge (Chazz Palminteri), who is shot in the ensuing fight. With this shock comes the realization that the "Hat Squad" is pregnable, government and military authority stretches further into the state and domestic realms than was ever the case when Max first started out on the job, and that L.A. is changing as a city, and is being reshaped by a postwar redevelopment which is more regulated and yet less certain of what the future might hold. The "Hat Squad" is finally broken up at the conclusion of *Mulholland Falls*, Max unsuccessfully attempts reconciliation with his wife (Melanie Griffith), and the military men who are the perpetrators of murder have become victims themselves—but, without any justice, the story never provides redress. Even in resolution, L.A. is not prepared for revelation or apostasy.

For Jake Gittes, a similar denouement unfolds. His retreat from the Chinatown neighborhood he patrolled as an officer, in the picture's backstory, is as a result of his inability to protect a vulnerable woman he cared about. Now, Evelyn Mulwray, who he similarly wanted to protect, is dead. The villainous Noah Cross has literally got away with murder, and Escobar (Perry Lopez), initially intent on pinning charges on Gittes for withholding information and perverting the course of justice, is no longer interested in Gittes or the case. Like Hoover, Gittes seems bewildered by his job, the authorities, and a city that is shifting rapidly before his eyes. "How could this happen?", he mutters under his breath while standing next to Evelyn's dead body in the car, slumped over the steering wheel. The LAPD cannot and will not touch Cross in Chinatown or anywhere else, just as they are redundant in the military cover-up involving government agencies in *Mulholland Falls*, and negligent in their pursuit of the lost and missing children of *Changeling*. The simplicity of the work, the logical sense of the place, appears redundant and contrived as each protagonist contemplates their future at the close of the respective narratives.

As Fine only further emphasizes, literary crime in Southern California, like its cinematic and real equivalents, was often "hidden behind a respectable façade" and provided wealth and anonymity in equal measure, making the innocent victims and the perpetrators unaccountable.[21] But if the LAPD is made to appear complicit in their failure to contain or even explain crime in these films, then the tarnishing of the fabric of the Southland through these years is as a result of more individual affirmation. The *Los Angeles Times*—but more especially its proprietors Harrison Grey Otis and, later, Harry Chandler—were the natural heirs of the frontier "boosterist" tradition that harked back to the state's incarnation and which infiltrates every pore of the three films in its self-aggrandizing manner. Promoting the Pacific Electric Railway as the most extensive transit system in the world in the early century, Otis was, as Stephen Schwartz notes, "fanatical about the promise of sunshine and the profits of real estate."[22] Together with the railroads and oil boom, the *Times* and, first Otis and then Chandler consolidated L.A.'s growth and confirmed its superiority over northern rival San Francisco.

Yet, while Mulholland, Otis, Chandler, and police chiefs such as Davis and William Parker have shared much of the limelight in the roll call of L.A.'s luminaries, fixers, and notorious apostles, Fred Eaton has remained on the periphery of this pantheon and yet is really the inspiration at the heart of all that surrounds the history underpinning the films. Mayor of Los Angeles at the turn of the century, Eaton is most noted for his relationship with Mulholland and the Los Angeles Department of Water and Power. Mulholland was recognized as both semi-autonomous and "an indefatigable go-getter and joiner."[23] That go-getting involved transportation networks, too. Subsequent *L.A. Times* owner Chandler had an investment in the Pacific Electric Railway's newest development just like Eaton, which railwayman and real estate developer Henry Huntington owned as the trolley car system, and both were mammoth patrons of the city's boosterist rhetoric, again just like Eaton. But even they could not claim the connections or murky involvement with the city's emergence to which their friend and associate subscribed.

As well as encouraging and investing in the Pacific Electric, it was Eaton that aimed ultimately to use the Owens Valley as the chief water source for the city. He made huge profits along the way from both negotiating the city's rights to acquire the land while channeling the water across a huge aqueduct towards L.A., *and* buying up crucial areas of the Owens Valley at the same time that he himself would then sell on at a price to the city authorities. Estimates suggest that Eaton made over half-a-million dollars from the sale of the land—in direct conflict of interest, as he was acting as the city's negotiator at the same time. A confluence of events and people was thus established that linked the power and independence of civic authority, the drive of self-made men, and the vitality of water as pointers towards a conspiracy in which "public ambition and private self-interest mingled murkily," and which became the catalyst for Towne, Polanski, and producer Robert Evans's film seventy years later.[24]

Eaton was a man who saw the limitless possibilities that the state, the Pacific Ocean setting, the fresh water supplies cascading off the mountains, and the fledgling city could have, and his thirst for a controlling stake in all that potential knew little bounds. His was a Californian mentality that has also come back to the movies from generation to generation. It is there in Gibson Gowland's interpretation of Frank Norris's McTeague in Erich von Stroheim's adaptation, *Greed* (1924); and the character is revisited as Daniel Plainview in Paul Thomas Anderson's realization of that other crusading writer Upton Sinclair in the novel and film *There Will Be Blood* (2007).

The films in focus here, however, share another facet that is also relevant and equally pertinent to the ambitions of the city's patrons. They each share an almost timeless quality of referentiality for Los Angeles as it once was, or at least as one might imagine it to look like, almost as though, in *Chinatown, Mulholland Falls,* and *Changeling*, the characters, stories, and imagery seek to dictate and dominate the historical debates about the city's construction of its past. It is that sense of the prophetic quality in each of the pictures that gives a clue to their role as historical signifier for a series of developments that somehow delineate the identity and outlook of California in general, and Los Angeles in particular. Some might argue this as a manifestation of postmodern filmmaking in the manner argued by John Cawelti and Fredric Jameson, particularly in the construction of the West and nostalgia.[25] But one might suggest that they instead offer up proto-modern visions of L.A.'s social and economic dilemmas to come—be they criminal, political, or cultural. The films also hint at the liminality of space and time that slowly, subtly, in the postwar years began to delineate and differentiate the city's haves and have-nots, the separation of its infrastructure and identification from the greater rump of its citizenry as frontier boosterism gave way to reality and a reputation that would later be besmirched by riots and racism.

Michael Eaton claims that *Chinatown* frames its emotional and ideological concerns as ultimately flawed but that the detective genre "has some faith in the eventual victory of human rationality."[26] *Chinatown, Mulholland Falls*, and *Changeling* each offer this reach for sense and logical perspective. In *Mulholland Falls*, Max realizes the ambiguity and illogical premise at the heart of the "Hat Squad" and its determination to mend the city by acting almost as badly as the criminals. In *Changeling*, Christine's plight is aided by Detective Ybarra (Michael Kelly), who begins to piece together her story with reports of other missing children that lead him out to the run-down hen farm on the city's edges and the evidence of Northcott's abductions. But, Eaton goes on to say, the idea of the detective traditionally returning what has previously been hidden back into the light, of recovering the past, is also somewhat subverted by Polanski's film. Although Gittes as the "private eye" is not infected by city cop corruption, Steve Neale presupposes that *Chinatown*'s constant fixation on sight, viewing, and vision results in all sorts of cinematic as well as psychological tricks, suffusing the philosophical and psychological arc of the story and metaphorically charging L.A. with deceit and obscurity. Evelyn's eye is shot at the close, binoculars and glasses are constantly invoked for seeing or discovering things, Jake loses a lens in his sunglasses at one point, and so on. In *Mulholland Falls* and *Changeling*, an awareness and understanding of action, reaction, cause and effect, revelation, and cover-up are similarly usurped by literal and figurative interventions that capitalize on L.A.'s immersion and subversion of evidence, reality, and optimism.[27] Each denouement is not simply ambiguous and unwilling to offer satisfactory closure; each actually inculcates the growth, expansion, and untrammeled rhetorical persuasion of the place with the concealment and protection of the institution's elite community and all the contradictions and misapprehensions they harbor. "We are not just crossing into a liminal space," surmises Eaton, "but instead a state of mind which is completely impossible to escape. We are entering an atonement-free zone, a site in which the possibility of any species of redemption would be laughable, totally out of the question."[28]

All three films do more, therefore, than merely condemn the city, its founders, and the spatial explosion of community, place, and resources that the early twentieth century resulted in. Ultimately, Hollywood's representation of Los Angeles over time might be seen as its revenge on a city whose patrons always held an ambivalent attitude towards the movie industry. The early years set up celluloid Los Angeles as an idyllic haven of opportunity and paradise, and the city's elite praised the studios for the free advertising and consumption of the "edenic myth" to which they themselves were only too happy to conform. But the studios also had a wanton disregard for private property as the needs of their expanding industry grew ever more voracious. As Bill Barich observes, "Whenever [the city] then tried to exert more control, the studio heads would threaten to move elsewhere."[29] Ultimately, the two recognized that they needed each other as much as they needed the geography around them, and a mutual understanding broke out whereby the excesses of each were largely concealed, and/or appropriated at certain times for particular publicity.

In *Changeling*, that pattern of observance to the rituals and demands of Hollywood, and the industry's grip on the city's economic and political will, as well as the imagination of the populace that shared the paradise in which it worked, is reconfirmed by the bookended narrative. The story begins with a family recollection of a visit to see a Chaplin film as the silent era reaches its climax (*The Circus*, 1928). It concludes with Christine betting on Frank Capra's *It Happened One Night* (1934) to win Best Picture at the Oscar ceremony being broadcast on her wireless in the office at work, thus signifying the beginning of a legendary and almost unassailable period in American filmmaking. Hollywood is the pervasive discourse even of this faded and long since passed vision of L.A., it seems to say. As Philip French concludes, Eastwood stretches the iconic signifiers so far as to begin the credits of *Changeling* with the "golden planet" logo that was Universal's actual studio symbol at the commencement of its films in the 1930s, almost as though dragging his audience back to that time and context even before the film, in its proper sense, has begun.

"It was the beginning of a golden era for Hollywood," confirms French in assessing these cinematic reference points that Eastwood wishes to confer so readily on his own work.[30] But, by implication, it was also the initiation of an ongoing history of cover-up and obfuscation for the city, of dark episodes and itinerant personnel who never wanted to participate in the myths the city concocted. The stories of Christine Collins, of Evelyn Mulwray, and of Alison Pond tell individual tales of life and loss. But they also tell of Hollywood's obsession with the City of Angels and the constructions, parables, fables, and fabrications that passed into "reel," historical, and celluloid legend.

Notes

1. David Fine, *Imagining Los Angeles: A City in Fiction* (Reno: University of Nevada Press, 2000): 17–18.
2. Kevin Starr, *Coast of Dreams: A History of Contemporary California* (London: Allen Lane, 2005): 546.
3. Kevin Starr, *Material Dreams: Southern California Through the 1920s* (Oxford: Oxford University Press, 1990): 79.
4. Robert M. Fogelson, *The Fragmented Metropolis: Los Angeles, 1850–1930* (London: University of California Press, 1993): 173.
5. Starr (1990): 79–80.
6. Starr (2005): 547.
7. The architects of the garden suburb scheme were Frederick Law Olmstead and Charles Cheney who designed a number of purpose-built communities around L.A. as examples of the sort of community living that could be achieved, and which were to be joined by the integrated transport network primarily serviced by the Pacific Electric trolley cars. See Fogelson: 157–9.
8. *Ibid.*: 547.

9. Starr (1990): 60.

10. Steve Neale, "*Chinatown* (1974)," in *Film Analysis: A Norton Reader* (London: Norton, 2005): 661.

11. Fine (2000): 148–9.

12. Catherine Mulholland, *William Mulholland and the Rise of Los Angeles* (London: University of California Press, 2002): 4.

13. Steven P. Erie and Harold Brackman, *Beyond Chinatown: The Metropolitan Water District, Growth, and the Environment in Southern California* (Stanford: Stanford University Press, 2006): 4.

14. Erie and Brackman: 33.

15. Philip French, "*Changeling*," in "Observer Review," *The Observer* (November 30, 2008): 14.

16. Briegleb is, like a number in the film, a real character, but no records cite him as ever being involved directly as a radio priest. He was a community activist and pastor in L.A. certainly, and he did know people from various ministries. One of these was Methodist R.P. Shuler who did broadcast on radio throughout the city in this period.

17. David Fine, "Nathanael West, Raymond Chandler, and the Los Angeles Novel," *California History* 68(4), (winter, 1989/1990): 196–200.

18. Fine, 120–5; see also Smyth, *Hollywood and the American Historical Film* (London: Palgrave, 2011): introduction, 18.

19. Starr (1990): 169–70.

20. Starr (1990): 171.

21. Fine (1990): 200.

22. Stephen Schwartz, *From West to East: California and the Making of the American Mind* (New York: Free Press, 1998): 159–60.

23. Mulholland: 44.

24. Starr (1990): 51.

25. John G. Cawelti, "*Chinatown* and Generic Transformation in Recent American Films," in *Film Theory and Criticism*, 2nd edn, edited by Gerald Mast and Marshall Cohen (Oxford: Oxford University Press, 1979): 200.

26. Michael Eaton, *Chinatown* (London: BFI, 1997): 40.

27. Neale: 674.

28. Eaton: 67.

29. Bill Barich, *Big Dreams: Into the Heart of California* (New York: Pantheon, 1994): 411.

30. French: 14.

12

Between Nostalgia and Regret: Strategies of Historical Disruption from Douglas Sirk to *Mad Men*

Vera Dika

Recently, I had occasion to view a 1978 photograph by the artist Laurie Simmons entitled "Woman Listening to Radio." The black-and-white print presents a miniature scene: a model radio, TV, and rug, in a model room, all recalling a 1950s past (Illustration 12.1). On a miniature couch within that room sits a plastic doll, her short legs not touching the floor. The stillness of the room is palpable, surely because of its constructed nature, a quality that paradoxically stirs memories and encourages reflection. The light from the supposed window, for example, fills the space with a sense of the warmth of day, while the allusion to music in the title brings a faintly audible, although imagined, tune into the represented space. A quality of returning to a long-receded space and time is created, a place of childhood perhaps, most specifically, a 1950s childhood.

I can recall the 1950s as a lived experience (for me, this picture is not *only* a representation) and so I have a personal response to what I see. I see my mother's world being evoked, my mother's day. Alone, after cleaning the house, after assembling its interior design, the woman, my mother, sits for a quiet moment, surveying the fruits of her labor and the conditions of her entrapment. This is the setting of her drama, her life. The house is still and she revels in the stillness, in the aloneness. Viewing Laurie Simmons's photograph in the late 1970s had had a particular impact on the women of my generation. This was a life we did *not* want to live. We vowed to break free from those chains. And in some sense, I believe I did. I am an academic and a writer, but I also have been a wife and a mother, and so now, in 2010, I can somehow identify with the little

Illustration 12.1   Laurie Simmons, "Woman Listening to Radio," 1978 © Laurie Simmons

plastic doll in the room. I know the pleasures of the home, as well as its encasement.

The photographic work of Laurie Simmons is part of an art movement called the "Pictures Generation." This practice emerged in the late 1970s and was initially seen as significant because it reintroduced recognizable images into art after a long period of abstraction.[1] At first this claim may seem somewhat strange in relation to Simmons's work, since the "recognizable image" had never significantly left photography. What is it then that "returns" in Simmons's work? As noted, a past time seems to return, as does a partially remembered place. On looking closer, however, what we see is really not all that personal. In the work of Simmons, as well as other artists of the Pictures Generation, such as Cindy Sherman and Robert Longo, it is images from past media sources that elusively return, especially those from old movies. Seen in this way, we can note that Simmons's photographs of narratively inflected interior environments are evocative of cinematic family melodramas. The films of Douglas Sirk come to mind, as do the 1970s critical discussion prompted by these works, ones that saw them as critiques of Eisenhower-era bourgeois society.[2] Simmons's photographs thus resound on a personal and a cultural level, in some ways bringing us a picture of a past movie memory, a "picture of a picture,"[3] and so not meant to reference the "real" as the documentary capabilities of photography might imply.

Works of art and popular culture that foreground their debt to a 1950s past are often referred to as "nostalgia." But when Simmons was asked about her work in this regard, she answered in this way: "People often say my work feels nostalgic, but I don't really like nostalgia—at least not the idea of nostalgia. I like the idea of regret, or what might have been."[4]

I am intrigued by the artist's notion of "regret," and would like to interrogate it further. Since Simmons does not expound on the term, I will attempt to extract her meaning from the work itself. In Simmons's photographs we see an edge of negativity when looking back, thus countering the reading of a longing for the past. We are instead offered a vantage point of criticality, of looking at childhood-like objects and images, but also at the social myths they embody, and the effects of those ideas into the present.

In Simmons's work the regret is formally evoked by the use of miniatures, plastic dolls of sadly fixed expression, and of fabricated environments, paper thin and manifestly not "real." The inherent still-ness holds a future that will never come because the fixed materials have no ability to move in time, a quality doubly articulated through the use of photography itself. The surface of the black-and-white image is still in its filmic graininess, revealing while embalming the past it registers. So if "nostalgia" is invoked, it is closer to the type first noted by Fredric Jameson.[5] That is, it is a quality inherent in the image itself, an image now bereft of "reality" by its artificiality, and by its manifest bond to a series of other representations.

In the present essay, I will further consider the notion of nostalgia and regret, now understood as formal strategies from which to engage the past, and extend them to describe a number of critically relevant works ranging from the 1950s to the present. On the level of content, the works I have chosen are linked to the influence of Douglas Sirk and melodrama, often addressing properties of the home and the dramas that take place in and around it. But these works also display distinctive qualities of the image and its relationship to history. Most recently, the television series *Mad Men* has mined the 1950s and early 1960s by referencing the cultural artifacts from that era, and importantly, its cinema history. In *Mad Men*'s compulsive return to nostalgic works, it shares an impetus evident in Todd Haynes's *Far From Heaven* (2002). Both works, in turn, recycle certain elements from Sirk's *All That Heaven Allows* (1955), and by extension, Rainer Werner Fassbinder's *Ali: Fear Eats the Soul* (1974). In all, however, we find a distinctive manipulation of the cinematic image, especially in relationship to historical trauma.

To trace pastiche works to their source material would seem to yield only limited critical insight. In the present essay, however, I will reconsider this particular group of nostalgia films, placing them within their historical contexts, thus bringing developments in art and film practice to the fore, as well as broader events in world history. We will see that the more recent works do not passively reflect the 1950s past and its cinema; neither do they simply embody a nostalgic wish to return to those pasts, nor even to conflate the past with the present by showing that "not much has changed." Instead these works, from Sirk to *Mad Men*, employ critical strategies that expose a life we may not want to live but in many ways must confront—a kind of regret for the past and the present.

Though "regret" is also a convention of melodrama—and therefore part of the narrative content of *All That Heaven Allows*, *Ali: Fear Eats the Soul*, and *Far From Heaven*—regret is also a feature of a number of "nostalgia films" from the 1970s. *American Graffiti* (1973) and *Badlands* (1973), for example, imply a historical regret, lamenting the loss of American innocence in a post-Vietnam era. Here, the past returns as a surface regret. As I have argued elsewhere, the dense picture surfaces in these "nostalgia" films destabilize the both the illusion of the fictive reality, and an uncomplicated access to an ideal past.[6] The access to the "real," if there is to be one, comes from the visual and historical ruptures created in the works, gaps that open up the fictive surfaces. But these strategies are not singular to the films given here. In the present essay, I will consider how contemporary filmmakers have reinscribed older strategies of historical disruption into their more current productions.

All That Heaven Allows

All That Heaven Allows is a seminal work of cinema that has received extensive critical attention. This film by Douglas Sirk has been heavily researched and documented, lauded for its use of melodrama, its importance to feminist film theory, and its distinctive use of *mise-en-scène*. We all know quite well, for example, that German Expressionism profoundly influenced Sirk, a German émigré, first in his work as a painter, and then in his subsequent theatre and film productions.

We also know how much this visual style provides a kind of abstraction, produced largely by its use of color, costume, and props, which places the viewer at a relative distance from which to appreciate the socially critical message of Sirk's films. I will, however, re-examine these claims. In one respect I will support accepted readings, in another, I will look for new permutations, questioning how and why artists and filmmakers, especially in our more contemporary period, have so often chosen *All That Heaven Allows* as a referential text, and how these strategies function anew in the later works.

The story of *All That Heaven Allows* is a simple one, and forms the nucleus of this American melodrama set in and around the middle-class family home. *All That Heaven Allows* tells the story of Cary, a widow, who makes a socially inappropriate love choice: she falls in love with her gardener, who is fifteen years her junior. The difference in age, as well as the differences in social position, causes Cary's suburban community to object to the union. As agents of a repressive society, the members of the country club, and even her closest friends and grown children, apply such pressure on the couple that Cary and Ron are finally forced to separate. The separation causes unhappiness and confusion, a state that ultimately leads to Ron's debilitating accident. As the film ends, the couple has been reunited, but because of Ron's impairment, the couple's future is unclear, and the mood can well be described as one of regret. There is regret for actions not taken, regret for missed opportunities, and surely regret for "what might have been."

The notion of regret, however, is also embodied in the quality of the image itself, one that harbors social and historical realties. First to note is that image in *All That Heaven Allows* stridently declares itself as a surface, but also as a representation, one never quite meant to represent the real world. The opening image is our introduction to this strategy. Here, we see a shot of a quaint clock tower against a blue sky, and watch the camera slowly pan across the gently flickering autumn leaves eventually to view a suburban street scene set in 1950s America. Small human figures go about their business, as women stroll with baby carriages, children play, and a 1954 turquoise Chevrolet station wagon makes its way up the center of the frame. To complete its mythic quality, the scene is accompanied by a languorous musical score.

Even for those who lived through the 1950s, the picture-perfect rendering at the opening of *All That Heaven Allows* foregrounds its qualities as a fabrication, a picture, and a widely circulated one at that. This is the image of the "American Dream" that was often featured in such publications as *Life* or *Look Magazine* during the period, and used to advertise consumer objects such as cars, homes, and appliances to returning to GIs and their families. This is also the image of American prosperity and cultural supremacy circulated after the conflagration of World War II, and one that in *All That Heaven Allows* is now rendered in Technicolor, a process dominated by deeply saturated primary hues of blue, red, and yellow. And although Technicolor was used in many films of the 1950s, it is the juxtaposition of the image's physical properties to other elements of *All That Heaven Allows* that give it its distinctive edge. In *All That Heaven Allows* it is the critical clash between what the surface of the image presents, and the historical reality that it both covers and implies. Through this clash another level of regret is thus embodied, for past actions revealed, or, for "what might have been."

On a production level, it is interesting to note that Sirk told Russell Metty, his cinematographer on *All That Heaven Allows*, that he wanted the colors of the film to be hard and "enamel like."[7] Here, we see that Sirk sought to create a hard reflective picture plane, one matched throughout the film by the use of such props as mirrors, windows, as well as other framing devices, such as doorways and screens. Shafts of colored lights were also used to articulate the surface of the image, a surface quality that further creates a barrier-like effect, and supports the themes of entrapment of the central character within the confines of the home, and of a restrictive society. This quality of surface is matched by the detail and precision of set design, costume, make-up, as well as acting style and delivery. The actors' bodies are held in often fixed, although not entirely unnatural, positions, while their voices are measured in their delivery, and often accompanied by strains of emotionally compatible music. And last, the pairing of the lead characters also helps to create this feeling of closure. The film's story tells us that Cary and Ron are separated in age, and by their differing social positions, but there is nothing in their looks or comportment that causes a visual disruption or disjuncture. In fact, both actors are beautifully matched in their star-quality good looks, and in their middle-class speech and manner, complementing each other in a way that facilitates their union. In the composite of these elements, then, there are no visual or aural inconsistencies that would topple the integrity of the image.

It has been noted that the use of expressive *mise-en-scène* in *All That Heaven Allows* facilitates our critical stance toward it. This quality, along with the use of melodrama, it is argued, mobilizes a critique of small-town American life, the constrictions of class, and from a feminist perspective, the dictates of patriarchy that limit a woman's ability to work and to love. I will claim, however, that this insistence on surface has historical implications as well, and while certain historical conditions are not directly featured in the film's content, they nonetheless underlie it, even structure it, through their absences. First to note is the disjunction between the regional American perfection presented in the film, and the historical reality that surrounds the work. As has often been noted, *All That Heaven Allows* appears to be steeped in the repressive politics of the 1950s, especially those regarding race, class, gender, and sexual preference. But a post-World War II era also underlies the film. Surely the picture-perfect surface keeps us from confronting most of those realities, but perhaps this is a distinctive feature. I will argue that as a representation, the film's glossy surfaces function as a form of "traumatic illusionism," a quality noted by the art critic Hal Foster in reference to painting but applicable here as a hardened barrier, a blocking, and a traumatic response to the "real" of history.[8]

This barrier, however, may not be entirely evident when the film is seen outside of its original 1950s context.[9] Today's audiences, for example, become uncomfortable when watching Rock Hudson, who plays Cary's love interest, and listen to his understated lines, some with the inadvertent sexual innuendo. There is often laughter when Hudson quietly tells Cary about his "silver-tipped spruce." The disruption, this "rupturing of the surface," if you will, comes from today's greater sexual explicitness in works of popular culture, but also from our knowledge that Rock Hudson was gay. And with this discomfort there is also a quality of sadness, or regret, for we also know that Rock Hudson died of AIDS in 1985. Hudson's image can no longer hold the cinematic closure it once did.

Barbara Klinger's study of Douglas Sirk's melodramas has documented the change in meaning that *All That Heaven Allows* and other Sirk films have undergone since their first release. In 1954, for example, the viewing audience did not know that Rock Hudson, the icon of male heterosexual allure, was gay. This fact, however, was nonetheless imminent in his image, and in retrospect, tears at its surface. One could speculate, for example, that Sirk knew of Hudson's sexual preference, or that Jane Wyman, his co-star, was aware of the fact. But one thing is for sure, Rock Hudson knew, and was well aware of the social and professional consequences this could pose. Hudson's sexual preference threatened his image. Homosexuality was illegal in the 1950s, and was listed by the American Psychiatric Association as a "disease," and as a sexual "deviancy." The anxiety of the image, then, its hard reflective surface, along with the double-edged dialogue, can now be seen to function as a barrier against the real. And it is here that later filmmakers, R.W. Fassbinder and Todd Haynes, will return, not only to this story, but also to this anxiety, raising it to the surface.

But there are other historical contexts to *All That Heaven Allows* that have not yet been explored. As noted, Douglas Sirk was a German émigré. Sirk was born of Danish parents in Germany where he was educated and where he first worked as an artist, and later, as a theater and film director. Just before leaving Germany, in fact, Sirk worked for the renowned German film studio UFA during the Nazi period.[10] There Sirk was known for his film melodramas, of which it is said that Joseph Goebbels was especially proud. It is important to note, however, that Sirk came to the United States because of persecution. Although Sirk himself was not Jewish, his second wife, Hilde Jary, was. When Sirk's first wife, Lydia Brinken, who had since become a Nazi, learned of Sirk's relations with a Jewess, she denounced them both publicly. Along with other rising tensions, leaving Germany was the only avenue left open to Sirk and his Jewish wife.

The end of the Holocaust and World War II predated the making of *All That Heaven Allows* by eight years. These events of both personal and world history cannot be ignored, and must be considered in relationship to the story of *All That Heaven Allows*, and to the quality of the film itself. The picture-perfect quality of the film's image, especially when juxtaposed to this catastrophic world trauma, takes on a different resonance, especially when one remembers that World War II left fifty-five million people dead, and millions displaced. Of course, these events took place on someone else's shores. This was America. In Sirk's film, the image of suburban America is ironized, intensified, calcified, and can be seen as a traumatic reaction to recent world events. Even the story can be read in terms of this double meaning, with the central conflict of *All That Heaven Allows*, the drama of a couple oppressed by a society that persecutes difference, as an allegory for Sirk's own experience in Nazi Germany. Of course, *All That Heaven Allows* presents this conflict in smaller, more manageable, or even, one might say, "inappropriate" terms.[11] But as Susan Sontag has pointed out, symbolic products of mass culture of the 1950s, such as the American science fiction films of the period, were able to embody society's memories and fears of disaster, of nuclear annihilation, now on a miniaturized or "trivialized" level. I think it is feasible to consider *All That Heaven Allows* in such terms.

The question of intentionality is at issue here, since the script of *All That Heaven Allows* was based on a story by Edna L. Lee, and the screenplay was written by Peg Fenwick. I am not claiming that the World War II interpretation is the one "true" meaning of *All That Heaven Allows*. The film is far too complex for such a conclusion. But once we look at Sirk's film from this historical perspective, a new layer of meaning accrues to it. Surely, the recent historical reality had underscored America's own mythological media images of itself during the 1950s. But historical context frames *All That Heaven Allows* in a profound yet immediate way because of Sirk's own experiences.

For this reason, claims that *All That Heaven Allows* is a "critique of American bourgeois society" should also consider a larger critique. Broader historical conditions come into play when considering, as the film itself states, those human situations "that bring out the hateful side of human nature." The dynamic of persecution cannot be separated from the events in Nazi Germany, and in the 1970s, as we shall see, Rainer Werner Fassbinder bought these particular historical reverberations to the fore in his own film *Ali: Fear Eats the Soul*. Fassbinder, of course, openly attributed the latter film to Sirk's influence.

Ali: Fear Eats the Soul

R.W. Fassbinder occupies an important place in the history of the German film. As a West German, he represented a post–World War II generation. His goal, and that of the other members of the New German Cinema, was to re-establish the national film practice that had been destroyed by World War II. During this period, Fassbinder belonged to a "Land Without Fathers," as Germany was called after the war, having lost so many of its men to that conflict. Fassbinder, too, had no father, and he turned to Douglas Sirk as his cinematic father, as a guide in the construction of his new cinema, and a new aesthetic. With an intention of making a critically involved cinema, and with Fassbinder's own strong Brechtian theater background, the young filmmaker could have turned to the politically confrontational cinematic model provided by Jean Luc Godard. Instead, Fassbinder moved in a new direction. He amalgamated both Godard and Sirk, striving to create a cinema that would make his audience think—but also feel. Fassbinder found a perfect inspiration for this endeavor in Sirk's melodramas. Fassbinder, however, radically altered Sirk's approach, while also being true to it.

In some ways *Ali: Fear Eats the Soul* is a "remake" of *All That Heaven Allows*, with its first level of confluence operating on the level content. Here, Fassbinder fashions a new story from Sirk's American version, setting his film in contemporary 1970s Munich, and offering an altered but still identifiable group of characters. The story of *Ali: Fear Eats the Soul* is centered on a much older woman, and one from a different stratum of society than that seen in *All That Heaven Allows*. In Fassbinder's film, we meet Emmi, a cleaning lady aged sixty-five who falls in love with Ali, a Moroccan guest worker thirty years her junior, and we watch as the German society around her profoundly objects to the union. Among those objecting are the women who live in Emmi's building, her co-workers, and even her grown children, all of whom respond to Emmi and Ali with exclusion, disgust, and condescension. The cumulative stress of this social response deteriorates the couple's relationship, and then even Ali's health. As the film closes, Emmi stands by Ali's hospital bed, and we are left to ponder what future she will have with this man whose health has been permanently marred by the sum total of his life in Germany.

The displacement of elements from Douglas Sirk's film on the level of character is then further extended to other layers of *Ali: Fear Eats the Soul*. First to note is the effect of changing the setting of the story from a 1950s American suburb to a location in Munich in the 1970s. Fassbinder's strategy in this regard infuses a new level of history into the film. In *Ali: Fear Eats the Soul* we are shifted from an immediate postwar period in the USA, and from a director who had escaped Nazi Germany, to a new context. In Fassbinder's film we are at a thirty-year remove from the war period, but we are presented with a film by a German director who is just coming into adulthood as an inheritor of the legacy of the Holocaust. This theme of culpability is central to *Ali: Fear Eats the Soul* and very much intended. Here, Fassbinder confronts the German audience of the mid-1970s, addressing its intransigent postwar amnesia, alluding to the past in the context of ongoing racially-based prejudices. Melodrama is the vehicle Fassbinder uses, as well as a number of aesthetic manipulations that further displace the visual and aural material of the Sirk film.

The opening sequence of *Ali: Fear Eats the Soul*, for example, radically inverts the visual and aural tropes of *All That Heaven Allows*. Instead of beginning with a high-angle overhead shot of a sunny day, as did the Sirk film, *Ali: Fear Eats the Soul* begins with a low-angle shot of a street at night. In fact, the camera lens is close to the ground in Fassbinder's film, focused on a muddy rain puddle at the side of the road, while the headlights of cars moving in the distance occupy the upper portion of the frame. As a German title appears on the screen reading "Happiness is not always easy," we hear the rise of an Arabic language song on the soundtrack. The distinctive undulations of the Arabic music and spoken word, now followed by the German title of the film itself, make a startling juxtaposition. The music continues through the remainder of the sequence, accompanying the scroll of German names, contributors in the making of the film we are about to see. In this way, the presence of the *auslander*, the foreigner, occupying a German space is made clear.

To introduce the central character, we are given a wide shot of the interior of a local bar. The camera is placed at the end of a long room, with the central doorway forming the focal point of the image. The door opens and Emmi walks through it. Emmi, a stocky elderly woman, waits there for a relatively extended period. To her right, we see a rug hung on the wall. It features a picture of gypsies in an animated dance, and we hear the Arab language song from the title sequence continue over the image. The placement of Emmi against the door frame redoubles her encasement within the film frame.

When the reverse shot to this opening sequence finally comes, it underscores the tableau strategy to be evident throughout much of the film. The allusion to Arabic culture is now confirmed by the characters that occupy the other side of room. A grouping of young Arab men and women is presented, all of whom now rigidly hold their poses. The picture-like quality is redoubled by the inclusion of other framed pictures within the shot. The gypsy rug on one side of the room is matched by three other framed pictures in the reverse field. These include two large dioramas of vacation landscapes in the rear of the room, and a framed image of a fat satyr with his nymph behind the bar. The atmosphere of this scene of *Ali: Fear Eats the Soul* is imbued with stillness, yet it holds incipient threat, and sexuality. The characters who occupy the foreign side of the room are young and part of a group. Emmi, the German on the other end, is old and out of place.

What is striking about this sequence is Fassbinder's use of framing devices, recalling Sirk's own strategies. Here, as will occur throughout the entirety of the film, doorways and framed pictures—and later, grids, shafts of colored lighting, and even geometric fabric design—are used to indicate the characters entrapment by society and by history. The images presented in *Ali: Fear Eats the Soul* also recall the use of color in Sirk's film. In *Ali: Fear Eats the Soul*, however, the colors of the image have been shifted in the portrayal of working-class characters and objects within the frame, and delivered by a grainier, lower budget type of cinematography. The "Technicolor" reds, blues, and yellows of *All That Heaven Allows*, for example, are now embodied in the interior design and objects of a seedy bar. The vibrant tertiary tones are also present, such as the turquoise of the car, and the orange of the autumn leaves, only now they have been displaced onto the skirt and tank top of a female character. The characters themselves, however, form a disjunction from the original film. In keeping with the strategy of visual disjunction, the characters in *Ali: Fear Eats the Soul* do not possess the star quality good looks of Sirk's Hollywood film. Not only is Emmi an elderly working-class woman, and Ali a Moroccan day laborer, but also they have the unglamorous look of ordinary people, as do all other characters of this film.

The visual elements of *Ali: Fear Eats the Soul* are thus used to destabilize the image, rejecting the glossy hard edge surface of the Sirk film, and replacing them with a kind of realism. It is from this vantage point that *Ali: Fear Eats the Soul* then launches its political work. In the opening sequence, this begins with a conversation between Ali and Emmi in the bar. The two leads dance to a song entitled "The Black Gypsy." Here, they exchange a form of tenderness in words and in manner that gives rise to an immediate exchange of truths between them. Ali has come to Germany to work, but has little else. He explains that Germans and Arabs are different people, as is made clear to him at his place of employment, and in society: "German master," he concludes, "Arab dog." A red light washes over the couple as they dance, and the music and lyrics of "The Black Gypsy," a racist song, rises to light the genocide of gypsies, and by extension, Jews, homosexuals, and political dissidents, making explicit what is latent in the dialogue. The references to "work," and to the "master" race, in the context of German history, are strong, and pointed.

The film will continue on this double register, telling the story of contemporary German racism, in the haunting shadow of its past. On a visual level, this is further made clear by the choice of location for the film, and by continued verbal statements that rupture the surface of the fiction. *Ali: Fear Eats the Soul* is set in Munich, a city that has important historical connotations. On one hand, Munich is the place of Fassbinder's birth, his "home town." On the other, it is also the location of the birth of the Nazi party. Hitler had once lived in Munich, and even made his early fiery beer hall speeches there. In fact, Fassbinder has shot his film *Ali: Fear Eats the Soul* in locations well-known to German audiences to have been frequented by Hitler during the early days of the Nazi party. In one scene, for example, Emmi and Ali go to a restaurant, *Osteria Italiana*, to celebrate their marriage. Alone and isolated, again framed within doorways and underneath framed pictures, they are condescended to by the waiter, who obviously does not condone the racially-mixed couple. On entering the restaurant, however, Emmi had mentioned that this establishment was one of Hitler's favorites. This statement is historically correct. Called *Osteria Bavaria* in the Nazi era, this very restaurant was indeed the site of Hitler's frequent visits. The visual impact of now shooting the *Ali: Fear Eats the Soul* in the exterior and interior of this location, and then presenting it to a German audience, destabilizes the image, under-scoring what is said in the scene, and the attitudes displayed there, with unavoidable historical reverberations.

Ali: Fear Eats the Soul is about Germany's racial prejudices, past, present, and future. The purpose of the film, however, is not to equate racial attitudes, but to set them within an historical framework, one which, especially in the 1970s, was often denied though a kind of mass amnesia. Fassbinder structures the dialogue and the actions of the film so that they allude to these different historical moments, condemning the racial attitudes that unite them, and so indicting his audience. The pointed messages are carried variously by Emmi, and by Ali. One subtle reminder of the past is Emmi's age. If Emmi is sixty-five in 1973, she was thirty-five in 1943. As an adult member of German society, what was she doing? Emmi supplies that information herself, admitting, for example, that she was a member of the Nazi party. She then adds matter-of-factly, "as almost everyone was." This accosts the viewers, especially those in the audience approximately Emmi's age. Do they remember their participation in the Nazi regime? Do they acknowledge their tacit willingness to support racial laws?

On the other end of the age-spectrum of *Ali: Fear Eats the Soul*'s audience were those Germans who in 1973 were in their thirties, as was Ali, and Fassbinder himself. The film thus reminds contemporary audience members of the foreign workers who entered Germany during the post-World War II period. These laborers, primarily from Turkey and North Africa, came as "invited guests" of the government. Germany was able to rebuild its shattered country with the help of these laborers, and eventually, to realize the "economic miracle" that has since made it the third strongest economy in the world. These guest workers, however, have continued to stay in Germany, with their number currently rising into the millions of individuals and their families, many of whom have only resident status.

Ali: Fear Eats the Soul is thus prescient, looking to the future of an internal racial unease within Germany (and within Europe), one that insistently reminds the audience of the Germany's history of racial hatred. It also belies another hatred, now of homosexuals, a sexual orientation that also warranted being sent to a concentration camp during the Nazi period. Fassbinder himself was gay, and "out" in the 1970s, as was his lover, El Hedi Ben Salem M'Barek Mohammed Mustafa, the actor who plays Ali in *Ali: Fear Eats the Soul*. This, too, is a knowledge that accosts the viewer through the image. Fassbinder forces the viewer both to feel and think about various aspects of German history through its displaced images and story elements, confronting the audience with what in 1973 was threatening to be repressed.

An amalgam of cinematic strategies and themes drawn from both Douglas Sirk and R.W. Fassbinder now strongly feature in Todd Haynes's 2002 film *Far From Heaven*. Considerable differences, however, must be noted.

Far From Heaven

Todd Haynes's *Far From Heaven* is a film melodrama that appears at a particular moment in film and art history. As we have noted, this film comes after the works of melodrama presented by both Sirk and Fassbinder. In some ways, *Far From Heaven* is a "remake" of those earlier works, especially drawing from Douglas Sirk's content and visual style. As we will discuss, however, *Far From Heaven* endeavors closely to copy the visual properties of the Sirk film, in the opening sequence especially, almost as a "tracing"[12] of the original. But this, too, should be seen in historical context. Haynes's film is preceded by nearly thirty years of precisely this style of film and art making; that is, a style of pastiche that copies the visual surface of older films, resulting in works that have the semblance of bygone cinematic products.[13] First noted by Fredric Jameson, and dubbed the "nostalgia" film because of its use of past styles, images and themes, this early practice can now be seen as a "first generation." Examples have been drawn from such commercial films as *American Graffiti* (1973) and *Badlands* (1973), and even *Halloween* (1976),[14] but this style is also prevalent in punk films, such as Amos Poe's *Unmade Beds* (1976) and Kathryn Bigelow's *The Loveless* (1982). The early practice has since continued, and mutated, in both content and form, into a wide number of works across the thirty years of its evidence. A few examples in later commercial film are *Last Exit to Brooklyn* (1986) and *Pleasantville* (1998), as well as Gus Van Zant's *Psycho* (1998), a shot-by-shot restaging of Alfred Hitchcock's earlier film.

The question now arises: why would Todd Haynes return in 2002 not only to a past era of filmmaking from the 1950s, but to the "nostalgia film" itself, and to a practice that largely predates the artists and filmmakers of his generation? The above-noted nostalgia filmmakers, for example, are Baby Boomers born in the late 1940s or early 1950s. Todd Haynes, on the other hand, was born in 1961, and so holds no direct memory of the past he is recounting. But Haynes does have knowledge of the films of the 1950s, as well as the more recent "nostalgia" films, both through their repeated showings. Haynes has a degree in semiotics from Brown University, and his work seems quite aware, not only of film and art history, but also of the critical literature that has accompanied postmodern practice over the last several decades. The critical writings of Roland Barthes, Fredric Jameson, Guy Debord, Hal Foster, and Jean Baudrillard come to mind. The theories of Baudrillard, in particular, are evidenced in Haynes's work, with the notion of the simulacrum, the exact copy, the original of which has been lost or decayed. As copies proliferate in our "society of the image," Baudrillard claims, we experience a "loss of the real."[15] Haynes's work is very involved with the notion of the copy, and with the possibility of accessing the "real" through trauma; again, a critical position much discussed in the 1990s.[16] But to what purpose does Haynes put these historical and critical insights?

I will begin our discussion of Haynes's work by looking at the way he manipulates sounds and images of *Far From Heaven*. *Far From Heaven* presents a familiar love story about two sets of socially mismatched characters in the 1950s. Haynes favors Sirk's visual style in his film, and returns us to the American suburban location. In fact, the opening sequence of *Far From Heaven* begins with a pointed replication of *All That Heaven Allows*, as well as a set of notable alterations. The film begins with a musical accompaniment that is evocative of 1950s melodramas, and written by Hollywood veteran composer, Elmer Bernstein.[17] The music is languorous, and one might say "nostalgic," perhaps for the past, but certainly for past movies. But what percentage of the general audience can still remember either the lived 1950s, or the original 1950s films? By 2002, this number has certainly receded. What the audience does remember, however, is current nostalgia film practice. And it is here that Haynes begins his layering of cultural references, ones that tend to underscore the film itself *as* a representation. The use of color, for example, is important in this regard. The deeply saturated colors, and their Technicolor-like vibrancy, are here rendered in autumnal tones. Moreover, the image manifestly looks like a "picture," and at times, like a painting. This practice of picture making, one that straddles the look of painting and photography, has many precedents, in the later color photography of Cindy Sherman, for example, or the highly constructed color sets of Laurie Simmons, or even in the "unreal" Las Vegas locations presented in Francis Coppola's *One from the Heart* (1983). This quality of the copy, of the decidedly obvious one that tends to discontent with reality, is then manifested in the title design of the Haynes's film. The style of the font in *Far From Heaven*, as well as the colors used, declare it as a copy through over-statement, and look almost "cartoon-like;" that is, "drawn." And it is this quality of the *representation*, that will then carry over, not only into the use of costumes, props, and locations in *Far From Heaven*, but also in the style of the acting, the tone and delivery of the lines, and the quality of the writing.

Far From Heaven begins with a blank screen that fades into a still image of a quasi-abstract rendering of tree branches with orange, yellow, and red leaves. This painting surface soon dissolves into a moving image of autumn leaves. A soft breeze animates the image as the leaves move gently across the frame, and a slow camera pan moves down over a small American town. The style of the clothing, the vintage of the automobiles, the small business establishments alert us that not only are we watching a scene from small town USA of the 1950s, but also, more importantly, we are watching a copy of the era, a nostalgia film. As *Far From Heaven* continues, the play of color, as well as the sources of the material, begin firmly to establish themselves. An insistent palette of autumnal tones, secondary colors of orange, greens, and contrasting blues, will dominate the image. As the opening camera movement initiated, the continuing wide shots, medium shots, and close-ups will present us with the seamless world of classical Hollywood filmmaking.

Within this obvious representational structure, disjunctions will begin to appear in *Far From Heaven*. The style of acting is on the edge of artifice, with lines delivered in hushed tones, in a stilted manner, and with minimal body movement. The content of the dialogue, when matched with these repressed tones, begins to crack beneath its weight. When we first meet the main character, Cathy Whitaker (Julianne Moore), for example, she has driven her turquoise blue Chevrolet station wagon up to her upper-middle-class suburban home. Getting out of her car, Cathy is greeted by her maid, Sybil. "Has Mr. Whitaker called?" Cathy asks. "No, he hasn't," is the answer. "How do you like that guy" comments Cathy, in the pleasant non-inflected tone of the presumed picture-perfect picture world of the 1950s. Since the availability of her husband, Frank Whitaker, will be a structuring tension within the film, this delivery can be seen to be a deeply ironic statement.

But this is only the beginning. To this "picture plane" we are confronted with further qualities of disruption. Cathy's maid is an African American woman. On showing this film to lecture groups in both the United States and abroad, I have found that audiences often feel a sense of "discomfort" with this image. Why? In one sense, we could say that this image disrupts our sense of surface, of representation, and puts us in contact with "history,"—here, understandable as the history of racial prejudice and class privilege in America. But how can we claim that this figure within the image is so disruptive? If we think of the reality of the United States, we can note that many people who work as domestic servants, especially in the New York and Los Angeles areas, are people of color. So, while not exclusively so, the presence of an African American maid could be a reality in an American suburb, both today in 2010, and in the 1950s.

But now let's look to film history. If we look back to films of the 1930s to the 1950s, for example, African American servants are often present. The maid character is centrally featured in *Imitation of Life* (both in the 1934 version by John Stahl and Douglas Sirk's 1959 remake), while African American servants appear in countless other films of which *She Done Him Wrong* (1933), *Gone with the Wind* (1939), and *Stella Dallas* (1937) are only a few examples. So, why should the inclusion of a black servant make us uncomfortable today? Perhaps it is because this image has been elided from most contemporary American films and, most pointedly, from the nostalgia film of 1973 to 2002. Nostalgia films tend to exclude African American characters altogether. This is largely true of *Grease, Badlands, American Graffiti, Happy Days*, all the way to *Pleasantville*. When African American characters do appear in 1950s nostalgia films, they are portrayed as extremely marginalized, as is the black couple at the school dance in *Grease*, or the upwardly mobile neighbors in *The Truman Show* (1998).

By including an African American maid on this obviously constructed picture plane of *Far From Heaven*, one highly coded as a representation of a representation, while now alluding to other nostalgia films, Todd Haynes attempts a comment on the nostalgia film itself. As simulacral, one could argue, this picture plane constructed surface is now ruptured by the inclusion of the maid figure. Haynes thus makes a comment on the historical structure of the nostalgia film itself. His intention is to return history to this form of filmmaking. It should be acknowledged, however, that Haynes is not the first to make such gesture. This has been done before in a myriad of films that can be designated as "nostalgia" works.[18] As an example, *Last Exit to Brooklyn* (1986) takes as its content the class, gender, and racial inequalities of the 1950s as a pointed critique of the 1950s-revival film craze.

Haynes's strategy, however, in this early sequence of *Far From Heaven*, and throughout the remainder of his film, will be one of "rupturing" the visual surface, in a way that recalls Hal Foster's observations in *The Return of the Real*. Here, Foster discusses the physical fissures, or gaps, on the painted surfaces of Warhol's *Death and Disaster* (1962–1964) silk-screen paintings. In *Far From Heaven*, Haynes now extends this notion of a rupture on the film's visual surface, now on the semiological surface of the picture plane itself. The presence of the African American maid within this particular nostalgia image, in conjunction with our cultural and historical knowledge, causes a kind of unease. This isn't the nostalgic past we want to return to as entertainment. But then again, why should we not be so confronted? It is our present.

The pressing question, however, is one that finally impacts the rest of *Far From Heaven*. While it is true that there really are people of color at work in the world, the problem is that Haynes does not sustain his analysis of this condition throughout the film. Instead, he goes on to tell a different story, once again relegating the maid character to a marginalized status. African American maids have been elided from current nostalgia films (and current films) because their image is a very potent one. The image of the black servant, its history in American film, and its sources in American history, especially the history of slavery, is too violent, and its legacy ever-present in an ongoing societal struggle, to be reduced to an image, or an aesthetic trope. This character and her history overwhelm the image, and will be joined by other unstable meanings in *Far From Heaven*.

It has been noted by Sharon Willis that Haynes's politics within *Far From Heaven* ultimately "disappoint."[19] For Willis, this disappointment comes from the visual equation that Haynes makes in *Far From Heaven* between racial issues, which we have begun to discuss, and issues of sexual orientation. The racial issues in the film, ones that will extend from the character of the African American maid to Cathy's friendship with her African American gardener, are narratively and visually juxtaposed to Frank Whitaker's own love choice, now with a gay male. The equation of racism and homophobia, as Willis notes, destabilizes the film, and tends to reveal the subject of the discourse.[20] I must agree with this assessment. However, I will look further to *how* Haynes manipulates the surface of his images to evoke ideas and feelings, and so continue an exploration of his strategies. Haynes went to Sirk, and by extension Fassbinder, not only for his narrative inspiration, but also for a practice of image-making that declares a surface "pictureness," and for methods of referencing the historical off-field, of what is not said, but imminent in the image. In making *Far From Heaven*, Haynes saw an opportunity to draw on the historical reality that surrounded the 1950s—in this case, the suppression of gay rights and gay desire—and to raise it to the surface of *Far From Heaven*. Haynes also chose to address the historical context of racial hatred in this early civil rights era, one that had also surrounded Sirk's *All That Heaven Allows* and *Imitation of Life*. Haynes thus rewrote a story of race and gender issues based on Sirk's strategies for melodramatic tension.

In *Far From Heaven*, however, Haynes takes a different approach to his process of picture making than did Sirk, and to critical consciousness. This is evident in one sequence of proposed rupture in the film. In a much discussed scene, for example, Cathy, a lonely housewife whose husband is struggling with his homosexuality, tells Raymond (Dennis Haysbert), her African American gardener with whom she has formed a friendship, that she cannot see him anymore. The couple talk beneath a movie marquee, and Raymond asks Cathy if we ever see "beneath the surface of things" (Illustration 12.2). The referent is explicit here, to issues of race and skin color, to be sure, but also to issues of surface, of representation—and as the movie marquee implies—to film as a construction, and to the quality of "pictureness" evident throughout *Far From Heaven*. Haynes's strategy, as in the opening sequence, is to rupture the representational surface through trauma; that is, through historical trauma. This is carried out pictorially, as well as narratively. As Cathy turns to go, Raymond grabs her arm and says, "Mrs. Whitaker, wait." A close-up of his hand on her arm confirms the contact. At that moment a white man shouts from across the street, "Hey boy . . . hands off!" Here, the image literally fractures, as Sharon Willis has noted, with shots of various people along the street stopping to look at Cathy and Raymond. The shot of the man who had made the statement is presented off-kilter, and the ones of the people at odd angles. But it is the semiological context of the statement that sets us reeling. We profoundly fear for Raymond, precisely because of the very American setting we are confronting, and because of the whiteness of its community. Images and ideas from history may come to mind, of lynchings in the South, or of the racial violence in the film *The Birth of a Nation* (1915). We may also think of James Byrd, a black man dragged to his death in Paris, Texas in 1998, but also of Michael Griffith, Michael Stewart, or Brandon McClelland, victims of racial hate

Illustration 12.2   *Far From Heaven* and the constructed space (2002) © Vulcan Productions/ Focus Features

crimes in the past and present. One can say that there has been a break in the surface of the image, and in the orderly flow of the narrative, by these historical references.

But then the film closes up again. Cathy looks up at Raymond and says, "You're so beautiful." Cathy is exercising her social power, which is greater than Raymond's. Cathy takes Raymond as her object, with herself occupying the dominant position. We, as audience, are caught in a quandary. Since this exchange is shot from a camera position over Cathy's shoulder, fixing Raymond in the frame, is Haynes commenting on the structure of objectification in film? If so, this is unclear. We are nevertheless identified with Cathy, a character who even now, almost three quarters of the way through the film, has not allowed her special friend to call her by her first name. She is still "Mrs. Whitaker" to Raymond. As she walks away, Raymond's point of view shot is only of an empty street. Mrs. Whitaker is never held as the object of Raymond's gaze.

This difference in terms of social address forms another disjunction for the viewer, an inconsistency, a tear in the surface of the narrative. Cathy maintains social power through the hierarchy of vision, to keep Raymond in "his place." Sharon Willis has noted that Haynes accomplishes much the same gesture in his film as a whole. For Willis, Haynes objectifies and victimizes Raymond as the African American male in his film, ands so fails at the assumed attempt to offer a film in favor of racial equality. Here, too, I would agree. The strategies of disruption mobilized by Haynes, when effective, seem too brief, and even when well-intentioned, are not ironized enough to form a critical disjunction with the forces of history, ones too complex and treacherous to be fully contained by the film's representation. In the end, Willis claims that *Far From Heaven* reveals itself as a story told by a white man, and through a cinema dominated by white codes and a white industry. And while there is a strong argument for Willis's position, I will raise a number of additional points to further strategies of disruption.

If we look at *Far From Heaven* more closely, we realize that small ruptures have been occurring throughout. We can note oppositions in the way characters are presented. Frank's barely-contained state of explosive rage, for example, is countered by Cathy's picture-perfect rendition of blank acquiescence. The children are a mix of wholesomeness and of grotesquerie, while the maid eschews her usual media role of a maternal figure, addressing the family in a business-like manner. Raymond is presented as a model of exceptionalism, in the style of Sidney Poitier, and even as having profound opinions on

European abstract painting, a position not typical of African American males on film or, for that matter, of any American males on film.

Haynes is clearly working within and against type. Sirk, too, had utilized the stereotype in his films, destabilizing the viewer's expectations. Sirk had ironized his characters by the excessive techniques possible within melodrama, thus addressing social issues. Can we claim that Haynes's characters function in the same way? I believe not. The most important difference is the shift in historical context. *Imitation of Life*, for example, is closer to the historical source of its material, and the audience is closer to understanding of the racial conflicts it depicts. *Far From Heaven*, on the other hand, wants its audience to engage in a more convoluted mental activity regarding historical eras. We are supposed to view this era with an attitude I am here calling "regret," as a time of unjust actions, and missed opportunities. The implication in *Far From Heaven* is that today we have come so far, that we have superseded the past, but more importantly, that the limitations of the past may in some ways still be with us.

Haynes, however, presents *Far From Heaven* as a copy of copies, and so weakens our relationship to the past. As noted, the disruptions presented in *Far From Heaven* have not been able adequately to reveal the complex nature of 1950s social struggles. The history of African Americans in the 1950s, for example, has been largely presented as one of victimization, and not from the perspective of their leadership and commitment in the fight for civil rights. One need only to think of the action of an outraged African American parent, Oliver L. Brown, that launched *Brown v. the Board of Education* in 1954; of Rosa Parks not giving up her seat to a white man in 1955; or of the unfailing courage of black students in 1957 to integrate Little Rock Central High School in the face of vicious racism. So, while *Far From Heaven* alluded to elements of this struggle, making reference to the NAACP, and including footage of President Eisenhower's Little Rock speech, these moments are brief, and the easy conflation between past and present is, in the end, insubstantial.

Mad Men

In the popular television series *Mad Men* (2007–present) we are once again returned to the mythic 1950s, now portrayed as a late 1950s-early 1960s era. Not only is the image in *Mad Men* replete with period-specific props, set design, costumes and make-up from that era, but the color scheme of the series, and the references to previous movies overwhelm the image. As pastiche, *Mad Men* is not a sustained remake, but is formulated from a cacophony of cultural sources, ones that are, nevertheless, not necessary for the understanding of the series. In the glamorous lead couple of *Mad Men*, Don and Betty Draper, for example, I in some ways recognize Sean Connery and Tippi Hedren from Alfred Hitchcock's *Marnie* (1964), a film about a woman who repeatedly changes her identity. In other more obvious ways, Betty Draper is almost an exact replica of Grace Kelly, complete with elegant style of dress, only now confined to a middle-class suburban home. The color scheme of the show, the greens, the browns, the hot pinks and oranges, match the palette of *How to Succeed in Business without Really Trying* (1967), and even include the actor from that earlier film, Robert Morse, as a central character. And then, of course, there are those knotty pine cabinets and yellow appliances in the Draper's kitchen that take me back (once again) to my mother's house.

But as I have noted, none of these references is necessary for an understanding of the show. Instead, to a contemporary young viewer, *Mad Men*'s visual surface is a copy of a copy, a copy of a 1950s revival film or, perhaps, of 1950s films rented on DVD they have seen before. And like *Far From Heaven*, and the more contemporary 1950s revival film *Revolutionary Road* (2008), it is one that expects us to do a convoluted time comparison. It presents us with the 1950s as "the bad old days." These old days are not only presented as a time of our parent's adult lives, as for many in my generation, but now as a time of a younger viewer's grandparent's adulthood. And in this past, all kinds of objectionable things happen—actions and attitudes we have long superseded—but have we? The answer—the conclusion we are supposed to come to by watching *Mad Men*, and as has been written into the show—is, of course, that we have not. History here is not necessarily presented as progressive, and movement in chronological time does not necessarily take us to a better place.

Mad Men shows us a past that is purposefully superficial, and extremely overt. The intention here, again, is to play with surfaces, and with the concept of the simulacrum, and now to juxtapose it to some very bad behavior on the part of the characters. The producers of *Mad Men*, however, conclude that there is no real beyond this representation, no matter how many layers are revealed, and this too is written into the material. The notion of the simulacrum begins with Don Draper himself. Draper has taken a false identity. As man from the lower classes with a treacherous past and a secret life—unknown and unknowable to the viewing audience—Draper (even the name implies a cover or a disguise) passes himself off as the living copy of a dead fellow soldier. As this simulacrum, Draper then becomes a star in the advertising business, making pictures to sell lies to consumers. As a copy of the "Organization Man" of the 1950s/1960s, however, Draper has no qualms about occupying this corporate position. He doesn't want to be a fine artist like Steve Archer in *Imitation of Life*, or to be one's own true self, as does Ron Kirby in *All That Heaven Allows*. Now, Draper is on the rise in business. Similarly, he is a sexual predator. Not only does he have a Grace Kelly look-alike wife waiting for him at home, subservient and dependent, but Draper acts on his male privilege to take any woman he wants.

The women of *Mad Men* are, instead, marginalized and contained. Of course, this presentation is ironized, with the woman in particular being gross caricatures of a period style. Pink angora sweaters abound—as do orange skin-tight dresses on spectacularly curvaceous bodies, as well as impossibly nerdy hairdos and dated jewelry—on very young actors. The women in some ways look like they have been arranged in Cindy Sherman-type disguises, only now they are set within a narrative structure that overwhelms the meaning of this disguise. As opposed to Sherman's work, we are not encouraged to look at the make-up, the hair, and the costumes and deconstruct, through the stillness of the image and the double exposure of the presence/absence of the artist, the variance in the constructions of femininity within patriarchy. The narrative of *Mad Men* instead fuses an era-specific selection of such disguises back into fiction, one in which women are knocked up, raped, abused, cheated on and left. This is the spectacle of the show.

The level of lawlessness is particularly evident in season 1 episode 7, entitled "Red in the Face." Interestingly enough, the segment was written by a woman. And here perhaps, too, we are meant to look at this series, and all others, with the regret and distain of looking back at a superseded era in the 1950s/1960s when women were so abused. That's how we were back then, but we are better now. Also inscribed in the show, however, is the question, "Are we?" Here, we do have a female writer of this episode of *Mad Men*, and there are other female writers on the show and, to a lesser extent, even female directors. In the film and television industry as a whole, however, the number of female writers and directors number only a small percentage. So, while female story editors and development executives abound in the media industry, a level of equal representation in the creative ranks has not yet been achieved.

In episode 7, the rampant abuse of power is shown and exaggerated to extreme, though symbolic, proportions. In this segment, substance abuse, now "everyday" 1950s-style abuse, is the subject of the episode.

Don Draper and Roger Sterling are shown to smoke, drink, womanize, and cheat with abandon. Of course, this type of behavior on the part of Draper and Sterling, and of some of the women as well, is typical throughout the series. In "Red in the Face," however, it is devoted to foregrounding just these properties. The sheer excess of substance abuse, especially seen from our contemporary perspective, can only leave the viewer exclaiming, ". . . another cigarette!", ". . . another bottle of vodka!", ". . . another bottle of gin!"

Then, we cut away to Betty at home in the suburbs. Here, we watch Betty walk though the house in her long-line bra, with her child in one arm, and a cigarette in her other hand. And later, when Betty entertains her pregnant friend, we cringe as the two have a few more cigarettes, and then some red wine. The effect throughout, however, is not quite laughter (perhaps because of the sheer over-emphasis), but guffaw. All, of course, is presented in typical television style, often with a characteristic lack of depth in the image, and many medium-shots or close-ups of the actors themselves. And it is here that the true fascination of the show rests.

The actors of *Mad Men* are extraordinarily beautiful, especially the lead characters, Jon Hamm and January Jones, who play Don and Betty Draper. The close-up of these characters fascinates us, and their sexual liaisons in bed are intimate and realistic, as are the bodies and encounters of the other actors. The casting of these characters has brought to television a much better-looking selection of actors than typical of the form. Here, we have a Hollywood-style type of person—recalling, as I have mentioned, glamorous leading ladies and men from past films. In short, we are presented with a serial spectacle of over-indulgence and sexuality, with a kind of playfulness regarding the unruliness of the bad old days, and with a kind of guilty pleasure of over-indulgence.

Another level of meaning in *Mad Men* that must be discussed is its obvious reference to contemporary reality. The young actors presented in the show, all in their twenties and thirties, refer to a contemporary young America by the convoluted process of embodying a time period of nearly fifty years ago. This is a very big remove. It should be noted, for example, that in *American Graffiti*, the actors and filmmakers were reflecting on their own teen years in the early 1960s, and that of their generation. What is foregrounded in *Mad Men*, then, is a contemporary generation and their social conflicts. The question of corporate jobs, of personal freedoms, of materialism, still persist now as they did then, as do questions of possessions of houses, of cars, of the raising of children, and of the struggle with monogamy. One could say that these are perennial questions that have plagued many a generation.

The historical positioning of *Mad Men*, however, is important. We must note, for example, that *Mad Men* is a post-9/11 nostalgia narrative. Our first clue to the resonance of this fact on the present generation comes at the opening of the show. In the title sequence, we see a figure recalling the Pictures Generation artist Robert Longo's black and white graphite on paper drawings entitled *Men in the Cities* (1979). Characteristically featuring men in business suits and slender black ties, we now see a figure similar to these falling from a great height outside a New York City office building. It falls past large James Rosenquist-style advertisements. Whatever meaning corporate logos and businesses in New York City office buildings may have had in the 1960s, I think it is fair to say that the meaning, especially in relation to this falling figure, has significantly changed for us in the 2000s. It cannot fail to evoke the World Trade Center tragedy.

We now inhabit a very different world. I speculate that the wild abandon of overindulgence in *Mad Men*, of male domination, and of female subjugation, as well as the total disregard for such safety rules as the use of seat belts, of refraining from smoking, and of watching one's cholesterol, give testament, not only to our level of "repression" but to our glee, whatever the age of the viewer, in watching a world unfold where there are no consequences to actions. We now know, as the 1950s/1960s regrettably did not, about the life-threatening effects of cigarettes, drink, and high fat diets. We also understand the challenges of a life lived in isolation in the suburbs, and the lasting impact on children of cheating and philandering husbands. Interestingly, *Mad Men* comes at a historical time when we are similarly paying for the consequences of our leaders' actions, both those of the distant past in the 1950s and 1960s, as well as the not-so-distant ones of the Reagan and Bush administrations, by such conditions as global warming and economic downturn. While the series started in 2007, just before the economic "fall," it is prescient that it continues, just as does that falling figure—*after* the fall. And if we have regret now, it is not so much for the past, as for the present.

Notes

1. See Douglas Crimp, "Pictures," in *Art After Modernism: Rethinking Representation*, Brian Wallis (ed.) (New York: New Museum of Contemporary Art, 1984).
2. See Barbara Klinger, *Melodrama and Meaning: History, Culture, and the Films of Douglas Sirk* (Bloomington, Indiana: Indiana University Press, 1994).

3. Crimp, "Pictures."
4. Laurie Simmons, "Laurie Simmons: Color Coordinated Interiors 1983," interview with James Welling (New York: Skarstedt Fine Art, 2007).
5. Fredric Jameson, "Postmodernism and Consumer Society," in Hal Foster (ed.), *The Anti-Aesthetic: Essays on Postmodern Culture* (Port Townsend: Bay Press, 1983): 111–25.
6. Vera Dika, *Recycled Culture in Contemporary Art and Film: The Uses of Nostalgia* (New York: Cambridge University Press, 2003): 56–64, 89–95.
7. Douglas Sirk quoted by Thomas Elsaesser, "Tales of Sound and Fury: Observations on the Family Melodrama," in Bill Nichols (ed.), *Methods and Meaning* (Berkeley: University of California Press), vol. II: 165.
8. Hal Foster, *The Return of the Real: The Avant-Garde at the End of the Century* (Cambridge: MIT Press, 1996): 136–44.
9. Klinger: *passim*.
10. See, for example, Andrew Bonnell, "Melodrama for the Master Race: Two Films by Detlef Sierck (Douglas Sirk)," *Film History* 10(2), *Film, Photography and Television* (1998): 208–16.
11. Susan Sontag, "The Imagination of Disaster," in *Against Interpretation and Other Essays* (New York: Picador, 2001): 209–25.
12. Sharon Willis, "The Politics of Disappointment," in *Camera Obscura* 54, 18(3) (Duke University Press, 2003): 132.
13. Dika (2003): 1–2, 11–23.
14. Vera Dika, *Games of Terror:* Halloween, Friday the 13th *and the Films of the Stalker Cycle* (Fairleigh Dickinson University Press, 1990). Here, I argue that unlike earlier works of genre replication, *Halloween* and the films of the Stalker cycle undergo a reworking of visual and thematic elements taken from Alfred Hitchcock's *Psycho* (1960) and, to a lesser extent, from other 1950s science fiction films. This is especially striking in *Halloween*, which begins with an extension of *Psycho's* traveling point-of-view shot from the shower scene.
15. Jean Baudrillard, "The Precession of Simulacra," *Simulations*, trans. Paul Foss, Paul Patton, Philip Breitchman (New York: Semiotext(e), 1983).
16. Foster: *passim*.
17. Elmer Bernstein has composed nearly 200 motion picture scores from the 1950s to the present.
18. See Dika (2003): *passim*.
19. Willis: *passim*.
20. Willis, 168–9. See also Salome Aguilera Skivirsky, "The Price of Heaven: Remaking Politics in *All That Heaven Allows, Ali: Fear Eats the Soul*, and *Far From Heaven*," *Cinema Journal* 47(3), (2008): 90–121.

Further Reading

Research on Hollywood cinema, American history, and historical film practice began with the work of Robert Allen, Rudy Behlmer, Roger Dooley, Douglas Gomery, John E. O'Connor, Peter Rollins, Thomas Schatz, Robert Sklar, and Pierre Sorlin, with notable subsequent interventions by George F. Custen, Philip Rosen, and Marcia Landy.[1] Of the few wide-ranging surveys of Hollywood's engagement with American history, Mark C. Carnes's *Past Imperfect: History According to the Movies* showcases various historians' short and damning assessments of Hollywood accuracy. Peter Rollins's *Columbia Companion to American History on Film* provides succinct assessments of several "canonical" historical films about the USA, but few of the contributions are methodologically adventurous.[2] Several essays in more recent collected editions, *The New Film History* and *Behind the Screen: History at the Movies*, consider key films about the American past in an even-handed manner.[3] More recently, David Eldridge's *Hollywood's History Films* and my own *Reconstructing American Historical Cinema from* Cimarron *to* Citizen Kane explore the transgeneric phenomenon of studio-era historical film practice and its links to mainstream interest in political, social, and intellectual history, as well as women's history and literature.[4]

With the exception of William Uricchio and Roberta Pearson's study of Vitagraph's "educational" historical films, there is relatively little research on silent American historical films, with the obvious exception of Griffith's *Birth of a Nation*.[5] Melvyn Stokes's recent book, *D. W. Griffith's* The Birth of a Nation, is a comprehensive resource for the infamous epic and addresses its complex historical discourses.[6] While Custen surveyed the studio-era biographical film, Dennis Bingham has re-evaluated the genre's continued importance in contemporary cinema.[7] Michael Isenberg's classic *War on Film*, J. David Slocum's anthology, *Hollywood and War*, and Peter Rollins and John E. O'Connor's edited collection, *Why We Fought: Hollywood's Wars in Film and History* are some of the strongest resources on the war genre's connections to the American past.[8] There are four major edited collections on the Western's attitude toward American history: Ian Cameron and Douglas Pye's *The Book of Westerns*, Roberta Pearson and Edward Buscombe's *Back in the Saddle Again*, Janet Walker's *Westerns*, and Peter Rollins and John E. O'Connor's *Hollywood's West*.[9] Gaylyn Studlar and Matthew Bernstein's *John Ford Made Westerns* is an excellent resource on the work of Hollywood's most influential Western historian, and Arthur Eckstein and Peter Lehman's edited collection on Ford's *The Searchers* (1956) provides some useful contributions on the film's attitude toward race and history.[10] Linda Williams's *Playing the Race Card* also addresses the representation of African American history, while in *Hollywood's Indian*, editors Peter Rollins and John E. O'Connor explore the industry's projection of Native Americans' past.[11] M. Elise Marrubio's work has subsequently explored Native American women's image in cinema, and in *Edna Ferber's Hollywood: American Fictions of Gender, Race, and History*, I have explored Hollywood's wider commitment to women's historical narratives.[12] There are several strong studies of Orson Welles's explorations of the American past, particularly Robert Carringer's *The Making of* Citizen Kane and Ronald Gottesman's anthology, *Perspectives on* Citizen Kane.[13] Edward Maeder has surveyed the influence of the period Hollywood costume designer, and Susan Myrick has provided an interesting first-hand view of the historical advisor on arguably Hollywood's best-known American historical film, *Gone with the Wind*.[14] *Gone with the Wind* also inspired Alan David Vertrees's work on historical set design.[15] Robert Kolker's classic *Cinema of Loneliness* and Vera Dika's *Recycled Culture* have surveyed the phenomenon of the American nostalgia film and its complex relationship to the American past.[16]

The majority of monographs published in the past twenty years focus overwhelmingly on the post-studio-era Hollywood epic and the work of director Oliver Stone. Among the best are Robert Rosenstone's *Visions of the Past: The Challenge of Film to Our Idea of History* and *History on Film/Film on History*, Trevor McCrisken and Andrew Pepper's *American History and Contemporary Hollywood Film*, Natalie Zemon Davis's *Slaves on Screen*, Marnie Hughes Warrington's *History Goes to the Movies*, and Robert Burgoyne's *The Hollywood Historical Film*.[17] However, of these, only McCrisken and Pepper's work makes a fundamental distinction between Hollywood films about American history and those made primarily about Europe.

Notes

1. Rudy Behlmer (ed.), *Memo from David O. Selznick* (New York: Viking, 1966); Behlmer (ed.), *Memo from Darryl F. Zanuck* (New York: Grove, 1993), Robert Sklar, *Movie-Made America* [1975] (New York: Vintage, 1994); John E. O'Connor and Martin Jackson (ed.), *American History/American Film: Interpreting the Hollywood Image* (New York: Ungar, 1979); Pierre Sorlin, *The Film in History* (New York: Barnes & Noble, 1980); Roger Dooley, *From Scarface to Scarlett: American Films of the 1930s* (New York: Harcourt, Brace, Jovanovich, 1981); Robert C. Allen and Douglas Gomery, *Film History: Theory and Practice* (New York: Random House, 1985); Thomas Schatz, *Hollywood Genres* (New York McGraw-Hill, 1981); Thomas Schatz, *The Genius of the System* (New York: Pantheon, 1988); George F. Custen, *Biopics: How Hollywood Constructed Public History* (New Brunswick, NJ: Rutgers University Press, 1992); Philip Rosen, "Securing the Historical: Historiography and the Classical Cinema," in *Cinema Histories, Cinema Practices*, Philip Rosen and Patricia Mellencamp (eds.): 17–34 (Frederick, MD: University Publications of American 1984); Rosen, *Change Mummified* (Minneapolis: University of Minnesota Press, 2001); Marcia Landy (ed.), *The Historical Film* (New Brunswick, NJ: Rutgers University Press, 2001).

2. Marc C. Carnes (ed.), *Past Imperfect: History According to the Movies* (New York: H. Holt, 1995); Peter Rollins (ed.), *The Columbia Companion to American History on Film* (New York: Columbia University Press, 2003). Kenneth Cameron's *America on Film: Hollywood and American History* (New York: Continuum, 1997) is similar in scope and argument.

3. David Ellwood (ed.), *The Movies as History: Visions of the Twentieth Century* (Phoenix Mill: Sutton, 2000); Sue Harper, Mark Glancy, and James Chapman (eds.), *The New Film History* (London: Palgrave, 2007).

4. David Eldridge, *Hollywood's History Films* (London: IB Tauris, 2006); J.E. Smyth, *Reconstructing American Historical Cinema From* Cimarron *to* Citizen Kane (Lexington: University Press of Kentucky, 2006).

5. William Uricchio and Roberta Pearson, *Reframing Culture: The Case of the Vitagraph Quality Films* (Princeton, NJ: Princeton University Press, 1993).

6. Melvyn Stokes, *D.W. Griffith's* The Birth of a Nation (Oxford: Oxford University Press, 2007).

7. Dennis Bingham, *Whose Lives Are They Anyway? The Biopic as Contemporary Film Genre* (New Brunswick, NJ: Rutgers University Press, 2010).

8. Michael T. Isenberg, *War on Film* (Rutherford: Associated University Presses, 1981); J. David Slocum (ed.), *Hollywood and War* (London: Routledge, 2006); Peter Rollins and John E. O'Connor (eds.), *Why We Fought* (Lexington: University Press of Kentucky, 2008).

9. Ian Cameron and Douglas Pye (eds.), *The Book of Westerns* (New York: Continuum, 1996); Roberta Pearson and Edward Buscombe (eds.), *Back in the Saddle Again* (London: BFI, 1998); Janet Walker (ed.), *Westerns: Films Through History* (London: Routledge, 2001); Peter Rollins and John E. O'Connor (eds.), *Hollywood's West* (Lexington: University Press of Kentucky, 2005).

10. Matthew Bernstein and Gaylyn Studlar (eds.), *John Ford Made Westerns* (Bloomington: Indiana University Press, 2001); Arthur Eckstein and Peter Lehman (eds.), *The Searchers* (Detroit: Wayne State University Press, 2004).

11. Linda Williams, *Playing the Race Card: Melodramas of Black and White from Uncle Tom to O. J. Simpson* (Princeton: Princeton University Press, 2001); Peter C. Rollins and John E. O'Connor (eds.), *Hollywood's Indian* (Lexington: University Press of Kentucky, 1998).

12. M. Elise Marubbio, *Killing the Indian Maiden* (Lexington: University Press of Kentucky, 2006); J.E. Smyth, *Edna Ferber's Hollywood: American Fictions of Gender, Race, and History* (Austin: University of Texas Press, 2009).

13. Robert Carringer, *The Making of* Citizen Kane (Berkeley: University of California Press, 1985); Sarah Street, "*Citizen Kane,*" *History Today,* 46(3) (March 1996): 48–52; Ronald Gottesman (ed.), *Perspectives on* Citizen Kane (New York: G.K. Hall, 1996).

14. Edward Maeder, *Hollywood and History: Costume Design in Film* (London: Thames & Hudson, 1990); Susan Myrick, *White Columns in Hollywood* (Atlanta: Mercer University Press, 1982).

15. Alan David Vertrees, *Selznick's Vision* (Austin: University of Texas Press, 1997).
16. Robert Kolker, *A Cinema of Loneliness* [1978] (Oxford: Oxford University Press, 2000); Vera Dika, *Recycled Culture in Contemporary Art and Film: The Uses of Nostalgia* (Berkeley: University of California Press, 2003).
17. Robert Rosenstone, *Visions of the Past: The Challenge of Film to Our Idea of History* (Cambridge: Harvard University Press, 1995); Robert Rosenstone, *Revisioning History: Film and the Construction of a New Past* (Princeton: Princeton University Press, 1995); Natalie Zemon Davis, *Slaves on Screen* (Cambridge: Harvard University Press, 2002); Robert Burgoyne, *Film Nation* (Minneapolis: University of Minnesota Press, 1997); Burgoyne, *The Hollywood Historical Film* (Malden: Blackwell, 2008); Robert Brent Toplin, *History By Hollywood: The Use and Abuse of the American Past* (Urbana: University of Illinois Press, 1996); Toplin, *Reel History: In Defense of Hollywood* (Lawrence: University Press of Kansas, 2002); Trevor McCrisken and Andrew Pepper, *American History and Contemporary Hollywood Film* (Edinburgh: Edinburgh University Press, 2005); Marnie Hughes-Warrington (ed.), *The History on Film Reader* (London: Routledge, 2009).

Index

adaptation, xxiii, 33, 106–7, 138–9, 165, 169–71, 181 n15, 199, 204
Addams, Jane, 179, 182 n.33
African Americans, xxiii, 12–13, 18, 43, 54, 186–7, 223–5, 227–8
Agee, James, 77–8
Ali, Fear Eats the Soul (1974), 210, 215–19
All About Eve (1950), 171
All Quiet on the Western Front (1930), 146
All That Heaven Allows (1955), 211–18, 222, 225, 230
American Empire (1942), 30
American Graffiti (1973), 211, 221, 224, 231
Andrews, Dana, 43
Ankersmit, Frank, 185
Annie Get Your Gun (1950), 170
Arizona (1940), 30, 41, 45
Arthur, Jean, 41
audience, 5–9, 11, 33–4, 36, 41, 80, 95, 102–3, 108–9, 119 n122, 143, 155, 176–7, 214, 223
auteur, xvii, 178

Bad and the Beautiful, The (1952), xxi, 72, 81–5, 90
Badlands (1973), 211, 221, 224
Banky, Vilma, 78
Barrymore, Diana, 81, 85
Barrymore, John, 81, 85
Baudrillard, Jean, 221, 222
Belle Starr (1941), 41, 45
Bickford, Charles, 88
biopic, xxiii, 138–58, 165, 167, 171–2
Birth of a Nation, The (1915), xviii, xx, 11–25, 69 n10, 226
Blossoms in the Dust (1941), 169
Bonnie and Clyde (1967), 157, 164 n118, 169

Brownlow, Kevin, 28
bootlegging, 95, 98
box office, 41, 68 n1, 110, 155–6, 196
Brackett, Charles, 74–80
Bradshaw, George, 81
Brando, Marlon, 51
Breen, Joseph, 105–7
Breen, Richard, 144–8
Breil, Joseph Carl, 12, 19–21
Broken Hearts of Hollywood (1926), 87
Buffalo Bill's Wild West, 29
burlesque, 40–2

Cagney, James, 103, 142
Cahiers du cinéma, xvii
California, history of, 194–5, 198, 200–1, 204
Capone, Al, 98–100, 108, 115, n50
Capra, Frank, 8, 206
Cat on a Hot Tin Roof (1957), 50, 106
Cawelti, John, 204
censorship, 8, 12–13, 105–12
Changeling (2008), xviii, xxiii, 192–206
Chaplin, Charles, 80, 206
Cheyenne Autumn (1964), 123
Chicago, history of, 194–208
Chinatown (1974), xxiii, 192–205
Cimarron (1931), xix, 37, 45, 167, 170
CinemaScope, 85, 88, 90
cinematography, 14, 16, 51, 83, 218
Citizen Kane (1941), xxiii, xxiv, 82, 165, 169, 171–9, 181 n17
Civil War, xxiii, 11, 15–16, 39, 61–3, 83, 186–7
Clansman, The (1906), 13
Clarke, Mae, 103
class, 3, 38, 41, 51, 169, 189, 213–14, 223–4
Cold War, 1, 72, 166

Coppola, Francis Ford, xxii, 222
Cooper, Gary, 36, 44
Cooper, James Fenimore, 29
Covered Wagon, The (1923), 26, 28–30, 38
Crowd, The (1928), 7
Crowther, Bosley, xxv n5, 156
Cruze, James, 26, 28–9
Cukor, George, 86, 88

Davis, Natalie Zemon, 184
de Havilland, Olivia, 57, 78
Deleuze, Gilles, 26–8, 31, 36–7, 39, 42–3, 45
DeMille, Cecil B., 26, 30, 33–4, 74, 76–7, 79, 81
Destry Rides Again (1939), 26, 40–2, 45
detective fiction, 192, 195, 200, 204
Diamond, I.A.L., xxi, 96–9, 102–4, 109, 111, 115, n50
Dietrich, Marlene, 40–42
Dillinger (1973), 169
Dixon, Thomas, 13–14
document inserts, xviii
Dodge City (1939), 30
Donovan, Robert, 139
Double Indemnity (1944), 192, 197
Douglas, Kirk, 81, 83
Drums Along the Mohawk (1939), 168
Duel in the Sun (1946), xix, xxv n5, 41, 45, 167, 170

Eastwood, Clint, xviii, xxiii, 193–8, 203
Eldridge, David, xxi
Eddie Cantor Story, The (1953), 72
editing, xvii, 5, 33, 69 n 10, 165, 174, 177
Ellroy, James, 199
ethnicity, 36, 41–4, 60, 70 n20

Fail Safe (1964), 43
Fairbanks, Douglas, 78, 95
Fanfaren der Liebe (1951), 104

Far From Heaven (2002), xviii, xix, xxiv, 210–11, 220–9
Farmer Takes a Wife, The (1935), 168
fascism, 165, 167, 172, 176
Fassbinder, Rainer Werner, 210, 214, 216–21, 225
feminism, 170, 178–9, 211, 213
Ferro, Marc, xvii, 189–90
film as agent of history, 6–7, 21–3
film as interpreter of history, 5–6, 14, 72, 80–7, 120–35, 166, 173, 186–90
film as product of history, 2–4
film as reflection of history, xvi–xvii, 4–5
film criticism, 54, 178
film historiography, 6, 14
film history, 71–21
film noir, xxiii, xxiv, 43, 192, 197
filmic writing of history, xvii, 189
Fine, David, 192, 199–200, 202
flashbacks, xviii, 82, 84, 123, 173
Fleming, Victor, 26, 34–35
Fonda, Henry, 42, 168
Fonda, Jane, 166, 168–69, 173
Ford, John, xvi–xvii, xxi, xxii, 5, 26, 30, 37, 120, 122, 124, 142
forewords, 169, 172, 180 n11
  (*see also* intertitles)
Foster, Hal, 214, 221, 224
Fourcade, Marie Madeleine, 169, 172, 179
Foy, Bryan W., 139–157
From Here to Eternity (1953), 165, 169
frontier, xxii, 26, 30–42, 45, 46 n1, 47 n37, 122–3, 133, 192, 197, 202, 204

Gable, Clark, 57
gangster genre, xviii, 98, 100, 102–3, 165
Gardiner, Muriel, 166, 179
Garland, Judy, 86, 89
Gaynor, Janet, 86–7

genre, xviii–xix, 36–42, 46 n5, 72, 80, 96, 122, 168, 184–5, 195, 204, 233 n14
genre cleansing, xviii
Giant (1956), xix, 170–1
Gilbert, John, 78
Gish, Lillian, 16
Glory (1989), xxiii, 186–8
Gluck, Sherna Berger, 179
Godfather, The (1972), xxii
Goldwyn, Samuel, 78, 171
Gone with the Wind (1936), 55, 170
Gone with the Wind (1939), xix, xx, 49–68
Graham, Gloria, 83
Great Depression, 1, 5, 38, 78
Great Train Robbery, The (1903), 30
Griffith, D.W., xviii, 11–25, 32
Grindon, Leger, 96
Guadalcanal Diary (1943), 139

Hale, Alan, 29
Hall, Virginia, 166, 179
Hammett, Dashiell, 174, 176
Hart, Moss, 86–7
Haskell, Molly, 178–9
Haver, Ronald, 87–8
Haynes, Todd, xviii, 210, 214, 220–8
Hearst, William Randolph, 171, 178, 181 n17
Hellman, Lillian, 165–79
heroes, 120–35
historical fiction, 96, 167, 170, 181 n14
historicity, 14, 100, 101, 148, 167, 169, 179, 184, 196
historiography, 1–9, 11, 14–20, 26–8, 72, 77–8, 83, 87, 90, 96, 102, 165–7, 170, 174, 179
historiophoty, xvii
Hitchcock, Alfred, 82, 185, 221
Holden, William, 74–80
Hollywood history, xx, 71–93
homosexuality, 105–6, 108, 112, 214, 225
Horton, Andrew, 189

Houseman, John, 81
Howard, Leslie, 57
Hunter, Kim, 51

I Remember Mama (1948), 171
Imitation of Life (1934), 224
Imitation of Life (1959), 224–5, 228, 230
intertitles, xviii, 11, 14, 15–16, 28, 59, 170
Iron Horse, The (1924), 26, 30–31, 39
It's a Wonderful Life (1946), 79

Jameson, Fredric, xxiv, xxv n8, n11, 204, 210, 221
Jeanne Eagels (1957), 170
Jesse James (1939), 168
Jezebel (1938), 170
Jolie, Angelina, 193
Jones, Jennifer, 41
Jowett, Garth, 22
Julia (1977), xix, xxiii, 165–81

Kael, Pauline, 178–9
Kazan, Elia, xx, 69 n8
Keaton, Buster, 78–9
Kennedy, John F., 139–58
Kennedy, Joseph, 140–3
Kerrigan, J. Warren, 29–30
King of Kings (1927), 79
Kitty Foyle (1940), 171
Klinger, Barbara, 214
Kracauer, Siegfried, 72
Ku Klux Klan, 16–17

L.A. Confidential (1997), xxiv, 192, 198–9
La Rocque, Rod, 78
landscape, 26–9, 31–40, 44, 55, 57, 192, 195
Landy, Marcia, 189
Lang, Fritz, 82
Lawrence of Arabia (1962), 179, 154
LeFebvre, Henri, 6
Leigh, Vivien, 49–67
Legion of Decency, 107, 110, 112

Leites, Nathan, 71–2
Lemmon, Jack, 94, 104–5, 110–11
Lewton, Val, 82
Longest Day, The (1962) 140, 154
Longo, Robert, 209, 232
Loos, Anita, 171
Los Angeles, history of, 192–206
Lost Cause, 16–16, 62
Love Me or Leave Me (1955), 170
Luft, Sidney, 86
lynching, 32, 42–44

Mad Men (2007–), xxiv, 28–32
Malden, Karl, 52
Maltese Falcon (1941), xxiv
Man For All Seasons, A (1966), 167,
    179
Man Who Shot Liberty Valance, The
    (1962), xix, xxi, 120–37
Mankiewicz, Herman, xxiii, 171,
    173, 178
March, Fredric, 86
Marion, Frances, 171
marketing and publicity, 7, 22, 28,
    117 n 91, 140, 152, 154–6
Marnie (1964), 229
Marsh, Mae, 16
Mason, James, 86
Maverick Queen (1956), 170
Mayer, Louis B., 72–4, 80–1
McCrea, Joel, 44
McDaniel, Hattie, 63
Meet John Doe (1941), 78
Meet Me in St. Louis (1944), 44
melodrama, xviii (*see also* women's
    picture)
Milestone, Lewis, 146, 149–56, 161
Milliken, Carl Jr., 147–8
Minnelli, Vincente, 44, 81–2
miscegenation, 13–16
Mitchell, Margaret, 55, 170
Mitchell, Thomas, 37, 60
Monroe, Marilyn, 101, 104, 106, 109
montage, 26–27, 90
Moon Over Miami (1941), 102
movement image, 27, 42

mulatto, 14–15
Mulholland, William, 195–6, 201,
    203
Mulholland Falls (1996), 192, 199–205
Murch, Walter, 174
Murder, My Sweet (1944), xxiv
Murnau, F.W., 73
musical, 75, 86
musical score, 19–21, 52
*Mutual Film Corporation v. Industrial
    Commission of Ohio* (1915), 12
My Darling Clementine (1946), 43
myth, 2, 29–30, 39, 46, 50, 172, 194,
    199, 205

National Association for the
    Advancement of Colored People
    (NAACP), 13, 22, 141, 228
Native Americans, 28–9, 31
"New Western History," xxii
Nietzsche, Friedrich, 27–8
Nilsson, Anna Q., 78–9
Normand, Mabel, 78
Nosferatu (1922), 73
nostalgia, xxiv, 45, 55, 58, 62, 102,
    131, 176, 210–11, 221–5, 232
Nun's Story, The (1959), 165, 169

objectivity, 11, 26, 121–9, 134, 165–7,
    186–7, 190, 199
Once Upon a Time in the West (1968),
    30
One From the Heart (1983), 222
oral history, 167, 169, 170, 172, 179
Organization Man, 230
Out of the Past (1947), xxiv
Ox-Bow Incident, The (1943), 26, 42–4

Paramount Studios, 75, 78, 80
Parkman, Francis, 26, 28
Pasley, Fred, 98–9
postwar Hollywood, 72
Pete Kelly's Blues (1955), 98
Pidgeon, Walter, 82
Pinky (1949), 170
Place, J. A., 135

Plainsman, The (1936), 37
plantation myth, 53–6
plantation suture, 56, 58, 61–2
Polan, Dana, 42
Polanski, Roman, xxiii, 194, 197,
   200, 203–4
popular history, 71, 98, 110
postmodernism, xxi, xxv n11, 204,
   221–2
Powdermaker, Hortense, 71
Powell, Dick, 82
Prairie Madonna, 30
prestige Western, 36
Prisoner of Shark Island, The (1936), 169
Production Code Administration
   (PCA), 105–7, 112
Prohibition, 94, 97–8, 110, 112,
   114 n. 25
progressive history, xiv, xxi, 26–7
PT 109 (1963), xxiii, 139–58
Public Enemy, The (1931), 98, 102–3

Queen Kelly (1929), 79–80

race, 12, 15, 43–4, 56, 58, 187, 219,
   225–6
Raft, George, 97, 100, 101, 103, 108
railroad, 30–31
Ramona (1936), 170
reception, 68 n5, 156, 178
Reconstruction, 11, 15–19, 61
Redgrave, Vanessa, 166, 177–8
regret, xiv, 210–213
relativism, 167, 173, 179
remakes, 71–2, 86–7, 104, 216, 221,
   224, 229
research, xix, 23, 97–8, 147
Resistance, 165–7, 176, 178
revisionism, 43, 54–5, 75, 136 n8,
   165–6, 170, 185, 213, 216, 224
Revolutionary Road (2008), 229
Robards, Jason, 174–75
Robertson, Cliff, 146, 152–6
Robin Hood of El Dorado (1936), 37
Robinson, Edward G., 100
Roosevelt, Theodore, 26, 28

Rosenstone, Robert, xvii xx, xxvii
Rotha, Paul, 72

Samson and Delilah (1949), 76–7
Santa Fe Trail (1940), 30
Saratoga Trunk (1945), 170
Sargent, Alvin, 171, 173, 182 n26
Sarris, Andrew, 178
Scarface (1932), 98, 100–01
Schary, Dore, 80
Schnee, Charles, 81
Schreck, Max, 73
screenwriters, 74–80, 166, 171, 178,
   197
script development, xviii, 75–7, 105,
   148–52, 173, 178, 195
Search, The (1948), 165, 169
Searchers, The (1956), 123
Second World War (World War II) 26,
   38, 41, 45, 71, 152, 154, 165, 169,
   194, 201, 212, 214, 215, 216, 220
Seitz, John F., 78
Selznick, David O., 81, 85
Selznick Lewis J., 85
Sennett, Mack, 80
Serpico (1973), 169
Seven Brides for Seven Brothers (1954),
   79
Seven Year Itch, The (1955)
Shaw, Robert Gould, 186
Sherman, Cindy, 209, 222, 230
Show Girl in Hollywood (1930), 87
Shurlock, Geoffrey, 106–9
silent Hollywood, 5, 71–4, 76–80
silent historical film, 11–25, 28–35,
   234
Simmons, Laurie, 208–10, 222
Singin' in the Rain (1952), 5
Sirk, Douglas, 170, 210–30
Sklar, Robert, xxvi, 234
Slocombe, Douglas, 176
Smyth, J. E., 98, 102
So Proudly We Hail (1943), 171
Soldier Blue (1971), 170
Some Like It Hot (1959), xix, xxi,
   94–119

sound bridge, 174
sound era, 35, 78
Southern belle, 50, 52, 65, 83
Southern space, 49–50
Southerners in Westerns, 32–40, 43
space, 49–68
Spirit of St. Louis, The (1957), 97
St. Valentine's Day Massacre, 97, 108
Stagecoach (1939), 37–40, 42, 45
star biopics, xxi
Star, The (1952), 72
Star is Born, A (1937), 72, 85–6
Star is Born, A (1954), xxi, 72, 85–90
Stevens, George, 171
Stevens, George Jr., 143–5
Stevens, Thaddeus, 17–19
Stewart, James, 40
Stewart, Paul, 82
Stokes, Melvyn, 12, 22
Story of Alexander Graham Bell, The (1939), 168
Story of Will Rogers, The (1952), 72
Streetcar Named Desire, A (1951), xx, 49–53, 63–8
Stroheim, Erich von, 79–80
studio era, xix, xx, xxiv, 26–46, 71–90, 94–112, 169–70
subjectivity, 49–52, 170
Sunset Boulevard (1950), xxi, 5, 72–80, 90, 170
Surtees, Robert, 83, 146, 155
Susman, Warren, xvi, xvii, xx
Swanson, Gloria, 73–80

Technicolor, 44, 77, 85, 109, 140, 212–13, 218
television, 7, 88, 90, 138, 231
Ten Commandments, The (1956), 79
They Were Expendable (1945), 142
Tierney, Gene, 41
time-image, 43
Titanic (1953), 97, 144
To Kill a Mockingbird (1962), 171
Toland, Gregg, 174
Tolson, Melvin B., 54, 69 n13
Toplin, Robert Brent, 96, 184

Towne, Robert, 195, 203
transsexuality, 112
Tree Grows in Brooklyn, A (1945), 170–1
Trumbo, Dalton, 171
Turner, Frederick Jackson, 26, 37
Turner, Lana, 81
Twelve Angry Men (1957), 43
Twentieth Century-Fox, 75–6

Union Pacific (1939), 30

Valentino (1951), 72
Valentino, Rudolph, 78
Vertigo (1958), xxiv
Vico, Giambattista, xxi, 1–2, 4
Virginian, The (1914), 26, 33–4, 42, 45
Virginian, The (1923), 26, 34–5, 42, 45
Virginian, The (1929), 26, 34–7, 39, 42, 45
Virginian, The (1946), 26, 44–5
voiceover, xxiii, 73–4, 76–8, 82, 169–71, 177

Wachsfigurenkabinett Das (1924), 78
Walsh, Raoul, 144–5
Warhol, Andy, 224
Warner, Harry B., 78–79
Warner, Jack, 86, 138, 140, 142, 145–6, 149–50, 154, 156
Warner Bros., 86–7, 139–58
Wayne, John, 37, 39–40
Welles, Orson, xxiii, 171, 173–4, 178
West, 27–38, 124, 128–34, 172, 192, 204
Western, xviii, 26–48
What Price Hollywood? (1932), 87
White, Hayden, xvii
Wilder, Billy, xxi, 5, 71–80, 94–116
Williams, Tennessee, 49–51
Willis, Sharon, 225–7
Wilson, Lois, 30
Wilson, Woodrow, 12
Wister, Owen, 31–32
Wolfenstein, Martha, 71–72

women, audiences, xxv n9, 34
women and Westerns, 40–1
women's history, xxiii, 167, 169–70, 179
women's picture, xviii, xxiii, 75, 165–81

Young Mr. Lincoln (1939), xvii, 43, 136 n4, 168–9

Zanuck, Darryl F., 75, 140, 168, 171
Zinnemann, Fred, xxiii, 145–6, 165–82